Adult Children of Divorce

Confused Love Seekers

GERALDINE K. PIORKOWSKI

PRAEGER

Westport, Connecticut
London

Library of Congress Cataloging-in-Publication Data

Piorkowski, Geraldine K.
   Adult children of divorce : confused love seekers / Geraldine K. Piorkowski.
      p.   cm.
   Includes bibliographical references and index.
   ISBN 978–0–313–34600–2 (alk. paper)
   1. Adult children of divorced parents—Psychology.   2. Adult children of divorced
parents—Family relationships.   I. Title.
   HQ777.5.P56   2008
   155.9′24—dc22   2008023765

British Library Cataloguing in Publication Data is available.

Library of Congress Catalog Card Number: 2008023765
ISBN: 978–0–313–34600–2

First published in 2008

Praeger Publishers, 88 Post Road West, Westport, CT 06881
An imprint of Greenwood Publishing Group, Inc.
www.praeger.com

Printed in the United States of America

The paper used in this book complies with the
Permanent Paper Standard issued by the National
Information Standards Organization (Z39.48–1984).

10 9 8 7 6 5 4 3 2 1

To my Family—husband **Frank,** son **Paul, and** daughter **Julie. In gratitude for their sustaining love, loyalty, and support.**

Contents

Acknowledgments

Special thanks are due to the following people who were extremely helpful in guiding this book on its journey to publication: Jane Kerner, who was an enthusiastic cheerleader for this book from its inception and provided hours of editorial direction to its development; Christine Holland, a senior graduate student in the department of psychology at the University of Illinois at Chicago, who was a masterful sleuth at unearthing relevant psychological and sociological literature; and Debbie Carvalko, my editor at Praeger, who had faith in the merits of this book. Also special appreciation and admiration are due to the scores of psychotherapy clients who provided many insights into the beguiling quality of romantic love.

Introduction

Romantic love is an elusive, fragile, and tenuous state—eagerly sought after and yet difficult to maintain. Nourished by fantasies and unrealistic projections, romantic love is easily deflated and readily discarded when the slings and arrows of interpersonal disappointment, conflict, and emotional assault hit hard. The 45 to 50 percent divorce rate in the United States is a powerful reminder of the massive ineptness in contemporary society when it comes to romantic love.

The American public is deeply conflicted about the value of divorce, but divorce appears to be a permanent fixture on the social scene. In fact, divorce rates around the world are on the rise. In spite of the increases, however, people worldwide tend to be ambivalent about divorce; they applaud the opportunity it provides for unhappy spouses to end marital misery and find happiness elsewhere, and at the same time they agonize about the life disruptions and loss of stability it bestows upon children. The tension between personal happiness and obligation to others, including spouse, children, church, and community, has spawned decades of public and private discourses on the subject of divorce that show no sign of abating.[1]

Similarly, public opinion about the consequences of divorce for children is as spirited and divided as the debate about divorce itself. Research has generated scores of articles that support the premise that children are negatively affected by divorce in a variety of ways. Compared with children from intact families, children with divorced parents score significantly lower on measures of academic achievement, conduct, psychological adjustment, self-concept, and social relations in hundreds of studies dating back to the early eighties.[2] As for more debilitating problems, Hetherington[3] reported that 25 percent of children from divorced families have serious social, emotional, or psychological problems compared to 10 percent from intact families. In addition, a large-scale survey of adults from divorced homes[4] found that even in the best of families, children of divorce were a alone lot, did not feel emotionally safe, and felt highly conflicted about their divorced parents' different lifestyles and new families.

In spite of the predominantly negative findings about the effects of divorce on children, Hetherington[5] and others, including Ahrons,[6] the author of *The Good Divorce*, have pointed out that approximately 75 percent of the children of divorce do eventually recover from its turmoil. And a small but important group of studies even suggests that positive outcomes, such as increased maturity, enhanced self-esteem, increased empathy toward others, and more androgynous attitudes[7] occur for some children of divorce.

A more recent controversy regarding children of divorce deals with the impact of divorce upon adult intimacy. Wallerstein and others[8] have written about "the sleeper effect," that is, the long-term effects of divorce that are not apparent until adolescence or early adulthood when cupid appears on the scene. In their twenty-five-year follow-up study of ninety-three adults (ages twenty-eight to forty-three) from divorced families and a comparison group, they found that the adult children of divorce were significantly more anxious than their counterparts about love relationships, less trusting, more likely to choose dysfunctional partners, more likely to have divorced if they married before age twenty-five, and more likely to have never married (40% of their divorced group had never married). Whereas some of the "never married" group was cohabiting and others had serial lovers, still others were leading solitary lives.

A number of other investigators documenting the higher divorce rates among adult children of divorce have reported that parental divorce approximately doubles the odds of offspring divorce.[9] Amato and Cheadle[10] found that divorce even extends into the third generation, where it correlated with parents and grandparents' lower educational attainment, higher levels of marital discord, high divorce rates, and greater tension in parent–child relationships.

Because of the contradictions and conflicts witnessed in their own families, adult children of divorce, currently comprising about one-fourth of the adults in their twenties, thirties, and forties in the United States,[11] appear to be more baffled by romantic love than their peers. Lacking a model or template of a satisfying marital relationship derived from their experiences with their parents, they are left to their own imaginations to create one, or else avoid romantic relationships altogether. As Wallerstein and colleagues have noted: "Their lack of inner images of a man and a woman in a stable relationship and their memories of their parents' failure to sustain the marriage badly hobble their search (for love, sexual intimacy, and commitment), leading them to heartbreak and even despair."[12]

Borrowing heavily from popular culture, those adult children of divorce who pursue romantic unions are often left with idealized, confused, and contradictory ideas about what love is all about, and have difficulty in discerning love from related emotional states, such as need, passion, and fantasy. In addition, their choice of romantic partners is frequently determined more by a reparative or mastery motive, that is, the desire to repair old emotional wounds, rather than by the objective qualities of their partners.

Cultural factors also play a role in how romantic love is depicted, realized, and maintained. In the United States, romantic love tends to be overvalued, distorted, linked to sexual prowess, and overpublicized in the media. In contrast, friendship, family allegiance, church/synagogue/mosque membership, and community participation are not given equivalent importance by society. As a result of the dearth of meaningful alternatives to romantic love, it (romantic love) holds sway culturally as the supreme, and yet surprisingly elusive, value. Overwork, geographical mobility, and the isolation of urban environments, all contribute to the widespread loneliness that hungers for romantic love to meet emotional needs. When that doesn't happen, profound disillusionment sets in.

This book, *Adult Children of Divorce: Confused Love Seekers*, is based on my forty years of clinical experience working with young adults in a variety of settings. As Director of two university-counseling centers in the eighties and nineties, I have seen many young clients profoundly disturbed by an aspect of abusive love that occurred in their lives, such as betrayal, courtship violence, date rape, infidelity, stalking, and run-of-the-mill rejection. While all young adults suffer from these emotional assaults, adult children of divorce have been particularly wounded and confused by these attacks on their self-esteem. In my search to understand the special vulnerability of these young adults, the research literature on adult children of divorce provided a conceptual framework for understanding these clinical observations. In addition, the young married couples I have counseled throughout the years, many of whom are children of divorce, continue to be a rich source of clinical data.

Adult Children of Divorce: Confused Love Seekers has been written to elucidate the complexities of romantic love in contemporary society and the problems of intimacy faced by a growing segment of the American population, namely, adult children of divorce. In addition, the book examines the role of popular and national culture in strengthening, or conversely, weakening marriages around the world. Chapter 1, entitled "The Fragility of Love," provides an overview of the American love scene, including the reasons for divorce, and examines the unrealistic expectations of romantic love that tend to create unhappiness when they are not met. From the Bible to poetry, *love* tends to be viewed as an all-consuming, eternal, magical, mystical, transformative, generous, and unselfish emotion.

Whereas these portrayals of *love* resonate with the human longing for unconditional love, these idealistic definitions, unfortunately, often set the standard for what is acceptable in a love relationship. Some of the attitudes or behaviors that are difficult to reconcile with love for adult children of dysfunctional relationships are sexual apathy, angry/critical outbursts, disloyalty, the partner's enjoyment of independent activities apart from the relationship, lack of conversational intimacy, absence of romance, and insensitivity.

In Chapter 2, entitled "Which Love Is *Love*?" the paradoxical and confusing nature of *love* is discussed. Although the concept of *love* is an enigma to most adults, it is especially perplexing to adult children of unhappy marriages. Because the subjective decision that one is "in love" is profoundly influenced by other variables, such as psychological vulnerability, self-esteem, and familial roles, adults from tension-filled families have difficulty sorting out these factors. Unable to distinguish love from sexual attraction, infatuation, needs for completion and validation, or duty/obligation, these adults frequently make poor partner choices.

Chapter 3, entitled "Love's Poor Choices," deals with the maladaptive partner selections made by children of unhappy marriages and the psychodynamics underlying their choices. Romantic partners selected on the basis of mastery motivation tend to make poor intimacy partners. For example, young women attracted to paternal, older men as a way of compensating for an absent father are often disappointed by the lack of companionship or sex in their marital relationship. Other maladaptive partner selections are blamers, conflict avoiders, emotional hermits, immature types, narcissists, oppositional types, and passive-aggressive personalities, all of whom have difficulty with mutuality, empathy, and altruism, which are considered essential ingredients for healthy relationships.

Chapter 4, entitled "The Fears and Risks of Love," addresses the fears of intimacy and how these serve to interfere with normal closeness. Because of their observations of dysfunctional love in their families and their often disappointing, personal experiences with love, children of divorce have particular difficulty with vulnerability and emotional intimacy. Afraid of making a mistake and being unhappily married like their parents, children of ill-fated marriages are often paralyzed by indecision and unable to commit to anyone. They are also especially fearful of rejection, betrayal, and abandonment, all of which were common occurrences in their families-of-origin. Other fears, such as fear of exposure, disappointment, abuse, and guilt, along with concerns about losing control and/or autonomy, serve to limit the degree of closeness, thus operating as safety valves to reduce psychological pressure.

Chapter 5, "Too Few Cultural Alternatives to Love," focuses on the lack of cultural alternatives in the contemporary American society to compete with the emotional power of romantic love. Because of too few friendships, excessive reliance on technology for social interaction, and sporadic group involvement, there is limited opportunity for corrective social experiences to reduce the idealization of romantic love and provide for the gratification of emotional needs. As a result of emotional isolation, people rely heavily on the fantasy of romantic love as an antidote to loneliness.

Chapter 6, entitled "Role Models of Romantic Love in Popular Culture," examines the role of movies, television shows, and romantic novels in perpetuating unrealistic standards about romantic partners and love. In the media, ideal women are beautiful, curvaceous (and thin), sexually uninhibited, and coquettish or provocative, while ideal men are virile, masterful, professionally highly successful, and adept at outwitting the wiliest of foes. Romantic love is portrayed in American culture as tumultuous, sexually passionate, and intense, which leaves little room for the quieter, gradually developing kind. Media myths[13] dealing with the transformative power of love, "love at first sight," predestined or fated love, and pyrotechnic sex, all contribute to society's obsession with and confusion about love. To the extent that young children of divorce rely on popular culture for a definition of romantic love, their expectations, ideals, and standards of love are likely to be distorted.

Chapter 7, entitled "Love by Arrangement," and Chapter 8, "Love Marriages Around the World," both examine international marriages. Chapter 7 looks at arranged marriages, the predominant form of marriage in Eastern and African nations, and highlights arranged-marriage practices in India, several Muslim countries (Egypt, Sri Lanka, and Turkey), and Kenya. In arranged marriages, family loyalty, suitable partner selection, and religious commitment, all play important and contributing roles to marital stability—factors worth noting in the Western world's angst about rising divorce rates. Although forced marriages resulted in scores of abuses over the centuries, the modern version— the semiarranged marriage—gives the final decision about a partner to the adult children. The task of initial screening for suitability (a role delegated to computer dating services in the United States) still remains with the parents or a matchmaker.

Chapter 8 focuses on the role of national culture upon marriage and examines marriages in Russia, China, Japan, Italy, Spain, and the Netherlands. The values and norms of a country can serve to stabilize (or destabilize) marriage, as does the degree of social upheaval. Countries in the midst of profound social turmoil, such as Russia, have high divorce rates, while stable countries with strong religious overtones and/or family values (Italy, Spain) have much lower ones. China, while essentially an irreligious society, does value family allegiance, discipline, hard work, and seriousness of purpose—characteristics that promote marital stability. Its divorce rate relative to Russia and the United States is low. Countries with a more materialistic, hedonistic flavor, such as Japan, have seen their divorce rates climb over the last decade and get close to their Western neighbors.

The last chapter, Chapter 9, entitled "Lost in the Land of Married Love," is focused on adult children of divorce and the factors that promote marital satisfaction, such as adaptive communication, reasonable expectations/perspective, strong commitment, similar values and background, healthy sex, and equitable distribution of household tasks. At a disadvantage because they don't have a road map of a fulfilling marital relationship derived from their families, adult children of divorce frequently stumble around the romantic scene looking for answers. Exposed to faulty communication and conflict-resolution strategies in their families-of-origin, they are more likely to repeat those same patterns in their adult relationships, to their own detriment. Most importantly, however, they lack perspective on what is important in a romantic relationship. They are likely to expect the worst, and via self-fulfilling prophecies, see the worst come to fruition. Likewise, their hopes for the best, in the form of overly high ideals, can lead to predictable disappointment.

In contrast to adults from unhappy, intact families, adult children of divorce experience many more losses, that is, loss of one (or both) parent(s), friends, extended families, economic stability, school, and other possessions. In addition, there is often a major disruption in parenting brought about by the divorce as parents try to cope with their own heartaches. Plus all of the serious family ills, such as alcohol/drug abuse, domestic violence, and infidelity, are more likely to be a part of divorced (and divorcing) families than of intact ones, creating additional burdens for the children and heightened vulnerability in adult intimacy.

Part of the hope in writing this book is that all adults, but especially children of divorce, will be able to modify (in an emotionally healthier, more realistic direction) their own expectations, ideals, fears, commitment concerns, and partner choices in romantic love. By so doing, they should be able to alter the vicious cycle of marital unhappiness currently being passed down from one generation of love-seekers to the next.

CHAPTER 1

The Fragility of Love

The story of Icarus, the son of Daedelus who flew too near the sun in his attempt to escape from Crete and fell to his death when his wings melted, is a striking parallel to love-seekers throughout history. Often reaching for the moon and stars in their quest for *love*, love-seekers fall hard when their dreams are shattered by the harsh reality of day.

Throughout the centuries, troubadours, poets, and modern-day songwriters have extolled the beauty of love in one breath, and then in the next they have bemoaned its treachery. In song and poetry alike, images of arm-locked lovers strolling through sun-drenched fields are juxtaposed next to somber, grey-tinged scenes of angry misunderstanding, emotional distance, and betrayal. The "many-splendored" image of love often appears fleeting, ephemeral, and as hard to hang onto as a wisp of smoke or a cool summer breeze. And yet, in spite of ample evidence of *love's* transitory quality, love-seekers throughout history have continued to reach for the heavens when it comes to love.

In their quest for *love*, love-seekers, especially those from dysfunctional families, often hope for unconditional positive regard, total understanding, unwavering support, encouragement, unremitting affection, protection, and validation of self-worth in their romantic relationships. Looking for the ideal combination of lover, best friend, playmate, companion, and all-loving parent, these love-seekers frequently strive to find a source of unequivocal strength in troubled times, a never-ending provider of literal and figurative chicken soup during moments of physical and/or psychological depletion, and a constant companion on life's often steep and rocky journey.

In addition, adult children of divorce and other unhappy marriages frequently expect romantic partners to provide what is lacking in their own personalities; for example, that she'll be an outgoing soul to compensate for shyness or a goal-oriented person to provide direction for a chaotic life. If the personal ads were rewritten to emphasize the emotional expectations brought to intimacy by lost love-seekers, they would sound like this: "WANTED: Lively, humorous man who could bring joy to my gloomy days and save me from a lifetime of depression" or "WANTED: Woman with self-esteem lower than mine. With her, I could feel superior and gain temporary boosts of self-confidence from the comparison."[1]

When expectations of romantic love arise from sources other than observations of healthy and happy relationships in the family, they tend to be derived from the portrayals of love in literature, music, and popular culture. For example, if *love* is defined in literature and the media as the supreme value in life, then it follows that it should satisfy all of one's longings. "For love is heaven, and heaven is love," wrote Sir Walter Scott[2] sometime ago. The Bible, in its elaboration of love in 1 Corinthians 13:4–7, proclaims that love is nothing but virtuous: "love is patient, kind, does not envy, does not boast, is not proud, not rude, not self-seeking, not easily angered, keeps no record of wrongs, delights not in evil but rejoices in the truth, always protects, always trusts, always hopes, always perseveres."

Besides all these virtues, *love* is viewed in poetry as an unchanging force that is impervious to the other's moods and vacillations. "Love is not love which alters when it alteration finds or bends with the remover to remove; O, no! It is an ever-fixed mark that looks on tempests and is never shaken," wrote Shakespeare[3] sometime ago. In addition, *love* is limitless, boundless, and infinite:

> "How do I love thee? Let me count the ways.
> I love thee to the depth and breadth and height
> My soul can reach . . . "
> I love thee freely, as men strive for Right;
> "I love thee purely, as they turn from Praise . . . "
> "I love thee with the breath, smiles, tears of all my life!—
> and, if God choose, I shall but love thee better after death.
> —Elizabeth Barrett Browning[4]

Further elaborating on love's eternal or permanent nature is Robert Burns's[5] poem entitled *My Love is Like a Red, Red Rose.*

> "And I will luv thee still, my dear
> Till a' the seas gang dry.
> Till a'the seas gang dry, my dear,
> And the rocks melt wi' the sun:

I will luv thee still, my dear,
While the sands o'life shall run!!"

Love is also all consuming, according to Edgar Allan Poe's[6] *Annabel Lee.*

"And this maiden she lived with no other thought
Than to love and be loved by me..."
"But we loved with a love that was more than love—
I and my Annabel Lee..."
"But our love it was stronger by far than the love of
those who were older than we..."
"Of many far wiser than we—
And neither the angels in Heaven above,
Nor the demons down under the sea,
Can ever dissever my soul from the soul
Of the beautiful Annabel Lee."

And Ralph Waldo Emerson[7] in *Give All to Love* further reflects on love's all-consuming nature and behooves us to be generous with love.

"Give all to love;
Obey thy heart;
Friends, kindred, days,
Estate, good fame,
Plans, credit, and the Muse—
Nothing refuse."

In addition, love is seen as beautiful and transformative. From Lord Byron's[8] "She walks in beauty like the night of cloudless climes and starry skies" to Shakespeare's[9] "Shall I compare thee to a summer's day? Thou art more lovely and more temperate," the poets see beauty everywhere. It radiates from their beloved's countenance and from themselves, because they love what they have become when they are in love.

"I love you
Not only for what you are,
But for what I am
When I am with you..."

"I love you because you
Are helping me to make
Of the lumber of my life
Not a tavern
But a temple!..."

"I love you
Because you have done
More than any creed
Could have done
To make me good
And more than any fate
Could have done
To make me happy."
        (*Love*, by Roy Croft[10])

From the poets to the Bible, *love* is viewed as eternal, mystical, virtuous, invincible, all consuming, and transformative. *Love* warms the heart, touches the soul, and transforms the mundane into the sublime.

The problem with poetic, idealistic definitions setting the criteria for *love*, as they do for children of divorce, is that they set unreasonably high standards that are doomed to fail. The lackluster, mediocre version of love one experiences sitting before the television set is such a far cry from the poets and moviemakers' depictions that it's difficult to reconcile the two. The angry, impatient man who has had a hard day at the office looks nothing like the love-smitten Romeo who speaks poetically to his Juliet. Likewise, the harried, overweight housewife bears little resemblance to a Meg Ryan or Julia Roberts. Ordinary modern lovers have little in common with the ideals of Hollywood or Shakespeare's poetry.

A young married couple, on the verge of splitting up after a physically abusive altercation, tried to talk about what went wrong between them. After hours of discussion in which they tried to unravel the painful reality of how their love went astray, the wife confessed that she never again felt close to her husband after she found out that he had a one-night stand with an acquaintance very early in their courtship days. She could forgive him, she said, but couldn't forget; she felt their love was forever tarnished by his early betrayal. For her, his infidelity during his college years permanently altered the quality of their love and it could never be restored to its once pristine state. An idealized love was forever shattered by one youthful indiscretion.

"If you loved me, you would never betray me," she seemed to be saying. His early infidelity contradicted her very definition of *love* and so she concluded, "he doesn't love me at all or he doesn't love me the way I need to be loved." Her idealized image of romantic love contained unrealistic expectations of herself and her partner, but also showed confusion regarding the meaning of *love* itself. Adult children of unhappy marriages, which she was, often fail to distinguish among the various components of love, such as affection, sexual attraction, sexual passion, and emotional intimacy. Further adding to their confusion is the reality that in Western culture, the phrase, "I love you," lacks universal meaning and can connote anything from lust to spiritual connection. Utterances about love can relate to duty, self-enhancement, gratitude, and vulnerability, and are affected by the emotional ambience of the setting. As is well known, the "I love you" uttered in the heat of nocturnal passion often evaporates quickly in the sobering light of day.

In addition, for adult children of unhappy marriages, *love* tends to be viewed as a constant state rather than a variable emotion that can fluctuate experientially as a function of other psychological states and/or competing priorities. For them, *love* tends to be viewed rigidly and dichotomously, that is, "you love me or you don't," with idiosyncratic criteria regarding its existence (e.g., if you loved me, you would never shout at me, prefer to be with your friends, look bored when I speak, watch TV endlessly, roll over and fall asleep right after lovemaking, etc.). As a result of such absolutist beliefs regarding romantic love, many potentially workable relationships have been terminated, essentially because romantic partners are convinced their own subjective criteria are valid. Often, however, their standards about loving behavior are based on their limited family perspective and thus, lack universality. For example, if one's parents fought frequently and later divorced, the sight and sound of an angry partner often raises unnecessary red flags about the union's durability. The questioning partner appears to be saying, "If you loved me, you would never get angry at me." Similarly, if one's parents were unhappily married and emotionally distant, extensive time apart can be associated with undue concern about the relationship's durability.

OVERVALUING ROMANTIC LOVE

Lacking a healthy model for adult romantic relationships in their nuclear families, adult children of unhappy marriages are especially vulnerable to the cultural models they encounter. In contemporary Western society, romantic love, especially sexual passion, tends to be overvalued and idealized in movies, romantic novels, and soap operas. In contrast, friendship, family involvement, church/synagogue membership, and community participation have not been given the media attention or emotional significance that romantic love has. In modern America, adults spend inordinate amounts of leisure time alone with their electronic gadgets (TV, computers, iPods, iPhones, etc.) or in romantic relationships rather than in significant interpersonal relationships of other kinds.

As a result of the dearth of emotionally meaningful alternatives to romantic love, romantic love holds sway culturally as the ultimate, and yet surprisingly elusive, value. Cultural alternatives (church, civic and political groups, PTA, charitable organizations, etc.) are available, but they are not utilized to the same extent they were thirty years ago.[11] Urbanization, geographical mobility, overwork, social isolation, and excessive reliance on electronic devices have contributed to the diminished significance of cultural alternatives to romantic love and the elevation of romantic love to its current status as *value supreme*. In addition, it is only within the last century in Western society that romantic love has been promoted to its present position as *sine qua non* for marriage,[12] a requirement that has contributed indirectly to marital unhappiness and divorce. Too much has been expected of romantic love in Western societies, and as a result, it falters. While the East is still heavily invested in more traditional marriages, including those arranged by parents and other elders, Eastern parents have been witnessing their adult children's experiments with the West's version of romantic love and marriage, much to their chagrin.

As early as 1963, Burgess, Locke, and Thomes[13] wrote in reference to American marriages that the traditional marriage was weakening as a result of industrialization and urbanization, and predicted that a new model of marriage, which they termed "companionate love," would become increasingly popular. "In contrast to traditional marriages, based on economic necessity and masculine and feminine sex roles, companionate marriages are contracted and endure on the basis of the partners' emotional ties, such as their love for each other and friendship," wrote Ellen Berscheid[14] more recently. In describing companionate love, Berscheid is referring to the more enduring, quieter form of marital love that ideally replaces romantic love when novelty and fantasy fade away.

Romantic love defined as "any intense attraction involving the idealization of the other within an erotic context"[15] is notoriously ephemeral and unstable most of the time. Even when romantic love is defined more substantially by the addition of emotional intimacy to the erotic pot,[16] it has been known to diminish within three years of marriage.[17] Romantic love, variously termed infatuation or romantic passion (akin to what is called "being in love"), is intense, turbulent, and ecstatic, whereas companionate love based on long-term association is more peaceful, relaxed, and fulfilling. As a result, companionate love is more "a matter of easy pleasure than ecstasy."[18]

The fragility of romantic love can be attested to by a whole host of U.S. national statistics on everything from courtship violence to divorce. In a nationwide study of courtship violence surveying 2,602 college women at thirty-two colleges and universities, 32 percent had experienced physical aggression from a date or other intimate partner.[19] In nationally representative surveys conducted a decade apart, more than 25 percent of the couples studied reported at least one incident of physical aggression during the course of their relationship.[20] Similarly, in a sample of 543 couples, Leonard and Roberts[21] found that at least one instance of premarital male-to-female aggression was reported by 28 percent of women. As for more destructive violence, more than three out of every one hundred, or 1.8 million women in the United States, acknowledged severe assaults in the year prior to the survey; that is, they were punched, kicked, choked, hit with an object, beaten up, threatened with a knife or gun, or had a knife or gun used on them.[22]

Besides domestic violence, the ever-present threat of divorce casts an ominous shadow on marriage, with the 50 percent divorce rate for first marriages still holding sway (some experts contend that the breakup rate has stabilized in recent years at 40 to 45 percent). The divorce rate for second marriages is estimated to be 60 percent.[23] While the U.S. divorce rate in 2006 is at its lowest level since 1970 (3.6 divorces per 1,000 people compared to 5.3 in 1981), the drop appears to be due to the fact that fewer people are getting married (the marriage rate has dropped by nearly 30 percent in the last twenty-five years) and more people are living together without marrying (the number has increased tenfold since 1960). Furthermore, the number of never-married adults has more than doubled since 1970 and accounts for 23 percent of all adults at present.[24] Thus, it is apparent that the U.S. population is staying away from marriage in large numbers and that those who venture into that hallowed state are divorcing and redivorcing in large numbers (the percentage of women redivorcing after remarriage has increased from 28.4 to 36.4 percent from 1980 to 1990).[25]

REASONS FOR DIVORCE: DEMOGRAPHIC FACTORS

For those who do get married, why do they divorce? The answer depends at least in part on the person or scientific discipline answering that question. Sociologists have focused primarily on structural and life-course predictors, such as social class, race, and age. With respect to age at marriage, for instance, individuals who marry at younger ages tend to report more marital problems and experience a greater risk of divorce than individuals who marry at older ages,[26] most likely because of psychological immaturity, unstable employment, and limited dating experience. Women who are younger than eighteen when they marry have twice the risk of a failed marriage as women who are twenty-five years or older when they marry (48 versus 24%).[27] With respect to duration of marriage, divorces occur more often in the early rather than the later years of marriage, most probably because romantic love has faded and "irreconcilable differences" have been discovered in the light of reality. Over a third of divorces occur for couples married for less than five years, with the largest proportion of divorces occuring for couples married for three years.[28]

As for socioeconomic status, it is inversely associated with the risk of divorce and correlated with the reasons for the divorce. Kitson,[29] for example, reported that divorced individuals of high socioeconomic status complained about lack of communication, changes in interests or values, incompatibility, and the self-centeredness of their ex-spouses. In contrast, low socioeconomic status individuals were more likely to complain about physical abuse, excessive time spent with friends, neglect of household duties, gambling, criminal activities, financial problems, and erratic employment.

Some other interesting sociological findings related to divorce deal with race, remarriage, and parental divorce. African-American couples are more likely than Caucasian couples to divorce during the first fourteen years of marriage[30] and there is greater risk for divorce among interracial couples, who have a 10 percent higher chance of failure in the first ten years than same-race marriages.[31] Also, the likelihood of divorce is significantly higher in second marriages than in first, especially for African-American women, women younger than twenty-five at the time of the remarriage, and women from separated or divorced families. And for couples where both members come from divorced families, the risk of divorce increases by almost 190 percent (by 70% if only the wife's family was divorced[32]). Parental behaviors most likely to predict problems in the offspring's marriage included being jealous, domineering, critical and moody, getting angry easily, and not talking to the spouse.[33]

In addition, being religious is a barrier to divorce, but by no means a fool proof one. A recent review of ninety-four studies indicates that greater religiousness facilitates marital functioning and decreases the risk of divorce, but the effect is small and almost disappears when education and income are controlled. However, adults who are affiliated with a religion are less likely to engage in premarital sex, more likely to marry someone if they move in together, and are more likely to see marriage as a lifetime commitment. Frequency of religious attendance has the greatest positive effect on marital stability, particularly when both spouses attend religious services together.[34]

REASONS FOR DIVORCE: RELATIONSHIP AND PERSONALITY FACTORS

In contrast to sociologists' broad strokes regarding causative or correlated factors for divorce, psychologists have more narrowly concentrated their research efforts on marital interactions, such as negative communication patterns,[35] dwindling interdependence[36] (the level of dependence on the relationship for fulfilling unique emotional needs), and personality problems in divorcing couples, such as neuroticism or chronic negative affect.[37]

Gottman's[38] work on marital interactional patterns during arguments has been shown to have predictive value insofar as divorce is concerned. The absence of positive behaviors during a conflicted discussion such as warmth, collaboration, and compromise, and negative behaviors such as anger, defensiveness, criticism, and contempt, have been related to the likelihood of divorce. Distressed couples who wind up in divorce courts are more likely to engage in defensiveness, criticism, contempt, and stonewalling than in positive strategies for resolving conflict. Negative-affect reciprocity, that is, responding to anger and criticism with increasing volumes of the same, and poor problem-solving skills are characteristic of divorce-prone couples, according to a number of investigators.[39]

Thus the top ten risk factors for divorce[40] during the first ten years of marriage are young age (less then twenty-five), low income (less than $25,000 per year), race (being African-American or marrying someone of another race), rape (having been raped), religion (none), children (having children at the time of marriage or unwanted children), divorced parents, education (less than a college degree), work status (being unemployed), and poor communication skills (nagging, stonewalling, escalating conflicts). When several of these factors exist, the probability of divorce spirals upward. For children of divorce, the presence of one or more other factors adds to an already precarious situation insofar as their likelihood of divorcing is concerned.

Rodrigues, Hall and Fincham[41] cite personality problems as one of the major reasons for divorce with neuroticism as the leading factor. While there are a number of definitions of neuroticism, the term typically refers to a general tendency to experience high levels of anxiety and other emotions along with excessive worry, phobias, and other emotionally based symptoms, such as compulsions and/or somatic distress. Higher levels of neuroticism have been consistently linked to elevated rates of divorce in a number of studies,[42] but the overall research in this area is not conclusive.

Other personality variables that have received some research support are a low degree of agreeableness,[43] a high degree of extraversion,[44] which is often associated with impulsivity and reckless behavior, and lack of conscientiousness.[45] Hostility in husbands and wives, limited perseverance, and a propensity to get angry are also linked to divorce potential.[46] As for more serious psychiatric disorders, there is ample evidence that all psychiatric disorders, with the exception of social and simple phobias, are associated with increased odds of divorce during the first marriage.[47]

From the subjective perspective of those who have divorced, the answers about why they divorced seem more to the point, irrespective of the biases inherent in subjective data. In Amato and Previti's[48] study of 208 divorced persons, the ten most common reasons given for divorce (in order of frequency) were infidelity (21.6% of individuals reported this item), incompatibility (19.2%), drinking or drug use (10.6%), grew apart (9.6%), personality problems (9.1%), lack of communication (8.7%), physical or mental abuse (5.8%), loss of love (4.3%), not meeting family obligations (3.4%), and employment problems (3.4%). While several of the categories are vague and difficult to anchor in behavioral terms, for example, incompatibility, grew apart, lack of communication, and loss of love, others represent the universally agreed upon death blows to romantic love such as infidelity, excessive drinking or drug use, and physical or emotional violence.

In other studies[49] just as in Amato and Previti's survey, infidelity has been cited as the leading cause of divorce with estimates of its occurrence in divorced couples ranging from 25 to 50 percent.[50] In addition, infidelity has been causally linked to domestic violence[51] and clinical depression in partners. Typically interpreted as a fundamental betrayal of trust by both men and women in the United States, infidelity undermines the self-esteem and sexual self-worth of partners, who often see it as a failure in themselves—a sign that they're missing some vital ingredient insofar as sexual appeal or behavior is concerned. The reality, however, often has nothing to do with the sexual competence of partners but rather reflects overall marital unhappiness (for unfaithful women) and sexual wanderlust (for unfaithful men).[52]

Drinking problems and alcoholism, one of the major causes of divorce, create their own brand of problems for the entire family, which includes domestic violence, child abuse, and incest. Alcoholics are four times as likely to divorce or separate as nonalcoholics[53] —a finding essentially supported by an eight-nation study correlating high divorce rates with high alcohol consumption.[54] According to James Milam and Katherine Ketcham, who wrote *Under the Influence*,[55] alcohol is involved in 60 percent of known child abuse cases, while Claudia Black[56] estimated that 66 percent of the children of alcoholics have been physically abused or witnessed such abuse in the family. In addition, she estimated that over 50 percent of known incest victims come from families where at least one member abused alcohol. Even in families with less serious problems, the unpredictability of the alcoholic parent (whose behavior vacillates significantly depending upon whether he or she is drunk or sober) creates high levels of anxiety, hyper vigilance, stereotypical role behavior, and lowered self-esteem among family members. As for the propensity of children from alcoholic families to become problem drinkers themselves, Piorkowski[57] wrote: "When these children grow up and have to contend with the demands of intimacy, they will find that a multipurpose drug like alcohol is a particularly appealing first choice for self-soothing and conflict resolution."

While physical or emotional abuse was cited by only 9 percent of the women respondents (5.8% overall) in Amato and Previti's survey[58] as the reason for divorce, domestic violence is a dramatic infringement of the rights of family members that severely impacts their health and well-being. In contrast to Amato and Previti's findings, which may have been a function of different socioeconomic status samples, Kurz[59] found that physical aggression was the primary reason cited for divorce by wives. Irrespective of the frequency of domestic violence in cases of divorce, physical abuse is potentially the most life threatening of all the cited factors and severe aggression has been most spectacularly linked to divorce in at least one study. In Lawrence and Bradbury's study[60] of physical aggression at the onset of marriage and its subsequent outcome, they found that 93 percent of the couples reporting severe physical aggression at the start of their marriage experienced severe distress and marital dissolution within the first four years of marriage compared to 46 percent of couples in moderately aggressive marriages. Thus, severe marital aggression condemns a marriage to dissolution within a relatively short time.

Stress is another major factor that contributes to marital breakdown.[61] Severely ill children, unemployment, poverty, overwork, and/or unequal distribution of household chores can overburden a marriage and tax it to the limits of its durability. When a weak commitment to marriage as a lifelong partnership is added to the mix,[62] the stage is set for divorce to be considered a viable option.

ADDITIONAL SOURCES OF RELATIONSHIP CONFLICT

Besides the tangible, clearly visible signs of marital dysfunction, such as infidelity, alcohol/drug abuse, and domestic violence, all of which are serious marital maladies, many more muted signs of emotional disengagement call into question the very nature of the relationship for some adults. Children of unhappy marriages in particular, who lacked differentiated models of long-term marital happiness, that is, positive models containing all the nuances and vicissitudes of life over the long haul, are prone to see defective love or problematic behavior where only human fallibility exists. Citing reasons for divorce such as incompatibility, growing apart, lack of communication, and loss of love, they are often unaware of how and where their emotional disengagement from their partners began and what maintained their alienation.

Incidentally, lack of love is one of the most frequently cited reasons for divorce in several studies.[63]

The behaviors that contribute to emotional disengagement are often the small, almost unnoticeable events such as failure to give compliments, spacing out during a conversation, falling asleep right after lovemaking, or forgetting important personal events, such as birthdays or anniversaries. Such mundane occurrences are often perceived as synonymous with insensitivity, disregard, and indifference, and thus incompatible with love. No matter how trivial the behavioral transgression appears to the culture at large, a long-lasting rupture in the relationship can occur when any particular act violates salient, and often very subjective, aspects of one's deeply held and idealistic view of romantic love. The less serious attitudes or behaviors that are difficult to reconcile with *love* for adult children of dysfunctional relationships, who are particularly sensitive to relational insults, are sexual apathy, angry/critical outbursts, disloyalty, the partner's enjoyment of activities apart from the relationship, lack of conversational intimacy, absence of romance, and absentmindedness or negativism about a variety of issues.

SEXUAL APATHY

Sometimes romantic partners equate sexual ardor with love; then when sexual passion is in short supply, they question the very foundation of the relationship. While sexual passion is a key component of romantic love and typically reigns supreme during the early stages of a relationship, its diminution is often quite complicated and unrelated to the most commonly assumed causes, that is, finding the partner sexually unattractive or decreased feelings of love.

"Not being in the mood" is the generic phrase that covers a whole host of emotional factors for sexual disinterest, but unfortunately the phrase doesn't differentiate the serious—emotional disengagement from the relationship—from the more mundane or typical causes. Among the more common factors for sexual apathy are boredom, overwork, fatigue, stress, performance anxiety, excessive alcohol or drug consumption, depression, physical illness and/or unresolved marital conflicts.

Boredom and/or lack of erotic stimulation in the context of marriage frequently result in long droughts of inter-spousal sexual activity. Alessandra Stanley[64] writing about one typical American couple with young children in the television HBO series, *Tell Me You Love Me*,[65] describes them as follows: "Katie and David haven't had sex in a year, but nothing appears to be wrong.

They are a loving if repressed couple deeply and equally involved in raising their children, from grocery shopping to Little League practice. David is not impotent; he masturbates with furtive relish when his wife leaves the room. Yet, neither seems able to summon desire for intercourse or take the initiative. A clue to their problem spills out during a therapy session, when the mild, buttoned-up David unleashes a rant about the lust-numbing domesticity of his life. 'I guess, yeah, I should be in the mood every time I clean out the gecko case,' he hollers, his sarcasm turning to rage. 'Everybody else is, it seems. I'll tell you what turns me on: Buying Cheerios is really hot, and then of course getting shoelaces or fantasizing about minivans, that's sexy, too.'"

Lost in the hectic, often humdrum, child-oriented aspects of their married life, Katie and David, like many other American couples, put sex on a back burner, only to be haunted by a vague sense that something is fundamentally wrong with their marriage. Not sure how to label their sense of uneasiness, they begin to question how much they love each other and whether their relationship is doomed. For children of divorce, this questioning leads all too quickly to the conclusion that divorce is inevitable because they witnessed such an ending in their own families. Unless couples similar to Katie and David deliberately work to put sexual liveliness back into their marriage, their frustration and disappointment with their sex life will lead to emotional disengagement from their relationship and loss of love—common precursors to divorce.

Overwork, fatigue, stress, and physical illness all take their toll on sexual arousal by diverting the body's available physical energy into nonsexual channels, while depression reduces both overall energy and the capacity for pleasure. A moderately depressed person can barely muster enough energy to handle survival activities and work requirements. Therefore, sexual behavior falls to the bottom of the priority list insofar as energy and enthusiasm are concerned.

An example illustrating the interaction of physical factors with emotional causes in sexual apathy is Jean (thirty-four) and Jeff's (thirty-seven) relationship. A very intelligent and professionally successful couple, they came into counseling because of Jeff's lack of interest in sex. Over the past several years of their eight-year relationship, their sex life was reduced to three or four occasions a year, most of which were unsatisfying to Jean. Trying to reconcile her feelings of disappointment and anger with her love for Jeff, she nevertheless felt that her sexual self was dying from neglect. At the time she came in for counseling, she was considering a divorce. The positive aspects of their relationship, that is, their affection for one another, enjoyment of each other's company, and meaningful conversations, were being outweighed by the lack of physical intimacy. She reasoned that if Jeff loved her in a romantic, hetero-sexual manner, he would desire her physically. It seemed obvious to her that she was no longer attractive to him.

What Jean didn't know was that Jeff had low testosterone levels and a strong case of performance anxiety related to his lackluster sexual performance. Over time, his fears about not performing adequately enough to please Jean over-whelmed his sexual feelings to the point that he experienced almost no desire. Even though he continued to find Jean attractive and told her so, he failed to initiate sexual activity with her, thus confirming her belief that she wasn't attractive to him. Jeff loved Jean intensely, but his anxiety was stronger and led to his avoidance of sex. Fortunately for them, medical and psychological treatment of Jeff's problem saved their relationship.

Sexual-performance anxiety typically follows a series of sexual encounters that were criticized by the partner or deemed "inadequate" by the performer. When the person involved begins to fear that substandard sexual behavior will reoccur, he/she may develop sufficient anxiety to interfere with sexual arousal. In these instances, the path of least resistance for the couple is avoidance of all sexual activity. In couples where performance anxiety is the primary causative factor for sexual apathy, the initial focus of psychological treatment is on stimulating sensual pleasure without any sexual performance component, and in that way reducing the anxiety involved.

Excessive alcohol or drug use, especially the abuse of depressant or tran-quilizing drugs, reduces physical and sexual energy, thus rendering effective sexual behavior less likely. The person who drinks too much, for example, is attempting to withdraw from stimulation rather than increase it because life is experienced as overwhelming, that is, too stimulating or demanding. In this instance, sexual activity can become another demand, rather than an oppor-tunity for pleasure or comfort. Also, the person who is overusing alcohol or other drugs often is retreating from interpersonal contact as a way of avoiding marital or romantic conflict, a strategy that does not promote sexual intimacy.

Chronic marital conflict, where one partner (or both) feels criticized, con-trolled, emotionally abused, misunderstood, unheard, and/or unappreciated, can also drain physical and sexual energy from the relationship. For exam-ple, if one partner consistently swallows disagreements and stops talking, the conversational retreat can lead to emotional and sexual withdrawal. Consis-tent inhibition of one's own feelings serves to dampen sexual desire and shut down sexual responses in much the same manner as external negative stimuli, such as criticism, humiliation, and belittlement. Sexual arousal is particularly sensitive to a whole host of emotional factors both within and outside the relationship.

With Margaret (fifty-five) and Edward (fifty-six), a child of divorce, their infrequent sexual contacts over the past three years stemmed from Margaret's sarcastic and overly critical manner, which focused on Edward's lack of responsibility for housekeeping chores. In response to Margaret's verbal attacks, Edward would swallow his resentment and conveniently forget what Margaret wanted from him both within and outside of the bedroom, that is, her requests for certain sexual behaviors as well as her demands regarding household chores. While their early relationship years were sexually passionate and mutually pleasurable to them both, their unhealthy style of dealing with anger sabotaged their bedroom pleasures. Only when they learned to be more direct, less caustic, and more tolerant in dealing with one another over mundane transgressions did their mutual enjoyment of sex gradually return in the course of couples therapy.

THE ANGRY LOVER

At first glance, the concept of an "angry lover" appears to be an oxymoron. While imagining a person being angry and loving at the same time is impossible, it is clear that the emotions of love and anger can be short-lived and follow one another in quick succession. Loving feelings can change rapidly in response to the other's behavior or an internal frustration and can be replaced by anger. However, because angry words are often hurtful and damaging to the self-esteem of the partner, the partner has difficulty reconciling the earlier loving words and manner with the rage directed at her. The injured partner understandably wonders, "If he really loved me, how could he be so angry?"

For the children of unhappy marriages that were filled with bitter, antagonistic exchanges, love and anger appear to be especially contradictory. Typically, when anger dominated the emotional climate of the household, warm and affectionate interchanges were in short supply. Instead, angry outbursts were followed by days and weeks of tension-filled silence in the family where the smoldering hurt and resentment were palpable. For these adults, angry behavior from their romantic partner elicits anxiety. Fearing that their relationship is intrinsically flawed and headed ultimately for dissolution when their partner is angry, these adults have difficulty in taking their partner's anger in stride and even more importantly, in evaluating whether their partner's anger is normal or excessive—a crucial distinction that can signal either hope or despair for the viability of the relationship.

Often a partner's anger rises out of circumstances apart from the romantic relationship. Frustration with one's job, friends, parents, or children can be more important than frustrations arising from the relationship itself. In addition, there are significant personality differences in how individuals deal with frustration, ranging from the intropunitive person who blames himself for most interpersonal conflicts to the externalizer, who is adept at shifting the responsibility to others when problems arise. With children of unhappy marriages, many tend to fall in the internalizing, or self-blaming category, most likely because they were blamed too frequently for their parents' conflicts. As a result, they are all too willing to take on more than their share of responsibility for the anger and frustrations of intimate others. As children they reasoned that if they were better behaved, their parents wouldn't be so angry. Similarly, in their adult romantic relationships, they reason that they should have been nicer, even when they played no part in their partner's anger. Excessive self-blaming often becomes their modus operandi.

In John (fifty) and Catherine's (forty-seven) case, John's anger was clearly a function of his job loss and inability to find another comparable position. He had been extremely happy with his position as an Engineering Manager for twenty years at a six-figure salary, and Catherine had grown accustomed to a lifestyle commensurate with his earnings. When his firm began to lose money and started to downsize, John's position was eliminated. Struggling with feelings of anger, humiliation, and inadequacy, John began to find fault with everything Catherine was doing. Always an externalizing, outer-directed man who complained vociferously about road traffic and incompetent drivers, he nevertheless had been a loving husband toward Catherine until the increased frustration brought about by his job loss needed a new, convenient outlet. While John's bitterness at having his stature and earnings pulled out from under him was understandable, his displaced anger at his wife, though clearly unfair, was unrelated to his deep, loving feelings toward her. In fact, it was as if his love and anger toward her were in two separate parts of his personality with impermeable boundaries separating the two.

LOYALTY AND LOVE

Whenever betrayal was a significant feature of their parents' unhappy marital lives, children of divorce and other unhappy marriages tend to require absolute loyalty in their idealized model of love. What is demanded is not just sexual fidelity or basic caring about one's welfare that is vital in all-loving relationships, but rather unswerving allegiance to one's views, opinions, and beliefs about a whole host of issues. As a result, children of unhappy marriages, who view loyalty as a central component of love, are often disappointed when their partners don't speak up strongly on their behalf or endorse their positions in any interpersonal debate. In one situation, a wife felt very betrayed that her husband wasn't more vocal in arguing with his family about their decision to invite his ex-girlfriend to a family picnic. While he had expressed his objection in clear, unequivocal tones, he had not been as forceful as his wife wished and she was angry. In another case, a wife felt betrayed that her husband didn't take her side in an argument with his mother when his mother attacked her for being selfish and not sufficiently loving toward her son. Instead, he pleaded the fifth, saying that he wasn't present at the time of the argument and tried to adopt a neutral stance, which infuriated his wife. She felt that if he truly loved her, he would have been her champion, ready to battle her enemies, including his mother, on her behalf.

When one partner fails to agree with the other about an important issue, the other often feels betrayed and questions the nature of the partner's love. How can he like my brother who is so hostile to me? How can she care about my father who's been critical of me all my life? Or, how can he dislike my church or political party when I feel so positively about them? In other words, if she loved me, how can she not understand and support me, is the basic question raised in the minds of those who equate unwavering loyalty with love.

Differentiation failures (not separating one's essential self from one's actions, attitudes, beliefs, minor characteristics, property, and family) are prime contributors to couple conflict early on in most romantic relationships, but most acutely in the relationships of children of unhappy marriages. These romantic partners tend to equate agreement with love, and disagreement with its absence. Not being complimented on a new article of clothing, having one's views of family life, music, politics, or religion challenged, or being criticized for some behavioral transgression, all feel like assaults upon one's self-esteem to the insecure person with an idealized view of love.

One young woman who grew up in an alcoholic family with an angry, often intoxicated father, recalled how upset she was when her brand new husband criticized the salad she made. As part of dinner, she had lovingly prepared a cucumber and onion salad, only to have it blatantly rejected as "too sour" by her husband. Her hurt feelings, brought about by her failure to differentiate herself from her culinary creations, were so intense and overwhelming that not even the mouth-puckering tartness of the salad (she had added too much vinegar) could diminish the intensity of her feeling unloved and unappreciated. Only time and growing maturity were effective in putting this incident into a realistic and laughable perspective.

The desire for unconditional love, that is, the wish to be loved totally warts and all, is a powerful underlying motive for many people, but for the children of divorce and other unhappy marriages it becomes a necessity in their view of love. Because their view of love tends to be inflexible, that is, it permits little deviation from its absolute requirements in dealing with the myriad disappointments of intimacy, its proponents are often severely disillusioned by romantic love.

While minor disappointments often become major betrayals for children of dysfunctional family relationships, infidelity—a devastating occurrence for most intimacy partners—can be an emotional deathblow for adults who experienced parental divorce, particularly when infidelity was the cause of their parents' marital dissolution. Having experienced vicariously the aftereffects of infidelity by observing their betrayed parent's anguish, they are traumatized anew when infidelity occurs in their own lives. Without therapeutic intervention of some kind, their own marriages in these situations tend to be lost.

INSEPARABILITY VERSUS AUTONOMY

For children of dysfunctional relationships, particularly younger ones, the partner's spending time in activities apart from the relationship is often viewed as a sign of imperfect love. The husband who prefers to stay home and watch television rather than join his wife on shopping expeditions is frequently perceived as self-centered and unloving. Likewise, the man who chooses golfing over home activities and the woman who spends hours on the telephone with her friends instead of her spouse are seen as minimally involved in the relationship. When inseparability is viewed as a central component of love, the pursuit of separate interests by one partner is threatening to the other.

While Mary (twenty) and Ted (twenty-one) had been dating steadily in college for over a year, Mary was becoming increasingly unhappy with the amount of time Ted was spending with his male friends. Twice a week Ted enjoyed playing cards, watching sporting events on TV, or drinking beer with his buddies. For Mary, spending time apart, when you could choose to be together, was a sure sign that Ted's love for her was flawed in some way. Since she preferred to spend every available moment with Ted, she believed that love itself demanded such exclusive devotion.

Because her own parents were unhappily married, fought a lot, and subsequently divorced, Mary's definition of love was heavily weighted with ideal qualities. She wanted a romantic relationship as different from her parents as she could imagine and to this end, permanence, freedom from conflict, exclusiveness, devotion, and inseparability were seen as essential elements. For her, love should be constant and all consuming, not filled with ambivalence, mood changes, and separateness. She didn't understand that the "dance of intimacy" in enduring healthy relationships requires time apart to solidify one's sense of self along with periods of closeness. Because she didn't have firsthand knowledge of the vicissitudes of long-lasting intimacy, she borrowed the ingredients for her concept of *love* from TV, movies, and books. In that way, she created a culturally sanctioned view of love that bore little resemblance to reality.

LACK OF CONVERSATIONAL INTIMACY

Women, who tend to nurture emotional intimacy by talking, often find lack of meaningful conversation with their partners distressing. They want to talk about their feelings, daily interpersonal events, and deep wishes, fears, or thoughts with their "soul mates," only to find their partner bored or disinterested. Because women have spent their lives talking with friends as a means of maintaining and strengthening emotional connections, and tend to equate talking with emotional support, the lack of conversational intimacy often signifies to them that something essential is missing in the relationship.

Men in Western culture, on the other hand, have been socialized to value physical activity and proximity as the means to emotional closeness. Boys bond with each other by playing games together, roughhousing, and teasing rather than talking seriously with each other. As adults, men frequently do things together, such as watching sporting events on TV or playing board games, and their conversation with each other tends to be limited to household repairs, investments, travel, or politics. Men also tend to prefer physical closeness with women, including sexual or affectional contact, than conversation; they provide emotional support by doing things for them rather than talking about how much they care.

One man said that he preferred "thinking about things in his head rather than chatting about nothing" with his wife. He wanted to do things with her, such as taking long walks, as a way of enjoying her company. His feelings about her didn't change as a function of the depth of their conversations; he felt uniformly close to her when he was with her no matter what they talked about. Physical proximity was clearly more important to him than verbal intimacy, whereas the reverse was true for her. She, like many women, felt disconnected from him when the conversation between them was minimal. Sitting in the TV room with him in semi-silence felt deadly for her, while for him, it was comfortable.

For women from dysfunctional families, the lack of conversational intimacy feels alarming, while for men who grew up in similar circumstances, sexual disinterest from their partner is the comparable anxiety-arousing factor that portends a negative outcome for the relationship. Not aware of gender differences in maintaining emotional connectivity and in providing emotional support, both sexes from dysfunctional families are quick to interpret any relationship shortcoming as a sign of defective love that is likely to fail.

THE UNROMANTIC LOVER: AN OXYMORON?

The absence of romance in the relationship may be the straw that breaks the camel's back for children from dysfunctional families, whose idealistic definition of love is heavily weighted with hearts and flowers. Candlelight dinners, tender embraces, surprise gifts, and spontaneous outpourings of song or poetry can appear to be the essence of love, rather than its celebratory moments, for these adults. Without such romantic flourishes, the relationship may appear lacking in vitality.

To a more pragmatic partner, romantic gestures may seem foolish, childish, or simply unfamiliar, and therefore may not readily come to mind. The more practical partner may have grown up in a household where fun, frivolity, and play were minimized in favor of hard work and seriousness. Acts of love in such a puritanical household might have consisted of works of labor, such as spending hours polishing the floor to please one's partner, rather than songs and flowers. Manifestations of love come in all shapes and sizes, and the concept of love is more complex and multidimensional than the dichotomous childhood game of picking the petals from a flower while chanting, "he loves me, he loves me not" would suggest.

Gary Chapman,[66] in his book, *Five Love Languages*, describes five different ways of expressing love in contemporary society: words of affirmation, quality time together, gift giving, acts of service, and physical touch. He maintains that each person has a dominant mode of communicating love, which is one's primary love language. The problem for all couples arises when each partner has a different preferred way of expressing love. For example, if one partner believes that words of endearment and compliments are the only valid way of expressing love, and the other partner tries to communicate love primarily by physical touch and acts of service, the stage is set for misunderstanding and disappointment.

Children of divorce and other dysfunctional relationships, who borrow heavily from popular culture for their own definition of romantic love, have a limited and rather rigid view as to what constitutes love. Because language and sex are seen as the primary modes of love expression within contemporary society, positive behaviors, including quality time together, small acts of kindness, and physical labor on behalf of one's partner are viewed as less important.

THE ABSENTMINDED LOVER AND OTHER TRANSGRESSIONS

The partner who forgets birthdays and other important occasions is often viewed as unloving by those who believe that sensitivity and thoughtfulness are cardinal features of love. The wife who complains that her husband lies around the house all day and doesn't do his share of household chores; the man who feels unloved because his wife is not affectionate nor appreciative of his efforts at the office; and the man who feels unloved because his wife is a terrible cook/housekeeper, are all operating from their own perspectives about love. "If you loved me, you would never...." each of them seems to be saying.

Besides love or its absence, what could be operating in each of these instances? The forgetful partner could be experiencing anxiety, depression, or a harried lifestyle. The man who is irresponsible about household chores could also be depressed about his professional status, could be physically ill, or too immature to comprehend family responsibilities. The cold wife may feel too vulnerable to show much affection, or too worried about her parents' deteriorating health. The woman who can't cook might have no interest or skills in this area and be unaware of the impact this failing has upon her spouse.

In all these examples, something more mundane, gender-based, or related to personality may be at the heart of the problem rather than imperfect love. The critical or demanding spouse, the alcohol-abusing partner, or the insensitive mate who retreats whenever conflicts arise may be experiencing dilemmas that have little to do with love. Feelings of inadequacy, insecurity, or emotional blocks to intimacy are often the causes.

For example, the person who doubts his own lovability or fears rejection in intimacy may have difficulty expressing the depth of positive feelings he has toward his partner. Overly concerned about the adequacy of his performance, he hesitates to express himself for fear of saying the wrong thing. Then, too, the expression of tender emotions may result in feeling too soft, vulnerable, and not in control. And so he avoids intimacy because it feels dangerous emotionally with the result that he appears cold and unloving.

The woman who is frightened by the depth of need she feels for her partner may also appear distant and unloving. Because her needs for closeness, support, and nurturance are overwhelming to her, she avoids occasions when these needs would be evident. Instead, she exudes an independent bravado that falsely conveys indifference and self-sufficiency. Her partner unaware of her neediness and vulnerability may conclude that she doesn't need, want, or care about him to any degree. He reasons, "If she loved me, she would be more affectionate, giving, and considerate."

While all romantic partners need to continually reassess and revamp their views of love in light of the realities they encounter, adults who grew up in dysfunctional households that led to divorce are hypersensitive to the relationship's shortcomings, ready to interpret the negative aspects as insurmountable obstacles or lethal flaws, and likely to terminate potentially viable relationships before reevaluating and reworking them to their realistic limits.

CHAPTER 2

Which Love Is *Love?*

The heroine of Billie Letts' novel *Where The Heart Is*[1] ponders the confusing nature of love: "Well, sometimes love seems easy. Like—it's easy to love rain—and hawks. And it's easy to love wild plums—and the moon. But with people, seems like love's a hard thing to know. It gets all mixed up. I mean, you can love one person in one way and another person in another way. But how do you know you love the right one in every way?" In a similar vein, Ingrid, in *White Oleander*[2] by Janet Fitch, writes to her daughter about the perplexing nature of love: "Love. I would ban the word from the vocabulary. Such imprecision. Love, which love, what love? Sentiment, fantasy, longing, lust? Obsession, devouring need? . . . Love is a toy, a token, a scented handkerchief."

The questions these literary figures raise represent the internal dialogues that take place within many lovers as they wrestle with romantic love. Such questions as, "Is it infatuation, lust, a passing fancy, or a love that is deep enough to base a lifelong commitment on?" frequently haunt the lover's quiet hours for months until a decision is reached. And even then, when the lover arrives at an inner certainty to say comfortably, "I love you," there is no objective yardstick that can be used to measure the quality or quantity of the lover's feelings.

In Susan Isaacs's[3] novel, *Any Place I Hang My Hat*, the heroine, in reflecting upon her realization that she loved John and he loved her, wonders what had gone wrong to have caused their parting. She speculates, "Maybe I just thought it was love because, for those couple of days, I needed a future. Or if it had been the real thing, maybe our relationship just dragged on too long and exhausted itself. Maybe it was LoveLite. Or maybe John and I were on such different cycles that we never loved simultaneously."

For the adult who grew up in a divorced or dysfunctional family, the uncertainty about what constitutes *love* is even more profound than for those growing up in intact families because of the contradictions and disparities regularly experienced in family life regarding love. Moments of affectionate closeness between parents followed by weeks of icy distance or turbulent conflict render the concept of love a mystery. The dynamics underlying sexual attraction described in this and the following chapter occur for adults from both divorced and intact families but are more pronounced and less tractable in dysfunctional families.

What makes it so difficult for most people to see clearly the nature of *love?* Besides the reality that romantic love is profoundly influenced by unconscious factors, it is not easily distinguished from related motivational and/or emotional components, such as needs for validation, completion, and/or nurturance. Robert Sternberg,[4] who wrote *The Triangle of Love*, postulated that romantic love has three separate factors (and yet they're often fused and indistinguishable from one another): *intimacy* (feelings of closeness, connectedness, high regard for, and the desire to promote the welfare of the other—a key component in all forms of love), *passion* (state of intense sexual longing for union with the other), and *decision/commitment* (an appraisal that one does love the other, and in the long run wants to maintain that love).

For the adolescent or young lover, romantic love tends to be identified solely with sexual attraction or passion because of the intense physiological arousal and sexual longing that are experienced, especially the first time around. In the throes of passion, the adolescent, who reasons that such intensity of feeling must be *love*, wants to merge with the other in both body and soul, and spend every waking moment in the company of his lover. When the other person is absent, obsessive thoughts about the other keep the lover alive and present each and moment. In one study cited in the *Monitor on Psychology*,[5] college students had difficulty in shifting their focus from their partner to an acquaintance; they couldn't stop thinking about their partners. "The great lengths the student had to go through to stop pondering her partner illustrates what a powerful force romantic love is," said Aron, a social psychology professor at Stony Brook, who believes that romantic love is a motivational state as fundamental as hunger and thirst.

Sexual attraction or passion, with all its biological imperative and consuming psychological preoccupation, transports ordinary men and women out of their mundane selves and catapults them into a more exciting, altruistic, and nobler state of being. The state of being "in love" is often described as alive, focused, energetic, optimistic, and euphoric. For most people, the state of being in love is a profound motivational state that is similar to an addiction with its intense cravings. And like an addiction, it can be viewed as highly desirable and difficult to control.

The state of being "in love" is clearly fueled more by one's imagination than by other person's reality. Because not much is known initially about the other person except what is readily apparent, one's own hoped-for-version of love keeps the fires aglow by embellishing the attractive qualities and ignoring the rest. Sometimes as one gets to know the rest of the person, the picture continues to be positive and the whole person is gradually loved. But more often, one's romanticization of the other person operates like blinders or tunnel vision in its focus on the positive to the exclusion of the negative. By sweeping all debris under the rug, the state of being "in love" is perpetuated until reality becomes strident in its demand for acknowledgment.

An extreme example of the blind aspect of being "in love" occurs in physically abusive situations. Women who have been beaten regularly by their lovers or husbands will return to the same abusive situation by telling all within earshot: "But I really love him." When asked to elaborate on what that means, they may blurt out: "We used to be so happy," or "I don't feel complete without him," or "He can be sweet and caring." While these responses have more to do with memory, need, or selective attention rather than love per se, they achieve a kind of nobility by being called *love*. Because loving someone is generally regarded as a higher-order activity that elevates humanity above its animal counterparts, the term *love* is used to cover a multitude of related feeling-states.

Infatuation, another variant of sexual attraction or passion, is often more idealistic than passion. In infatuation, which typically occurs in adolescence, for example, when a teenager becomes obsessed with an admired teacher or older family friend, the emotional longing and romanticization of the other person take precedence over sexual desire. These adolescent crushes tend to be magical, mythical, and transformative. Just as Sir Lancelot and Lady Guinevere achieved a nobler, more heroic stature by virtue of their love, so the infatuated person and his lover appear to be elevated to a grander status by their intense longing for one another.

Another confusing aspect of the topic of love is the distinction between romantic love and companionate love. In passionate or romantic love, intense, sometimes turbulent, emotional, and sexual feelings are involved, whereas in married or companionate love, trust, reliability, and friendship are the calmer ingredients. For some people, especially those for whom friendship was the beginning foundation of the relationship, romantic love is quieter and steadier, resembling conjugal love from its outset. For these more subdued lovers, concern about their lack of "in love" feelings, meaning the absence of obsessiveness, euphoria, and single-mindedness, leads them to question the overall depth of their feelings for each other.

NEED FOR COMPLETION

In both passion and infatuation, people tend to fall in love with their own projections and idealizations, that is, with qualities that would make them more admirable or complete. The mystery writer P.D. James[6] wrote: "I endowed her with qualities she didn't have and then despised her for not having them." The ideal qualities that one hopes will transform one's self are heaped upon this other person on the basis of limited evidence. An enigmatic smile, a tousled look to the hair, an expansive gesture, or a devil-may-care attitude is singled out for attention and a cascade of feeling follows. The stranger across the crowded room with certain characteristics is capable of setting one's heart afire. Whether one is attracted to beauty, power, high socioeconomic status, or sense of humor, one scans the world persistently in search of these valued qualities, essentially because these ideals are viewed as vital to one's well-being. And once those qualities are found, like the fetishist who's sexually attracted to things, one can be "in love" with the possessor of a particular trait.

When someone is asked the following question, "What attracted you to your partner in the first place?" the answers frequently reflect the idealized quality that is being sought. In the midst of stereotypical responses about physical attractiveness, comments such as "she seemed so lively," and "he appeared solid and trustworthy," pinpoint what is especially desirable. The shy, retiring person who is attracted to the extraverted, outgoing personality and the irresponsible, impulsive gadabout who finds the conscientious, hard-working type appealing are examples not only of the "opposites attract" principle but also of the search for subjective ideals.

The wealthy older man attracted to the beautiful young woman is hoping to find the youth and beauty that are fading in his life, while she is looking for the wisdom, stability, power, and/or money that are not a part of hers. When feeling lonely, empty, or inadequate, depressed persons often are attracted to vibrant, energetic, and confident persons in a hope that these qualities will rub off on them. Likewise, the emotionally inhibited and brilliant intellectual who falls for a spontaneous, carefree, childlike soul, and the organized, pragmatic woman who is attracted to a creative but chaotic partner, are both operating out of mutual needs for completion. The search for opposites or ideals is a quest for those qualities that are missing in one's self and yet, are highly desirable in the eyes of the family or the culture.

In other instances the ideals being sought after are opposite qualities to what was experienced in family life. The young girl who grew up with an angry, explosive father may search for a gentle, quiet man who doesn't manifest a trace of rancor. After finding a good approximation to that nonviolent ideal and marrying him, she may eventually discover that her docile partner has a dark angry side, or expresses anger passive-aggressively (e.g., by forgetting chores, being late for appointments, losing things). In short, her carefully selected partner may be miles away from her ideal.

The search for ideals can also lead to disillusionment when the ideal qualities are "too much" of a good thing. The man who is looking for stability to make up for the chaos of his family life may get bored over time by the predictability, coldness, and unemotionality of his stable partner. The woman who is searching for emotional excitement to compensate for the stoicism of her family is often dismayed later on to find that her partner's emotional liveliness is accompanied by irrationality and instability as well. The passionate quest for a compensatory trait often blinds the searcher to the total person; it's as if the seeker is so pleased to find the needle in the haystack that the qualities of the surrounding countryside are overlooked.

In a similar manner, the search for qualities to make up for personal deficits is often disappointing. The cautious introvert, who is uncomfortable being the center of attention, may initially admire the ease with which his outgoing partner holds court, but soon thereafter, may grow to resent her partner's incessant need for attention. Because the gregariousness of the extravert didn't transform the introvert into a similar social creature (and, in fact, may have made it harder for the introvert to shine), the quiet partner may come to resent the very quality that was the basis of the attraction. Likewise, the intellectual person sought after by a partner hoping for reasonableness in her life may later view his rationality as pedantic or distant. When one's expectations for self-transformation from the relationship aren't met, disappointment in the partner is likely to occur.

For the children of divorce, the ideals they're attracted to are heavily influenced by cultural icons. Because their own families failed to provide models of lovability for romantic love—parents who were loved regularly, permanently, and without reservation by their partners—they had to rely on the popular culture's definition of attractiveness or lovability for their own ideals. Whether it's thinness, good looks, fame, adventurousness, or sensitivity that the popular culture values, for adults who grew up in dysfunctional homes, these ideals have more validity than the contradictory and hypocritical values of their families.

Lovability, which is a component of self-esteem that is often overlooked, plays a key role in romantic love, where its perceived absence regularly manifests itself in therapists' offices after a broken love affair. The successful professional adult who is devastated by a lover's rejection and self-doubting as a result illustrates the distinction between lovability and competence as dimensions of self-esteem. At the time of the rejection, professional success may matter little to this sort of successful career man; what is of greater significance is that he was found unlovable or deficient in certain ways. He may feel that he lacks a key ingredient in his subjective rendition of lovability, for example, wittiness, charm, or conversational skill, and as a result is not intrinsically worthy of love. When the definitions of lovability and the ideals being sought after come from popular culture rather than the family, they are often rigid, exaggerated, and impervious to reality. Because the definitions and ideals have not been finely tuned by repeated personal experiences over time, they tend to operate as absolutes rather than as guiding principles.

Twenty-seven-year-old Susan, with a history of bulimia, depression, and alcohol addiction, was obsessed by thinness and dieting. She came from a high-conflict family where her parents fought intensely and regularly. When they finally divorced (she was in her early teens), she began her antisocial behavior and psychiatric history with violence toward her parents, school truancy, sexual promiscuity, and alcohol abuse. Throughout this period of time, she was obsessed by dieting and concerns about her sexual attractiveness, which revolved totally around her weight that fluctuated from normal to twenty pounds overweight. Illustrating the "opposites attract" principle along with the need for completion of her cultural and personal ideal of thinness, the "man of her dreams" was a very slightly built, bookish male who was totally indifferent to food, and like Susan, equated thinness with sexual attractiveness and lovability. When Susan came into therapy after stopping all alcohol and other drug use, she made significant changes in her lifestyle, entered graduate school, became less depressed, and improved her relationships with her boyfriend and family, but her preoccupation with her weight and the ideal of thinness appeared to be hardwired into her personality and remained resistant to therapeutic interventions.

SEARCH FOR VALIDATION

Another similar quest is the search for validation, which also enhances self-esteem, but, unlike the need for completion, the desire to make up for missing qualities is not as pronounced as dynamics. Validation occurs when another's attention heightens one's sense of attractiveness or lovability, and is most evident in situations where the lover has a valued commodity, such as power, prestige, money, or physical attractiveness.

In the experience of validation, the person who is flattered by the advances of the pursuer derives a measure of self-esteem from the attention and confuses being flattered with love. The young, struggling starlet who falls for the successful film star and the graduate student enamored of the tenured faculty member illustrate both the power of validation and ego-ideal gratification in romantic love. In both cases, the younger, less accomplished person is flattered by the attention of someone admired and seduced by the illusion that their own ideals (e.g., fame, academic status) are within their grasp.

While most people experience pleasure and ego gratification from being in the company of famous and/or talented individuals and may be charmed by them, typically they don't fall in love with these superstars. It is only when romantic love and self-validation are linked that the stage is set for love in vulnerable persons. Among these are adult children of divorce who were abused physically or verbally by a parent, blame themselves for the parental conflicts that led to the divorce, and as a result feel flawed or damaged insofar as lovability is concerned. The finding that the proportion of emotionally troubled adults is around three times as great among those whose parents are divorced comparatively to those from intact families, attests to the reality that self-worth is significantly damaged in many of these adults.[7]

The search for validation is manifested in its purest form in rebound situations when a rejected lover depleted of self-esteem is revitalized by the attention of another. The loving concern of a third party on the scene helps to soften the injury of being discarded and promotes the restoration of self-worth, regardless of the appropriateness of the new lover as a partner. In search of healing balm for rejection injuries, intelligent, hard-working, and decent people fall in love with all sorts of unreliable and inappropriate lovers (in terms of shared values and interests). Sociopaths, drug addicts, and narcissists represent the most extreme end of the continuum of inappropriate partners with lackluster, unmotivated, or unavailable persons occupying the largest space on this dimension.

A case in point was Greg's love attraction to Mary, a beautiful but unstable woman who seemed enamored of Greg's money. A narcissistic woman who had not been self-supporting for any length of time (she modeled occasionally and jumped from one money scheme to another), Mary managed to keep Greg involved with her vague promises of a future love relationship. In spite of many failed promises to this end, Greg, a brilliant money investor who was extremely overweight, continued to be seduced by Mary's beauty to provide her large sums of money for maintaining her extravagant lifestyle.

While most of Greg's family and friends warned him repeatedly that Mary was "a gold digger," he rationalized her acquisitive nature by portraying her in his own mind as a lost, waif-like soul in need of nurturance. What he failed to realize was the extent to which her beauty and charm provided him with validation of his lovability. At the time he met Mary, he was recovering from a failed love relationship that significantly bruised an already damaged ego. With Mary on his arm, he was hoping to heal quickly, but unfortunately Mary's emotional instability left him reeling with more disappointments than pleasure. After several years of dramatic ups and downs that rivaled those of the daily soap operas, their relationship ended bitterly when Mary left Greg for another wealthy man who was physically more appealing than Greg.

A psychoanalytic interpretation of both the needs (completion and validation) is related to the concept of self-object in self-psychology.[8] The term, self-object, is used to describe persons in the external world who are experienced psychologically as a necessary part of the self because of the functions they serve. Functions such as idealizing (need for an idealized parent), validation (need for positive reassurance), and twinship (need for companionable interaction), are viewed as crucial in facilitating self-cohesion and self-enhancement developmentally that lead to higher levels of personality integration. When parents are inadequate to the task of providing these functions, significant fixations can occur that result in pathological searches to find partners to complete the self.

When parents are unhappily married and embroiled in concerns about their own lovability, they have little emotional energy available to attend sufficiently to the development of their children. As a result, their adult children often seek out partners to validate and/or complete themselves under the guise of love. Unable to distinguish their own quest for self-completion from genuine affection, these adult children are convinced that their problems in romantic relationships stem from failures in their partners rather than their own unrealistic yearnings and expectations.

THE POWER OF FAMILIAL ROLES

The familial roles played by adult children from dysfunctional homes are typically rigid and intractable, but generally safe from assault and/or immobilizing conflict. These patterns of thought and behavior usually represent the best alternative available under the circumstances and, as such, are highly valued and difficult to relinquish. Whether the role is positive,[9] such as "the responsible one" or "the hero," or negative, such as "the scapegoat" or "the acting out child," familial roles are confining and restrictive of the self. Being superresponsible, for example, may gain accolades from parents and teachers alike, but it often results in the child's denial of his own playfulness, dependency, anger, and/or confusion. In contrast, in a safe, loving, intact family, there is more opportunity for role experimentation and less familial need for the children to carry out functions that belong to the parents.

In Marquardt's[10] study of the children of divorced parents, *Between Two Worlds: The Inner Lives of Children of Divorce*, she describes the role of "Little Adults," which these children often assume. Needing to protect their parents emotionally, especially the mother, and to make sense of their parents' different values and lifestyles in many cases, these children become adept at hiding their own confusion, isolation, and suffering from the adults around them under a pseudo-mature facade. In a comparison of late adolescents and young adults from divorced and intact families, Jurkovic and colleagues[11] found that the divorced group reported that they provided more emotional and instrumental caregiving to family members, that is, more tender loving care and more cooking/cleaning than the intact family group.

The two common familial roles among children in divorced families are the role of caretaker and its converse—the dependent child. Caretakers feel valued for their nurturant qualities and derive self-esteem from being in a superior position relative to others. While caretaking is highly regarded throughout societies for its altruistic and empathic properties, what is often overlooked is the self-enhancing function of caretaking. Caretakers tend to be viewed as more complete, more intact, healthier, and/or more competent than the people they serve—a perception that often fails to coincide with reality.

Accustomed to the caretaking role from an early age (usually the oldest child in a dysfunctional family where one or both parents were unable or unwilling to handle certain aspects of this role), caretakers frequently seek out impaired individuals as romantic partners to nurture, and as a result feel more competent and confident in the process. The tender concern that gets aroused by the helplessness and vulnerability of the needy partner is easy to misinterpret as *love*, even when the self-serving component—the boosting of self-esteem—is paramount. The problem with this version of *love* is that its one-sided nature undermines its long-term durability. The giver over time can become embittered and worn out, especially if there is little return on the loving self-sacrifice. Wallerstein and Lewis[12] in their longitudinal study of children of divorce, wrote: "A discovery at the 25-year mark (25 years after the divorce) was how frequently they installed the familiar caregiving role into their own adult relationships and how often they sought out needy, troubled partners whom they nurtured to their own emotional detriment."

The Henry Higgins-Eliza Doolittle romance in Shaw's *Pygmalion*[13] (later a play and movie entitled "My Fair Lady") and the Humbert-Humbert/Lolita merger (in the book and movie, *Lolita*, by Nabokov[14]) are classical examples in literature of the Parent (or caretaker)–Child pairing. In "My Fair Lady," Henry Higgins is the sophisticated, upper-class English professor who transforms the naïve, unschooled, lower-class Eliza into a sophisticated, well-mannered woman in British society. In the process of Eliza's elocution lessons with Henry, they fall in love, and as most fairy tales imply or explicitly state, live happily ever after. Unfortunately, their married lives ten–fifteen years hence, when Henry's role as father/mentor becomes obsolete because Eliza has grown up, are not portrayed in the novel, and so there is no opportunity to observe the kind of interpersonal changes that would need to be made for their relationship to survive.

Developing new, more egalitarian roles with one another would require the Henrys of the world to give up their superiority and dominance as parental figures in order to accommodate the maturation of their child partners into adults. Because this change in their relationship requires a loss of power and more vulnerability for the parental partner, this kind of shift is often very difficult for the dominant partner to make. Just as parents and teenagers engage in tumultuous battles during adolescence over the changing boundaries of power and control, so do Parent–Child marriages suffer the same kind of "sturm and drang" ("storm and stress") when the child partner begins to mature.

Adult children of divorce and other dysfunctional families often seek out replacement parents as romantic partners when one or both of their own parents were psychologically absent throughout childhood or vanished suddenly at the time of divorce. Women who marry substantially older men are assumed to be looking for a partner to provide the missing childhood ingredients—strength, direction, support, and nurturance—in their lives. Substitute parental figures, such as teachers, physicians, magistrates, or policemen, are often prime targets of their search—a common quest for women who experienced divorce in their families.

Patricia grew up in an alcoholic family with elderly parents, both of whom were impaired, but in different ways. A passive, emotionally absent, alcoholic father, a physically ill mother, and a twenty-year older brother, who was in the military for most of her growing-up years and returned home as a disgruntled, aimless alcoholic, constituted her nuclear family. Although both her parents died when Patricia was in her teens, they left her money for schooling, which opened many experiential doors that provided her with opportunities to meet her developing interests. Unfortunately, the parental omissions in her life created a need for a parental romantic partner that was stronger than her intellectual and emotional needs in other areas. When Patricia was in college, she met a fifteen-year older policeman at the car agency where she held a summer job. Even though they had nothing in common in terms of family background, educational attainment (he was a high school graduate, she was finishing up a degree in Biology and later got her Master's), interests, or values, he wooed her with attention and expensive presents until she agreed to marry him. While their marriage was not a disastrous one by most standards (although they had a schizophrenic son), their differences created a lonely and discordant environment for Patricia.

Whereas the role of child entails some obvious rewards, that is, attention, care, and support from the parental partner, like all familial roles it tends to be limiting. Thwarting the development of self-confidence, self-reliance, and maturity, the role of child in a romantic relationship perpetuates dependency and passivity for the role holder. Like Peter Pan's quest for perpetual childhood status, the journey can be comfortable and adventuresome for a period of time—until developmental stirrings for autonomy and self-sufficiency become strong. Then when conflicts with parental partners arise, significant role adjustments on the part of both partners need to be made in order for the relationship to survive. However, when people are locked into dependent characterological patterns, the many fears of maturity and the comforts of a childlike existence can drown out autonomous urges.

DUTY OR GUILT CONFUSED WITH LOVE

Just as *need* can masquerade as *love*, so can duty or guilt. Long ago, Dante[15] said it clearly when he urged those who are loved to return the love: "Love, which absolves no beloved one from loving." When people feel obligated to love others who profess love or need for them, the resulting commitment on their part can have the appearance of love but lack the genuine caring for the other that is love's hallmark. Long-term marriages maintained solely by shriveled old promises and obligations fall in this category, as do some romantic relationships that were initiated on disparate playing fields. An example of the latter situation occurs when one partner wants only a sexual union or a brief ego trip while the other person desires a long-term commitment. When the more committed partner expresses dismay at the incongruity of their motives and feelings for one another, the more casual partner may begin to feel guilty and attempt to make a commitment as a way of ameliorating the situation. This kind of commitment borne of guilt, responsibility, and a desire for atonement may seem noble and self-sacrificing on the one hand, but it can be hollow and passionless on the other. Without the spontaneous gestures of affection and kindness that naturally accompany genuine warmth and caring, the recipient of such duty-driven devotion frequently winds up feeling superficially loved and of minor importance to the partner.

Couple differences in romantic motivation typically become manifested when the topic of long-term commitment or marriage arises; at this point in the relationship, one member of the dyad may be eager to move forward

and make a deeper commitment, while the other member is hesitant and ambivalent. In the following example, John's ambivalence illustrates how guilt
can become confused with love and bring the momentum of the relationship
to a screeching halt.

John was recovering from the breakup of a long-term romantic relationship
when he met Amy, who adored him from the start. Amy's devotion helped to
alleviate the emotional pain and self-doubt John had been experiencing ever
since his steady girlfriend of three years abruptly walked out on him six months
earlier. John enjoyed Amy's company and was grateful for her validation at a
time when he was especially vulnerable, but he didn't feel "in love" with her.
Over time, however, his guilt at using Amy to soothe his wounded ego in the
face of her deep affection for him began to concern him, and he started to
confuse the amalgam of feelings he had for her with love. It was only when
Amy started to pressure John into making a marriage commitment that he
became more fully aware that gratitude and guilt were the primary components of his feelings for her. Whereas this kind of common relationship crisis
can serve to move the relationship to a new footing if one or both partners
discover hitherto unrecognized, positive feelings for the other, but in John
and Amy's case the relationship ended because of John's inability to move
forward.

Adult children of divorce are often guilt-ridden, especially when they were
blamed or took on responsibility for their parents' disagreements and turmoil.
Along with a pseudo-mature façade, these children often maintain a strong
desire to be in control, even when it means taking on blame unfairly rather
than feeling helpless and vulnerable. In one study[16] it was shown that adult
children of divorce had more problems with control and submission, that is,
they were over-controlling and had more difficulty in submitting to authority, than their counterparts from intact families. As adults, adult children of
divorce often feel overly responsible for interpersonal conflicts with family and
friends, and are quick to misinterpret their own upset in the face of conflict
as a sign of caring rather than guilt. Thus, because of the contradictions they
experienced with these feelings and conditions in their families of origin, they
are especially apt to confuse obligation and guilt with love.

OTHER CONFOUNDING FACTORS

Besides emotional needs and familial role behaviors, the state of being "in
love" is profoundly influenced by other variables, such as psychological vulnerability, self-esteem (particularly around lovability), and mastery motivation
(the latter topic is covered in Chapter 3), which affect love's timing, intensity,

and object choice. While self-esteem and mastery motivation relate more to object choice, psychological vulnerability is the timing and intensity factor that provides emotional energy or fuel to the chase. For example, when a person is feeling particularly lonely, depressed, depleted, and/or anxious, the stage is set for passion to develop.

A classical study[17] demonstrated dramatically how fear magnifies interpersonal attraction (e.g. walking across a shaky, unstable bridge intensified the appeal of the person on the other side), while other investigators have shown how physiological arousal in general enhances sexual responsiveness.[18] Whether people have difficulty in distinguishing one kind of arousal from another or whether there is a fusion of other emotional states with sexual arousal is not clear, but any overwhelming emotional experience can intensify romantic feelings and lead to mistaken judgments regarding choice of partners. As psychologist Arthur Aron[19] has noted with respect to people who meet and fall in love during crises: "It's not that we fall in love with such people because they're immensely attractive," he says, "It's that they seem immensely attractive because we've fallen in love with them."

In addition, when people meet and date under the regular influence of drugs or alcohol, they are likely to be inaccurate about the source of their romantic feelings. The positive feelings during the dating experience may be due to drug effects and not the unique interpersonal pleasures of the person involved. In other words, being high on drugs, alcohol, or adrenaline can lead to poor decision making with respect to romantic love.

A related phenomenon that contributes to the confusion among emotional states is called "misattribution of arousal" and has been documented repeatedly by social psychologists. In a number of experiments[20] it has been demonstrated that the arousal attributed to *love* might actually be physical arousal—such as a pounding heart from exercise or caffeine—rather than attraction per se. In addition, the experienced emotion might represent feelings from the past, unfulfilled needs, and/or self-esteem deficits. When it comes to interpersonal attraction and *love*, it is often difficult to discern the sources of such intense feeling.

In clinical interviews at a university counseling center conducted by the author, an extreme group of love-tormented individuals—stalkers—described their own depression or psychological upheaval that was occurring at the time they began to fixate on a particular person. Ordinarily in stalking cases, the turmoil and fixation relate to rejection by an ex-lover, but in other less common instances, the object of such intense passion is a casual acquaintance that becomes transformed into an angel of mercy or harbinger of salvation by the vulnerability of the stalker.

In the throes of depression and acute panic brought on by being away from his divorced mother and siblings for the first time, one college freshman stalker reported the first sighting of "the love of his life." Through a glass partition in the library, he saw a seated young woman dressed all in white, who was deeply engrossed in her studies. According to him, she looked like "an angel" and as he imagined their romantic possibilities together, his heart began to beat rapidly. Unfortunately, she wasn't interested in him, a reality that initially fanned his flames of passion and stalking behavior until he was summoned by the Dean of Students and threatened with expulsion if he didn't stop following her around. At that point, he left school and pursued psychiatric treatment in his hometown.

Psychological vulnerability in reasonably intact individuals is likely to oc-cur after severe losses, including rejection by a significant friend or lover, or important failures such as school or job dismissals. After such traumatic occurrences there is a high probability of becoming attached to the next avail-able person who shows promise of becoming a caretaker or has the capabil-ity of eliciting laughter. Emotionally fueled by disappointment or loss, such rebound romances have little regard for the objective characteristics of the participants, and therefore are likely to fail. Adult children of divorce who have been exposed to losses of all kinds (loss of a parent, home, friends, so-cioeconomic level, etc.) during their childhoods and/or adolescent years and sensitized to loss as a result are especially vulnerable to these occurrences in adulthood.

If all other emotional factors are of minimal significance, self-esteem tends to be a significant determinant of object choice. People tend to seek out partners at their own self-esteem level, provided they don't have strong emotional needs or role behaviors in other areas, and psychological vulnerability is not an issue at the time. Several investigators[21] have reported that children of divorce have lower self-esteem than children from intact families. In Marquardt's national survey[22] of over 1,500 adults between ages eighteen and thirty-five, half of whom were from divorced families and the other half from intact families, the adults from divorced families reported that they were alone a lot (53% versus 14% from intact families), did not feel emotionally safe as children (28% versus 6%), and felt their family life was stressful (64% versus 25%). In addition, adult children of divorce perceived their families as more emotionally distant and disorganized than children from intact families.[23] In other words, adults from divorced families are more likely to have been lonely, stressed, and emotionally vulnerable as children—all of which have a negative impact upon self-esteem. If they then seek out partners with equally low self-esteem, the stage is set for marital hardship and conflict.

Another factor that relates to adult romantic relationships is attachment style, that is, the kind of attachment one had with primary caregivers tends to influence the kind of romantic relationships one forms and maintains. Hazan and Shaver[24] identified three different attachment types: *secure* (representing 56% of the American population and characterized by happy, friendly, and trusting romantic relationships), *avoidant* (representing 24% and marked by lack of trust, fear of intimacy, emotional volatility, and jealously in their re-lationships), and *anxious/ambivalent* (representing 20% and characterized by extreme sexual attraction, obsession with love, strong desire for union with the loved one, as well as emotional volatility and jealousy). Following the ini-tial work on attachment style, Bartholomew and Horowitz broke down the avoidant category[25] into two subtypes—the fearful avoidant (those who adopt an avoidant orientation to prevent being hurt or rejected by partners), and the dismissing avoidant (those who adopt an avoidant orientation in order to maintain a defensive sense of self-reliance and independence).

In their studies, Hazan and Shaver did not find that parental divorce per se was related to attachment style, but quality of parental relationships with their children and with each other was related to attachment style. In other words, secure subjects, in comparison with insecure ones, reported warmer relation-ships with both parents and between their two parents. Avoidant subjects, in comparison with anxious/ambivalent subjects, described their mothers as cold and rejecting, while the anxious/ambivalent subjects saw their fathers as unfair. Thus, when parental divorce impacts negatively the quality of parent-child relationships, which it frequently does, their children's attachment styles become more insecure than secure.

In summary, some of the factors accounting for the romantic confusion of adults from divorced families relative to their counterparts from intact homes, appear to be need for completion and validation, psychological vulnerability and lowered self-esteem, loneliness, a sense of guilt for interpersonal conflict in intropunitive individuals, rigid familial roles (e.g., pseudo-mature caretakers), a tendency to have an insecure attachment style when their parental relation-ships are flawed, and unhealthy partner choice. The selection of romantic partners on the basis of similar vulnerabilities, self-esteem, and/or mastery motivation is likely to perpetuate the intergenerational cycle of marital un-happiness followed by divorce.

CHAPTER 3

Love's Poor Choices

One of the most baffling phenomena in love is the heartbreaking love affair that keeps being repeated over and over again. The endless repetitions may be with the same partner, or, more commonly, with psychological clones of the original heartbreaker. One adult child of divorce pursued and then left his second wife, Margaret, fifteen times (within that number are two marriages and two divorces) before she finally got tired of the pattern and left him permanently. Each time he was with her, he would settle down for six weeks or so before the urge to return to his first wife would overwhelm him. After being with his first wife for several weeks, Margaret would gradually reemerge in his consciousness as "the love of his life." He would return to pursue her with dramatic intensity, an example of which was his purchase of advertising space on a large city billboard on which he had printed "I love you, Margaret." A victim of a classical approach-avoidance conflict (where the positive or approach characteristics of a person or situation are much greater at a distance—while the opposite is true at close), he gradually learned in counseling to integrate his positive and negative feelings for Margaret into a realistic image—which was decidedly less idealistic than his fantasy—rather than continuing to shift back and forth between two opposite perceptions.

THE REPETITION OF THE PAST

In most maladaptive love choices, a failure of integration and family psychodynamics from childhood are in play. The competent woman who falls in love repeatedly with distant, unavailable men, and the successful man who is attracted to needy, low self-esteem women are repeating old issues. Likewise, the self-sacrificing woman who goes from one alcoholic partner to another, and the battered wife who keeps taking back her abusive husband are playing out dramas that originated in their nuclear families.

The tapes from the past keep getting replayed because the old familial issues they relate to have not been resolved. The battered woman who was abused in her family-of-origin, for example, is conflicted—on the one hand, she expects abuse from those she loves, and on the other hand, she keeps hoping that her lover will not betray and humiliate her once again. Even though the abusive behavior has been going on for years, she holds onto the dream that her love story will have a better ending. It is this hope for a better tomorrow that accounts for her genuine dismay when the abusive pattern is repeated once again. It's as if she's saying, "I can't believe you did this again, when I so hoped and prayed that this time around would be different."

Generally, this hope for a better ending to old family dramas is part of mastery motivation, that is, the desire to conquer, rework, and improve upon unresolved issues from the past. In psychoanalysis, "repetition compulsion" is the term that refers to the tendency to repeat earlier experiences or actions in an unconscious effort to achieve belated mastery over them.[1] By encountering anew the version of the original disappointment, the optimistic lover is attempting to gain control of an earlier, highly upsetting, or deeply confusing situation and replay it with a happier or clearer ending. Unfortunately, such profound hope—similar to magical thinking—operates like rose-colored glasses in maximizing the positive aspects and minimizing the negative or dark sides of reality.

One woman whose alcoholic husband had been drinking excessively for five years acknowledged years of disappointment and anger at him when she finally said, "he killed my dream." The dream of having a loving, intact family had sustained her throughout his abusive drinking years to such a degree that she couldn't see clearly the interpersonal damage wrought by his drinking. Having a close, loving family, in contrast to the tension-filled and loveless family of her childhood, was the dream that sustained her during the darkest hours of her marriage.

The hope for a new, positive ending to the same melodrama underlies the persistence of many unhappy romances. The man who keeps finding self-centered, unloving women who are unable or unwilling to give him much attention or emotional support is often genuinely perplexed by his "poor luck." What he does not understand is that he's drawn like a magnet to these women because of their similarity to an important, but unavailable, maternal figure in his early life. The quality that attracts him consciously is an appealing trait, like creativity, intelligence, or vivacity, but it is the constellation of their other personality traits (e.g., emotional unavailability, narcissism) that magnifies the appeal. It is the pot of gold precariously perched at the edge of a steep cliff that appeals to him, not just the gold per se. A pot of gold sitting safely within an arm's length would be diminished by its availability; for what he is really after is the opportunity to rewrite the original tragedy with a happy ending. He wants to believe that cold and self-centered women with sparkling wit and intelligence can be transformed into nurturing maternal types. Just as frogs can become princes, so witches can be subjected to metamorphosis and emerge as good mothers, or so he hopes.

Dan, a forty-five-year-old, twice-divorced, successful investment broker, was depressed over a string of unhappy romances at the time he came into counseling. His first wife lost all interest in sex after their first year of marriage, his second wife ran away when he was having financial problems, the "love of his life" had an affair with their mutual friend at the time she and Dan were living together, and all his other intervening romances ended just as badly. While such a history of romantic failures would suggest that Dan had major psychological problems or was a rogue of some sort, he was actually a very intelligent, caring, empathic, and good-looking man who devoted himself to pleasing his partners. His only apparent flaws were his excessive need to please others, a stoical denial of his own needs, and a conversational tendency to describe events in too much detail.

What was clearly amiss, however, in Dan's case was his choice of women. Like Henry Higgins, he picked young, talented ingénues who needed mentoring in the ways of the world. In addition, his choices were unusually self-absorbed women with a strong tendency to escape conflictual situations by literally running away. While Dan's romantic partners provided him with an opportunity to gain self-esteem from the role of mentor or father figure, these women did not appear to be loving, affectionate, or concerned about him. Like his own talented, but self-centered, mother who was a prominent lawyer, his choices appeared to have romantic potential on the surface, but basically lacked empathy and altruism. Prior to his mother's divorce, she distanced herself from her family by burying herself in an extramarital affair when Dan was a young teenager, leaving him to care for his younger brothers and sisters. Thus, Dan's choice of women was an attempt to win the love of women like his mother by being a giving-and-responsive caretaker. Unfortunately, narcissistic women like his mother are characterologically unable to be nurturant in intimate relationships, and as a result are disappointing romantic partners.

Mastery motivation is most likely to occur when the original source of disillusionment was an ambivalent figure, that is, someone who possessed sterling attributes in addition to highly injurious ones, or a beloved figure whose departure from the family scene was sudden or totally unexpected. In the former situation are caretakers who were admired for their professional success and renown but disliked for their critical, abusive, or distant behavior toward their children. Talented and brilliant parents can fall in this category, as can drug-dependent parents whose behavior vacillates dramatically depending upon whether they are sober or drug using at the time.

For example, alcoholic, depressed, and/or mentally ill parents are noted for glaring inconsistencies in their behavior that breed ambivalence in their children. The depressed mother, who is ordinarily kind and responsive but unavailable for days or weeks on end because of her depression, cannot be relied on nor easily understood by her young children. Similarly, the alcoholic father with dramatic mood swings and erratic behavior that varies as a function of his alcohol intake, is a source of confusion for his children. Extreme unpredictability of parental behavior and wide-ranging emotional states—extreme shifts from affectionate to angry or withdrawn behavior—tend to create the ambivalence that underlies mastery motivation. Parental consistency, even when almost totally negative, is easier for the child to resolve; in consistently negative situations, the child's option is to reject wholly the parental figure rather than struggle with seemingly irreconcilable feelings of love and hate.

When a child completely rejects a parental figure, he/she often creates an antithetical romantic ideal possessing opposite qualities to that of the rejected parent. It's as if the child emphatically decides: "I'll never become involved with or marry anyone like him." For example, when a parent was cold and rejecting, the sought-after romantic partner is often very affectionate and unconditionally accepting. Similarly, if the parent was angry, critical, and emotionally abusive, the ideal partner would be easy-going, highly tolerant, and loving. When an antithetical or opposite ideal is operating, it tends to be inflexible, that is, it requires absolute adherence, permitting little deviation. Thus, any divergence from the ideal, even normal responses such as mild annoyance or disinterest, on the part of the partner, can become the basis for disillusionment and ultimate disengagement from the relationship for the ideal's creator.

More frequently, however, strong ambivalent feelings toward a parental figure and mastery motivation are involved rather than an antithetical ideal. Carol, a twenty-seven-year-old, easy-going, nonassertive woman came into counseling trying to resolve her feelings for Dick, her live-in boyfriend of five years, whom she had recently left. Describing many incidents of being demeaned (called "stupid" or "slow"), of being controlled (strongly criticized for her friends, leisure preferences, etc.), and being betrayed (he had several affairs), she nevertheless had strong feelings of connection with him and remembered many happy moments with him throughout their dating history. Though Dick appeared to be an intelligent, energetic, and daring adventurer (he had many outdoor interests and friends) who was very much in love with Carol, he was jealous, boastful, and drank too much. Not surprisingly, Carol's physician father had a similar mixture of positive and negative qualities that included alcoholism, ambition, bravado, intelligence, and a quick temper along with a generous and playful spirit.

Carol's earliest memories of her father included one in which she was being pleasantly tickled by him but the tickling continued to the point where she felt frightened and out of control. Further reflecting anxiety about him was her memory of his scaring her and siblings by peering in through the window wearing a grotesque Halloween mask, and another particularly sad memory of her father's leaving the family for a month's stay at an alcoholism rehabilitation facility. The ambivalent fusion of affectionate admiration with anxiety created intense feelings that were difficult to resolve, and became the basis for her sexual and emotional attraction to Dick, who bore many striking similarities to her father.

In other instances, strong ambivalent feelings occur when a parent departs the family home precipitously, either through death, desertion, or divorce. The sudden loss of a parent from daily life can be incomprehensible to the child, especially if the parent was an ongoing source of comfort and care. Reconciling one's positive feelings with anger and sadness due to the loss can be a painful and time-consuming process of grieving for an adult, but for the child who lacks the necessary experiential background and cognitive abilities, it can be overwhelming. Trying to master the hitherto unmanageable jumble of feelings by repeating and gaining control of the original trauma in some form can be a lifetime goal for some children.

For the children of divorce, mastery motivation is often the primary drive behind the selection of romantic partners because of the broad range of traumas that often occur in divorced families. Not only are the most debilitating family traumas, such as alcoholism, child abuse, domestic violence, and parental mental illness, more likely to be a part of the family history in divorced as opposed to intact families, but the likelihood of less devastating familial conditions, such as emotional neglect, stress, and marital conflict, is also greater. Even in low-conflict, divorced families, the sudden departure of a beloved parent from the family scene results in feelings of betrayal and abandonment that are difficult to reconcile with loving images of the parent in question. With no preparation in the form of loud, hostile arguments and vitriolic parental exchanges, in a low-conflict family the parent's unexpected departure adds to the shock value of the leaving.[2]

When parents are unhappily married, the emotional spin-off affects everyone in the family. In an earlier publication,[3] writing specifically about the impact of alcoholism on the family (the comments are also applicable to other conditions that have widespread effects on family life), Piorkowski wrote: "One of the legacies of alcohol abuse is significant damage to the ability of family members to be intimate with others. Because parental alcohol abuse creates unpredictability and instability in the family system, nothing and no one can be trusted."

Besides the high probability of traumatic events in divorced families, mastery motivation is likely to be strong in children of divorce because of the difficulty in resolving ambivalent feelings about a nonresidential or absent parent. When a parent is not regularly a part of the child's life, there is little opportunity for a child to observe and experience the varied aspects of the parent and attempt to integrate different perceptions and feelings into a cohesive, realistic whole. In the vacuum created by an absent parent, the child is often left with unidimensional memories that become magnified over time. Distorted or idealized parental images that affect choice of romantic partners are often the result. Prime examples are the many adult women from divorced families who spend their dating years in search of a strong father figure to marry, only to find romantic partners with the same brand of immaturity that their own fathers had.

While any constellation of parental qualities can form the basis for mastery motivation, certain personality types with limited capacity for intimacy are more likely to be parental figures in family divorce dramas. These same types are then likely to reappear as romantic partners for the next generation, at least for those trying to master parental disappointments. In this way, *poor-risk intimacy partners*[4] perpetuate the intergenerational cycle of marriage and divorce.

In addition to severe psychopathological conditions, such as schizophrenia, manic depressive illness, bipolar disorder, borderline and sociopathic personality disorders, and clearly dysfunctional patterns, such as alcoholism, criminal behavior, and drug abuse, there are a number of less obvious, but common personality types in contemporary American culture that are unlikely to be stable and caring romantic partners. Such *poor-risk intimacy partners* have overwhelming emotional needs of their own, limited interpersonal or conflict resolution skills, severe emotional immaturity, and/or basic defects in altruism and empathy. Regardless of whether their personality liabilities are genetic or a function of familial exposure or damage, they tend to inflict emotional turmoil or distance upon their partners, generally creating unhappiness wherever they go. In contrast, more ideal partners calm troubled waters in family life and spread good cheer along the way. According to Firestone and Catlett,[5] who wrote

Fear of Intimacy, an emotionally healthy partner is (a) open and nondefensive, (b) honest and nonduplicitous, (c) affectionate and easy-going, (d) mentally and physically healthy, (e) independent and successful in his or her chosen career or lifestyle, and (f) aware of a meaningful existence that includes humanitarian values.

Poor-Risk Intimacy Partners vary in severity from the verbally and/or physically abusive "Blamers" at the more serious end of the scale to "Conflict Avoiders" at the opposite, more benign end. In between are "Emotional Hermits," "Immature Types, " "Narcissists," "Oppositional Types," and "Passive-Aggressive Personalities," all of whom have pronounced difficulties in navigating the complex terrain of intimacy. These seven types are not uniquely separate or distinctive from one another; rather they are overlapping categories that illustrate the different personality and/or defensive styles that can impede emotional closeness in romantic love. A particular individual may have a combination of characteristics from the different categories; for example, a conflict avoider might also be emotionally withdrawn and passive-aggressive, thus adding to the intimacy problems that are created.

BLAMERS

As the name implies, blamers seldom takes responsibility for their shortcomings, communication errors, or behavioral transgressions, and are quick to attribute the responsibility for missteps to others. If a stranger accidentally bumps into a blamer, for example, the blamer will be extrapunitive (accusatory), shouting or thinking "watch where you're going" rather than self-blaming (intropunitive): "Oh no, it was my fault" or neutral: "No problem." Likely to be domineering, defensive, and somewhat paranoid, the blamer is quick to deflect any criticism by counterattacking—"you think I'm stubborn, look at your bullheadedness," or "I'm stubborn because you're so demanding and controlling." Ever ready to put on protective armor to ensure that no critical barbs penetrate to a softer and more vulnerable core, the blamer appears invincible and self-righteous on the surface.

Because the blamer lacks a self-observing capacity—the ability to be self-analytical and self-critical—he is not likely to mature as a person. Forever fixated at an earlier developmental stage, the blamer is often isolated from others whom he does not readily trust. The blamer's excessive need for self-protection makes it difficult for him to engage easily in the reciprocity of friendships and intimate relationships.

As an intimacy partner, the blamer tends to be self-esteem damaging rather than ego enhancing to his partner. Because he displaces responsibility for relationship conflicts onto the other person, he is highly critical of his partner when conflicts arise. Thus, his partner is left bearing the total burden of accountability for their problems and, as a result, is often guilt-ridden. Furthermore, his failure to apologize for transgressions and his tendency to avoid conflictual areas of discussion can create an artificial, distant, and tense situation for both of them.

Ted, a fifty-year-old married man of low energy and passivity with strong undercurrents of resentment, didn't see anything wrong with his frequent angry and critical outbursts in the car at other drivers or his wife of twenty years for her failures, which included inattentiveness to his many demands. What was especially difficult for him, however, was handling criticisms of any sort directed at him. His wife's complaints about even minor failures, such as his lack of effort with respect to household chores, felt like assaults, to which he responded with scathing attacks against her. Even when he choked her on one occasion for shouting at him, he blamed her for precipitating the attack. His inability to take responsibility for his actions, no matter the provocation, led to his marriage failure and his further isolation from family and friends.

Blamers, like Ted, use emotional intensity to magnify their accusations. When blamers are charismatic and renowned to boot, their pronouncements reverberating with an arrogant, godlike certitude are difficult for their romantic partners to ignore. Ministers, CEOs, politicians, writers, movie stars, and other creative talents can fall in this category. Because their accomplishments give them star billing and top decision-making authority within their circles, they often lack the self-awareness and humility to acknowledge their contributions to intimacy conflicts. Rather, they often utilize the full power of their status to browbeat their partners into submission.

CONFLICT AVOIDERS

The conflict avoider is ordinarily an easygoing, passive person who avoids potentially unpleasant situations by going to inordinate lengths to appease others or by changing the subject to a safer, more neutral topic whenever a discussion begins to heat up. Because the conflict avoider fears that open conflict will escalate into chaos or dangerous warfare, he treads carefully, trying to avoid interpersonal fault lines. While conflict avoidance is characteristic of most of the poor risk types, in its purest form (uncontaminated by other dysfunctional behavior) conflict avoidance occurs in easy-going, eager-to-please personalities who are uncomfortable rocking any boats.

An extreme example of conflict avoidance out of fear of violence was an elderly woman's self-defeating strategies to avoid confronting her middle-aged, violence-prone, schizophrenic son who lived with her. Because he had a tendency to be argumentative and hostile with little provocation, she provided for all his physical needs, and never asked him to bathe, do household chores, or move his endless piles of newspapers and other belongings out of her way. Instead, she restricted her living space to the kitchen, a small hallway, and bedroom, while allowing him to take over the rest of the house. In this way, she achieved some peace of mind at the expense of her own autonomy, enjoyment, and social pleasures (for example, she couldn't entertain guests at her house because of its squalid and slovenly condition). In addition, by not providing boundaries or limits to her son, she promoted his demanding, narcissistic disregard for others and inadvertently discouraged any growth stirrings toward maturity and self-sufficiency on his part.

Often socially inhibited and hypersensitive to negative evaluation (similar to the blamer in terms of hypersensitivity but highly dissimilar in behavioral response to criticism), the conflict avoider works hard to avoid being shamed or ridiculed and tries to maintain a light and cheerful interpersonal atmosphere around him at all times. When emotionally upset, he is most likely to retreat into his turtle shell and wait for the emotional downpour to subside. While most of the qualities of a conflict avoider are likeable, and even admirable, the tendency to cope with demeaning and destructive situations by swallowing resentment often leads to depression and the erosion of positive feelings toward significant others.

Jim, a forty-four-year-old, successful auditor, came into counseling because of depression and guilt related to a four-year extramarital affair with a coworker, to whom he felt "a cosmic connection." In contrast, his eighteen-year marriage (both he and his wife were children of divorce) was described as lonely and loveless, but without acrimony. Describing facetiously the only conflict-resolution strategy he and his wife ever used in their marriage as "a cry and cave" approach (and they used it rarely)—she would cry and he would cave—Jim was proud of the fact that he and his wife never fought, just as his parents never did. Instead of trying to discuss their differences in order to reach resolution, whenever a conflict arose Jim and his wife stopped in mid-sentence and retreated into separate rooms before resuming cordial relations several days later. While he was effective professionally managing fifteen employees and had no difficulty confronting any of them when their work duties were being shirked, he couldn't tell his wife the sources of his own marital dissatisfaction.

Jim's list of complaints about his wife included inequitable distribution of housework, lack of quality time together, inattentiveness, lack of affection, and sex—a standard list in most unhappy marriages—except for the specifics of the first item. In contrast to the situation in most marriages, Jim did all of the housework, cooking, and child chauffeuring on the weekends, while his wife lay in bed reading novels. She was a schoolteacher, who was diligent about her own professional responsibilities, but totally indifferent to household and family chores. In addition, she was not interested in sex and regarded affectionate gestures disdainfully, saying "I'm not an animal; petting and pecking are not for me." While Jim and his wife were highly intelligent people, they, especially his wife, seemed unaware of how important the missing elements in their relationship were for marital satisfaction.

Ironically, Jim's marital situation was similar to that of his parents with respect to emotional distance and conflict avoidance. Describing his parents as "strangers in the house," he said they never exchanged even one angry word with one another. Predictably, they divorced when Jim was in his early teens. While he has been close to his mother throughout his life, he seldom saw his father after the divorce.

At this point in time, it is not clear whether Jim and his wife divorced (he dropped out of individual therapy and she refused to seek psychological help) but his lack of positive feelings for his wife (and vice versa) created unbearable loneliness that contributed to the intensity of his feelings for his coworker. However, his colleague was also married and felt guilty about their affair, making their future uncertain.

EMOTIONAL HERMITS

Another disappointing romantic partner, the emotional hermit, is similar to the conflict avoider in ignoring potential disagreements, but more emotionally withdrawn and more intellectual than his counterpart. More adept in the world of ideas and concepts than of feelings, emotional hermits are often very intelligent, talented scholars, bankers, engineers, lawyers, chemists, doctors, and other professionals. Frequently sought after as marriage prospects because of their financial and/or professional success, emotional hermits are skilled at hiding their emotional disability, especially during the early days of a romantic courtship when feelings are intense. In fact, during the early phase of a romance (when emotional hermits are overwhelmed by sexual and emotional longing), they may be quite sensitive and loving. While they withdraw in romantic relationships only when negative feelings begin to surface, their pronounced pattern of emotional withdrawal is evident in all their other relationships.

The common intimacy dangers (fear of abandonment, betrayal, criticism, disappointment, guilt, loss of autonomy, loss of control, and guilt) are especially hazardous for the emotional hermit because of his family background.

Either the emotional hermit grew up in an emotionally repressed household, where feelings were seldom talked about or manifested, or in a volatile family, where emotions flared up intensely and unpredictably. In the first situation, the emotional hermit had little experience with intense emotions, and learned to fear strong feelings because of their alien quality. In the second scenario, intense emotion did lead to dangerous outcomes in the family, so the development of protective armor became essential to survival.

Harry, a sixty-year-old CEO of a commercial real estate firm, and Sue, his fifty-eight-year-old lawyer wife came into couples counseling because they were ambivalent about continuing their twenty-eight-year marriage. Harry had been having a clandestine sexual affair with an out-of-town colleague for five years, and when Sue found out about it, she was devastated. When Harry finally ended the affair because his lover was cheating on him, he and Sue decided to try and improve their marriage. Sue's chief complaint about Harry was his emotional coldness, which extended into all aspects of their relationship, from sex to conversation (a complaint also made by his girlfriend, although Harry experienced more emotional excitement—"more bells and whistles"—in his relationship with her).

Harry's major criticism of Sue was her sarcastic and controlling manner, which he experienced as belittling and demanding. However, rather than confronting her about her behavior when he was upset, he withdrew for days on end into an icy demeanor that limited conversation to perfunctory comments about the weather. Unable to deal openly with his resentment at Sue's barbed retorts or perceived attempts to control him, withdrawal was his main strategy, which kept Sue anxious and uncertain about what was on his mind. In the wake of his affair, Sue felt she couldn't trust him, especially when he was silent, and pleaded with him to talk to her about his thoughts and feelings. However, in the power struggle between them, Harry had trouble giving up his only weapon—the weapon of silence—that effectively rendered her powerless. Fortunately, over time they were able to make significant shifts in their emotional responsiveness to one another to create a viable and more rewarding marriage.

IMMATURE TYPES

Immature personalities come in all shapes and sizes, from Peter Pan and Cinderella on the romantic, fairy tale side of the coin to Don Juan and Jezebel on the more dramatic, adventuresome side. Variations on this theme are young men in their thirties still searching for their first careers and young women inordinately attached to their depressed and/or tyrannical mothers and fearful of leaving them emotionally. In the American culture, if a young man or woman has not sorted out his/her adult identity by the time the thirtieth birthday is reached, the likelihood of ever-reaching maturity begins to diminish.

The Peter Pan–Cinderella types are essentially young men and women who are fixated at earlier developmental stages. Hoping to meet either strong maternal types (in the case of Peter Pan) or Prince Charming (for Cinderella), they are looking for someone to take over adult responsibilities for them. Basically interested in play, pleasure, and same-sex activities, such as sporting events, Peter Pans spend hours playing cards, hanging around the corner, or drinking with the boys. They may dabble at a variety of short-lived jobs, but do not pursue serious employment with any regularity. In addition, they are usually disorganized, messy, and indifferent to household cleanliness as well as other domestic chores.

Another variation of the Peter Pan syndrome is the "undiscovered genius," who believes that his hitherto undiscovered talents will be found, and that soon thereafter he will be headed for stardom. As a result of his belief in future stardom, he is disdainful of the mundane details of earning a living and cavalier about leaving this responsibility to his typically hard-working wife or live-in partner. One young, thirty-four-year-old man with a beautiful singing voice (according to his family and romantic partner) worked erratically as a waiter while hoping to be discovered as a singer. What made his behavior disconcerting to his partner, however, was the reality that he was not proactive in pursuing a singing career, for instance, he did not take singing lessons, audition for parts, and/or contact theatrical or musical agents. Since the early days of college when he had starred in several college musicals, he had essentially left his dream of being a singing star up to fate, chance, or destiny. In addition, he was slovenly around the house and generally irresponsible with respect to paying bills, filling up the car with gas, and other household chores. While generally loving to his partner, his manner of handling adult responsibilities was highly immature for an intelligent, educated man of his age and created significant financial and emotional hardships for his partner.

Cinderella, a more culturally acceptable version of immaturity for women, essentially waits for a rescuer to deliver her from her unhappy home or tedious, unfulfilling job. A passive and dependent woman, Cinderella has not developed self-initiative nor learned to rely on her own resources in solving life problems. Instead, she has invested a significant amount of psychological energy in the fantasy of romantic love and its transformative power. Once Prince Charming arrives, she believes her life will be dramatically different— she will live some version of "and they lived happily ever after." She will be protected, cherished, and provided for through no effort of her own. And if she is beautiful, her fantasy will be reinforced by the real-life Cinderellas who do meet sugar daddies to take care of them. However, for men who are interested in more than caretaking, Cinderellas with their limited resources are likely to lose their appeal over time.

Don Juan–Jezebel immature types are fundamentally untrustworthy because of their inability to commit to a single partner. Since they derive excitement and validation from conquests, once they're secure about a partner's involvement with them, they lose interest and are ready to move on. The process of collecting trophies or notches on their belts is the emotionally gratifying part of intimacy and not the relationship per se. Because emotional closeness resulted in traumatic betrayal and/or abandonment in the past, ongoing intimacy is an unreliable phenomenon for them. So, they sample intimacy for brief periods before becoming restless and eager to explore new territory with brand new partners.

NARCISSISTS

The narcissist, by definition, exhibits a pervasive pattern of grandiosity, an excessive need for admiration, and lack of empathy.[6] Aside from these qualities, the narcissist believes that he or she is "special," has an exaggerated sense of entitlement, that is, unreasonable expectations of special treatment or privilege, and appears haughty, boastful, and arrogant. Because narcissists lack the ability to recognize or identify with the feelings of others, they are markedly insensitive, callous to others, and interpersonally exploitative. As long as the conversation or interaction revolves around their perceptions, needs, and/or self-proclaimed accomplishments, they are content. But when the focus of attention shifts to another person or topic, they become distracted, envious, and/or unhappy. A fifty-five-year-old former model interrupted a philosophy professor's discussion of "Existentialism" with what she believed was a fitting segue, "speaking of existentialism, modeling is similar," before launching into a lengthy and rambling account about her own experiences as a model. Although a highly intelligent woman, her narcissism clouded her judgment about what was appropriate in many interpersonal situations.

By virtue of their exaggerated need for admiration and attention, narcissists frequently occupy center stage in the arts, drama, and music, where they successfully garner the applause they so desperately seek. While they may be superstars professionally because of their talents, their insensitivity to others, lack of observing ego, and sense of entitlement result in a demanding, emotionally labile interpersonal style that is difficult for others to appreciate. Typically egocentric and inattentive to others, narcissistic individuals take up most of the psychological space in a romantic relationship, leaving the partner in the role of adoring audience or disgruntled lackey. As a result, their romantic partners do not feel cared about or valued in the relationship, but rather feel used to gratify the narcissist's whims. In addition, because narcissists respond to most criticism with rage, their partners wind up feeling helpless about how to voice their concerns and be heard.

OPPOSITIONAL TYPES

Oppositional types have an inordinate need to be in control and manage to do so by contradiction, correction, and humor. Typically responding to another's comments by critical adjustments—"No, it wasn't Thursday, it was Wednesday night," or "the party was on Christmas Eve, not Christmas Day"— oppositional types believe these minor corrections to an anecdote are critical. Their belief in accuracy or precision of expression is so extreme that they feel compelled to correct even trivial discrepancies from their pristine version of truth.

Paradoxically, while carping is one of their interpersonal weapons, humor is another. Often adept at comic relief in the form of puns, oppositional types use humor to disarm and distract their intimate partners from serious concerns. Like their counterparts in medieval times—court jesters—they are skilled at shifting the focus from conflict to lighter and more amusing concerns. Because the focus on potential conflict is too threatening, modern-day court jesters, or oppositional types, move rapidly to humor whenever a moment of potential disagreement appears on the scene. By turning a serious moment into laughter, they take the upper hand and seize control. Because the change in emotional ambience may be confusing to the partner, especially when the partner had a serious relationship complaint in mind, he/she may begin to doubt the validity of the concern.

Often growing up in families where conflict was swept under the rug only to explode later in an unpredictable fashion, oppositional types learned to put on a happy face in the midst of underground family tension. However, while hoping that laughter would be the best medicine in reducing conflict, they came to believe that interpersonal disagreements were impossible to resolve, and that the best strategy was to maintain control at all costs. To this end, they avoid interpersonal contact when possible (often being loners), create distance by nitpicking, and use humor—most notably puns—to disarm perceived opponents and reduce the tension between them. For their romantic partners, intimacy, though interspersed with humor, is often discordant and argumentative. In addition, areas of disagreement tend to be chronic because of the difficulty oppositional types have in resolving problems.

THE PASSIVE-AGGRESSIVE PERSONALITY

Similar to the conflict avoider and the emotional hermit in sidestepping controversial issues is the passive-aggressive personality. Unable to express openly disappointment, frustration, or anger, the passive-aggressive person acts out his feelings indirectly by seemingly insignificant transgressions, such as forgetfulness, procrastination, or tardiness. While not all such behavior is passive-aggressive (some may be due to stress, distractibility, and/or depression), a chronic pattern involving these subtle, but irritating, lapses bespeaks of underlying hostility.

Repeated forgetfulness about chores, for example, is often a rebellious reaction to the partner's demands for compliance. Like the teenager who resents being treated as a child and rebels at parental authority, the passive-aggressive person is communicating by his actions, "You can't make me do anything. And furthermore, the more you insist, the less I'll do." According to psychologist, Scott Wetzler,[7] who wrote *Living with the Passive-Aggressive Man*, in addition to the above-mentioned qualities, passive-aggressive men are characterized by ambiguity, lying, sulking, fostering chaos, and fears of intimacy.

Because the style is deceptive, passive-aggressive individuals are difficult to deal with. The partner's dilemma is how to be reasonable about minor lapses, maintain control of the fury that gets aroused by repeated provocation, and yet confront the irritating behavior. No matter how serene, tranquil, or wise a partner may be, a string of broken promises can be exasperating and immobilizing. Very often, after swallowing years of resentment the partner winds up helpless and depressed because of the intransigent nature of the other's behavior. Frequently, the final stage to the marriage or live-in arrangement is the partner's emotional withdrawal from the relationship itself. After years of frustration have taken their toll, the road to divorce begins to appear less catastrophic and more promising than the years of struggle with an elusive enemy.

With these *poor-risk intimacy partners*, the dangers to a romantic partnership are varied, covering the gamut from emotional distance to partner abuse. Overt marital conflict, or marital discord, is most common in intimate relationships with action-oriented blamers, narcissists, and oppositional characters—while emotional distance is the most likely outcome with more behaviorally inhibited personalities—such as conflict avoiders, emotional hermits, and passive-aggressive types. As for unions with immature individuals, the out-come will depend on the type of immaturity displayed and on how disturbing or disruptive the maladaptive behavior is to the partner. Amato and Booth[8] found that overt marital discord was negatively related to their children's mar-ital harmony, and that the parental behaviors, most likely to predict problem-atic marriages among offspring, included jealousy, being domineering, getting angry easily, being critical, moody, and not talking to the spouse.

In all these situations, the partner's maturity and particular coping strategy in dealing with the dysfunctional behavior of their mate will affect the degree of overt conflict and the overall degree of relationship satisfaction. In addition, whether a particular "poor risk" relationship will lead to divorce or not is a function of a number of other factors. Among these variables are the attractive-ness, or rewards of the relationship, the barriers against divorce (e.g., religion, economic considerations), and the attractiveness of other alternatives, such as being single.[9] Thus, while an intimate relationship with a *poor-risk* partner may not necessarily lead to divorce, the chances of it being a growth-inducing and satisfying relationship are small.

CHAPTER 4

The Fears and Risks of Love

Love may be "a many-splendored thing," but the experience of emotional and physical intimacy can be dangerous in significant ways. Referring to the paradox of *love*, the Mills Brothers[1] long ago sang: "You always hurt the ones you love, the ones you shouldn't hurt at all." Because emotional intimacy involves a lowering of defenses and exposing the vulnerable parts of the self, the likelihood of being hurt in intimacy is far greater than in solitude. And for the adult children of unhappy marriages who witnessed intense emotional pain in one or both parents and experienced hurt and disappointment themselves, the dangers of romantic love are all too apparent.

In her study of the adult children of divorce, Wallerstein[2] wrote: "Anxiety about relationships was at the bedrock of their personalities and endured even in very happy marriages. Their fears of disaster and sudden loss rose when they felt content. And their fear of abandonment, betrayal, and rejection mounted when they found themselves having to disagree with someone they loved." And later Wallerstein said: "But no matter what their success in the world, they retain some serious residues—fear of loss, fear of change, and fear that disaster will strike—especially when things are going well."

Where does all this anxiety come from? Fears typically occur in response to (a) real-life events that caused psychic pain or injury, (b) threatening experiences that implied danger, and (c) objects or persons that bear a symbolic or transformed similarity to the original traumatizing source. At its most obvious level, if one grew up in a physically or verbally abusive household, the likelihood is high that one would be fearful of being abused again in a romantic relationship. No matter how different from the abusing figure a partner might appear, the psychological similarity, that is, an emotionally close relationship, often reawakens anxieties that were spawned in the nuclear family. People tend to fear the reoccurrence of those dangers that they witnessed or experienced. And for adults who grew up in dangerous and/or severely dysfunctional families, anxieties about romantic love can be debilitating.

What then is dangerous about love besides the obvious risks of abuse and abandonment? Among the many subtle and frightening aspects of closeness are betrayal, criticism, disappointment, guilt, humiliation, loss of autonomy, loss of control, rejection, and shame—discussed by Piorkowski in *Too Close For Comfort: Exploring the Risks of Intimacy*.[3] Earlier, Hatfield[4] had discussed similar dangers (exposure, abandonment, angry attacks, one's own destructive impulses, loss of control, and loss of one's individuality) as dimensions of "the dark side of love."

It is clear that when people get close to another person, or even think about getting close, they often fear that they will be betrayed by having their vulnerabilities revealed to others and/or used against them in some way. They may fear that they will be drained or suffocated by the demands of another and have no time to themselves. They may fear being used for sex when what they are looking for is love. But mostly they fear entering into a romantic relationship wholeheartedly, and having the rug pulled out from under them by rejection. According to one survey,[5] most Americans (56%) have had a very troublesome relationship in the last five years, so the feared dangers of intimacy are not imaginary. Although the fears may be exaggerated and inaccurate in new situations, they are usually based on some aspects of reality in childhood, adolescence, or early adulthood.

Fear of intimacy has been defined in the psychological literature in a number of ways. Descutner and Thelen[6] defined fear of intimacy as an inhibited capacity to share thoughts and feelings of personal significance with another highly valued individual, and as such, it appears to be related to fears of exposure and betrayal. A thirty-five-item self-report measure, called the Fear of Intimacy Scale (FIS), was developed by them to measure three components of the fear—content (the communication of personal information), emotional valence (strong feelings about the information being exchanged), and vulnerability (high regard for the individual receiving the information). Similar to the fearful attachment style, described as a desire for social contact inhibited by fears of loss or rejection by Bartholemew,[7] the FIS scale has been used in a number of studies.

For example, dating couples share the same level of fear of intimacy on the FIS, that is, low-fear individuals tend to gravitate to low-fear partners and vice versa.[8] In addition, women at the high end of the scale had shorter-lived relationships than those at the low end. Not surprisingly, men had higher fear of intimacy scores than women, and adult children of divorce feared intimacy more than adult children from intact families.[9] In another study,[10] lack of perceived fatherly affirmation was associated with low self-esteem for women and high levels of fear of intimacy. Also, fear of intimacy has been positively correlated with family conflict per se,[11] and in divorce situations it is associated with both pre- and post-divorce levels.[12]

Another interesting finding related to fear of intimacy is that it tends to be associated more clearly with shame-proneness, a more general, pre-Oedipal feeling of inadequacy, than guilt-proneness, a negative self-evaluation related to specific transgressions.[13] Shame-proneness entails a sense of deep humiliation for perceived inadequacies, whereas guilt-proneness, which occurs later developmentally—in the Oedipal phase—involves a sense of badness for behavior deemed inappropriate in some way.

According to Firestone and Catlett,[14] fear of intimacy is something more fundamental to personality. For them, fear of intimacy is a powerful psychological defense or internal voice that acts as a barrier to closeness. Formed in childhood and based on the internalization of parents' destructive attitudes and defenses, this internal perspective fosters negative distortions of the self and others that interfere with intimacy. This negative voice predisposes individuals to suspiciousness, defensiveness, distancing behaviors, and compulsive habits, all of which detract from closeness in romantic love.

Regardless of the definition, fears of intimacy are universal but vary substantially in terms of specifics and intensity. Physical violence, for example, which traumatizes approximately six million women beaten in their homes each year in the United States,[15] affects not only the actual victims but the family onlookers as well. Often intensely angered and upset by the sight of their mothers being beaten, adolescent boys frequently attempt to intervene in family disputes and end up injured, killed, or psychologically damaged themselves. Unbelievably, over 60 percent of young men incarcerated for homicide had killed their mothers' abusers.

The factors that contribute and/or relate to fears of intimacy are manifold, ranging from the mundane and universal, such as fears of disappointment, criticism, and rejection, to the catastrophic, that is, fears of physical abuse, death, and desertion. With adult children of divorce, who are more likely to have witnessed family tragedies than adults from intact families, fears of intimacy are widespread and run the gamut from commonplace concerns to more calamitous anxieties.

RISKS OF EXPOSURE, SHAME, AND HUMILIATION

The risk of exposing one's self and then being humiliated as a result is one of the common dangers of romantic love. Revealing one's worst failings to another person in utmost confidence, only to have it thrown back in one's face months or years later, "Yes, you really are cowardly or crazy or self-centered," is a significant breach of trust that confirms one's worst fears. Similarly, sharing one's whimsical or deep-seated desires with another person in a moment of closeness, only to be made fun of, results in a feeling of shame and exposure that further erodes trust and intimacy.

Ordinarily one's deep-seated inadequacies are hidden behind a veneer of competence that is designed to protect self-esteem and avoid humiliation, but in emotional intimacy where self-disclosure is the vehicle for promoting closeness, the risk of exposure is great. The imperfections and vulnerabilities that people fear exposing are physical/genital as well as psychological features, ranging from fears of being seen as too fat, too thin, too amply, or insufficiently endowed at the physical end of the continuum to anxieties about being viewed as too boring, lackluster, too angry, or too needy personality-wise.

Sometimes the inadequacy concerns revolve around the fear that something vital and necessary to a relationship is lacking in oneself. As Piorkowski[16] wrote regarding the feared missing piece: "the missing piece may be viewed as deep and central: 'The core of me is empty;' 'I'm incapable of love;' 'I'm just basically unlovable;' or 'She'll find out that underneath all of that tinsel is more tinsel—I'm a phony.';" Sometimes the fear is that some important quality, like conversational skill, assertiveness, or creativity, is lacking in one's self, as noted in the complaint "I'm just too ordinary—there's nothing exciting about me."

Children who grew up in unhappy households, where intimacy and trust were in short supply, often have unresolved inadequacy concerns that loom as major stumbling blocks to their attainment of romantic love. In unhappy marriages, the chances of a parent relating to his or her children in a sensitive and loving manner are diminished by the parent's own marital dissatisfaction and/or depression. Likely to be critical and/or withdrawn, unhappy parents, while often well meaning, have difficulty being consistently affectionate and supportive. In an Oprah Winfrey Special on Adult Children of Divorce,[17] a thirty-eight-year-old woman talked about her unresolved anger at her mother, who was extremely bitter and depressed after her husband left the family over twenty-five years earlier. On the show, the young woman said to her mother: "You shut us (the children) out because he shut you out. You should have loved us. We were still there."

As a result of a parent's withdrawal, children of unhappy marriages, especially those from divorced families, frequently feel unloved and are most disappointed with their paternal relationships.[18] They tend to feel less loved and less heard by both parents (in contrast to those from intact families) but particularly by fathers. In addition, because children of divorce saw their parents' marital relationship fall apart, often in humiliating ways, their fears of being demeaned in their own love relationships are strong. Therefore, they avoid the chance of being humiliated by staying away from romantic relationships altogether or by settling for superficial ones with little risk.

Betty, a forty-four-year-old, attractive, petite, professionally competent woman, came into counseling after a weekend romantic encounter ended abruptly. An adult child of divorce, Betty was devastated when her weekend Romeo told her at the end of the weekend that he was interested only in friendship, not romance, in spite of a long telephone courtship and a summer flirtation that seemed to promise otherwise. While understandably upset by the rejection, Betty was convinced that she was overweight and that her "fat body" was the cause of the breakup—a conclusion that had no basis in the objective reality of her appearance nor in any of her suitor's comments. Nevertheless, she felt humiliated and shamed by the devastating turn of events, and at the time of her first appointment for counseling, appeared headed for a serious depression, much like the one that had consumed her mother throughout Betty's childhood.

The noteworthy aspects about Betty's history were the severity of her mother's chronic depressive illness that necessitated several hospitalizations during Betty's adolescence, and the paucity of dating experiences in Betty's life. Even though she was clearly heterosexual and highly attractive, she had dated less than a handful of men, each of them for only a brief period of time. She was highly uncomfortable with both men and women—essentially because she saw them as potentially critical of her physical and emotional qualities, especially her "fat" appearance. In general, she preferred the company of her two sisters—who were a mixed source of social availability and criticality—rather than attempt other relationships. Her avoidance strategy, which was related to her fear of being shamed and humiliated, was pronounced, but fortunately, diminished as a function of counseling.

FEAR OF LOSING AUTONOMY

Another common fear in romantic love is the dread of losing one's autonomy, that is, losing one's integrity and/or independence. Fear of losing autonomy, or loss of self, tends to occur in relationships where one person, usually the dominant or powerful one, emotionally suffocates or engulfs the other. In families, it is most likely to occur in overly enmeshed families, where the privacy and boundaries of children are often violated, rather than in emotionally distant ones.

In both situations—romantic unions of unequal power or in enmeshed families—the more acquiescent partner (or child) tends to silence himself or herself in order to please the other and be liked. This silencing of the self, which entails suppressing one's own thoughts, feelings, and desires, occurs because disrupting the status quo of the relationship is perceived to be a precursor to its ultimate demise. The abused wife keeps quiet because she fears being beaten again if she speaks her mind; the henpecked husband bites his tongue because he fears losing yet another acrimonious battle; the submissive partner maintains a deferential stance in order to avoid criticism and conflict, all of which are seen as necessary to avoid abandonment and loss.

The fear of losing autonomy can occur if the partner demands so much time, energy, and closeness that little time or energy is left over for the self. All of the power and decision making in the relationship seem to belong to the other person by virtue of the other's louder and more insistent voice. Decisions about social activities, money, interpersonal contact, and recreational pursuits are made by the more dominant partner, leaving the more passive partner feeling unheard and ignored. In these situations, where one partner is highly dominant, requests for affection, handholding, and even sex can feel like infringements upon one's space by the more submissive partner. The phrase "I need more space" communicates loudly and clearly the speaker's sense of being suffocated and in need of fresh air emotionally, which usually translates into time alone to replenish one's resources.

Demands for time and attention also occur when one's partner is especially "needy," that is, regularly calling out for assistance because of his/her helplessness and inadequacy concerns. In this situation, the responsibility of being loving, caring, and attentive to an insecure spouse or partner can be burdensome. Trying to please an insatiable or high-maintenance partner drains legitimate energy from the self and results in a depleted sense of autonomy, especially for more introverted individuals who require time alone to solidify the sense of self—time to think through desires, thoughts, feelings, plans, as well as the day's events—in order to feel complete.

In the most extreme variation of this fear—namely the fear of merging—one is anxious that the boundaries between self and other will become blurred, leading to confusion about where a feeling or idea is coming from. One woman, an identical twin with strong fears about both abandonment and suffocation in intimacy, emerged from a state of panic about too much closeness with her husband, saying: "Things were distant but healthier between the two of them—they were less entangled." In one study[19] it was shown that adult children of divorce had more difficulty than others in maintaining a separate sense of self, or independence, without withdrawing from significant others.

In violent families, the likelihood of setting off a nuclear verbal or physical explosion by mild self-expression is so high that these children typically adopt false acquiescent manners to stave off the threat. Unable to express disappointment, vulnerability, or anger because of the threat of assault, the children in a violent family believe that the only safe manner of navigating one's interpersonal world is by good behavior, that is, by maintaining a smiling, obedient self. As adults, these children of violence fear not only violence itself in romantic love, but the loss of self that can occur as a means of preventing such assaults. The pseudo-mature roles[20] (hero or responsible one) adopted by children in alcoholic families are attempts to ward off dangerous parental behavior by extreme compliance.

The fear of losing autonomy is especially strong for men throughout the developmental cycle in Western culture (except for old age when the sex difference tends to be reversed), because self-reliance and competence are central components of the male self-image. Thus, emotional intimacy with women is often experienced as child-like and potentially regressive. For men who grew up in unhappy households where the father was dependent or emotionally abused in the marriage, the fear of becoming too close to a woman and losing one's self in the process can be strong and frequently results in commitment phobia.

Fears of commitment and losing autonomy also occur in situations where familial intimacy resulted in lack of privacy and restrictions on personal property. One very successful physician who grew up in a large, immigrant, Hispanic family with ten children described the close quarters they lived in and the amount of sharing of toys and clothes that took place between him and his brothers. While he valued the loving spirit of sacrifice and closeness in his family, emotional intimacy with women meant loss of freedom, privacy, and personal space. As a result, his fear of losing autonomy led to frequent interruptions and abrupt endings to his many romantic unions, and ultimately prevented him from making a marriage commitment to the woman he truly loved. Unfortunately, when he resolved his fears and was ready to propose marriage to the "woman of his dreams," she had moved on, forming a romantic relationship with a man she regarded as less complicated and safer than her unreliable lover of ten years.

RISK OF DISAPPOINTMENT

Disappointment, the most common of *love's* dangers, is as integral to intimacy as hope is to healthy living. Because romantic love is filled with fantasies, idealizations, and projections, disappointment is likely to rear its realistic head repeatedly. Not only are people disappointed by their partners' failings and transgressions but also by the many personality flaws unearthed gradually over time. For example, he may turn out to be less assertive, less articulate, and emotionally weaker than she had surmised during the early days of their romance. She, on the other hand, may wind up being much less generous, less affectionate, and more self-absorbed than he had hoped. And for both of them, disappointment ensues.

Very often, the quality that is the source of the greatest disappointment is the attribute that was originally highly valued and attractive. He may have admired her no-nonsense, solid character but is now bored by her lack of joviality and playfulness. She may have been dazzled by the fact that he was no ordinary neighborhood boy, but rather a dreamer with exciting plans for their future. Now she complains that he does not have his feet on the ground and does not provide adequately for the family's financial and emotional well-being.

Disappointment occurs whenever an expectation is not met, with the degree of disappointment varying as a function of the importance and ascribed meaning of the transgression. For example, if a partner has forgotten his spouse's birthday, the spouse's disappointment would be affected by the security (or lack thereof) she felt in the relationship and her perception of his motives for forgetting. If she felt very secure and interpreted his behavior in a benign manner ("Oh, he always forgets birthdays"), she would be less affected by his neglect than would an insecure woman who ascribed more malevolent motivation to this same behavior ("He's trying to hurt me").

While there is some uniformity or agreement in a given culture as to the seriousness of particular intimacy misdeeds (e.g. coming home late for dinner or forgetting to perform a particular household chore are generally regarded in Western countries as trivial compared to infidelity or abuse), individual differences with respect to expectations are primarily responsible for the experienced degree of disappointment. For example, a person with high expectations may require unconditional love and unwavering devotion from a romantic partner, and as a result, is frequently discouraged and let down. Whenever the partner is consumed by his own agenda and not particularly attentive to hers, the high expectation lover is not only disappointed but also frequently enraged. The partner may be preoccupied with a disturbing work situation at the time his wife is feeling in need of attention. Not able to shift gears quickly, he struggles to tune into her distress but manages only half-hearted attention, which leaves her feeling especially let down. Traditional homemakers eager to talk to their spouses after a long-day tending to children's needs are often disappointed and feel emotionally disconnected by their husband's reluctance to recount his day's experiences upon arriving home.

Expectations of *love* are derived from one's own personal experiences (including the observations of others) and from the culture at large, including books, formal education, movies, religion, and television. When family experiences with romantic love are unhappy ones, the children in these families begin to create their own expectations from romantic novels, television, and movies. Their parents, in contrast, become negative role models, that is, examples of what not to do, rather than positive models to emulate.

In a letter to a friend, one twenty-six-year-old woman, a child of divorce with an abusive and unfaithful father, wrote: "I know that my Mom was unhappy, but I did not know what it takes for her or anybody else to be happy. My version of what I would like to have in my life came from French romantic novels set in times of kings, queens, and nobility. Those were my ideal men, who would come on white horses to save their loved ones, who are strong as a rock, kind, powerful, and romantic. I knew that my father wasn't one of them. So, my goal became to never be with anybody who would in any shape or form resemble my father. Other than that, I didn't have a clue."

Children in happy families, on the other hand, are likely to adopt their parents' more successful standards and behavior regarding romantic love. While these children may modify them based on their own observations of other families, the resulting expectations will be more realistic than those created by their counterparts from unhappy families. In one study[21] comparing the relationship ideals of adult children of divorce with those from intact families, the investigators found that adult children of divorce had significantly higher relationship ideals than others, specifically around affection, acceptance, independence, and passion—a finding that suggests that adult children of divorce can easily be disappointed if these ideals are not met. Also, requiring heavy doses of passion and excitement in romantic relationships can lead to confusion regarding sex and love as well as boredom once the initial fires of sexual attraction die down.

Fears of disappointment in romantic love are widespread among those who have been deeply disappointed in a first love, a serious love affair, or in marriage. After disappointment and betrayal, the task of rebuilding trust and optimism sufficiently to attempt another relationship is arduous. One man's first marriage ended when his wife developed an aversion to sex and wanted to avoid sexual contact altogether. Not only was sex an important source of pleasure for him, but also it was validating and affirming to his sense of masculinity. Without sexual contact, life together seemed barren, and so they mutually agreed to end their marriage. However, the fallout for both of them from this disappointing marriage was the fear of trying again with someone new.

FEAR OF BETRAYAL

Whenever betrayal is added to the experience of disappointment—when a partner has been deceived or led astray in some manner—there is added damage to the relationship. Most commonly in Western culture, betrayals, in promised monogamous relationships, center around infidelity with its powerful assaults on sexual identity, sexual attractiveness, and self-esteem. No matter how secure the betrayed felt prior to the infidelity, he/she feels diminished afterward. Questioning one's own desirability or sexual sophistication for months following the discovery of unfaithfulness, the betrayed typically alternates between rage toward the partner on the one hand and self-blame on the other.

In addition to the partner's loss of self-confidence wrought by infidelity, the loss of trust is particularly damaging to the relationship. Those who have been betrayed often don't know how to reconcile the infidelity with their past perceptions of their partner nor with their memories of the relationship at the time the affair was taking place. One woman whose husband of thirty years was involved in a clandestine affair for five years kept saying in couples therapy: "But I always saw you as trustworthy. How could you lie?" His lying was unfathomable to her because she had consistently viewed him as an honest man. She also questioned the validity of her past views of their marriage because she had many happy memories of their life together at the time he was having the affair. For her, the restoration of trust was a very slow and gradual process that occurred over time as she began to experience him as trustworthy in their ongoing lives.

For the adult children of divorce, fears of betrayal are widespread. One couple whose histories contained ample evidence of infidelity—in her case (she was a child of divorce) with a philandering father and in his case with a cheating first love—saw betrayal lurking behind every corner. Whenever either partner would speak animatedly to a member of the opposite sex, the other partner would become anxious and/or incensed. Ordinary friendliness and gregariousness were perceived as seductiveness leading ultimately to betrayal. Following the breakup of this relationship, which did end with infidelity on her part, the young man spent the following five years in casual sexual encounters without any emotional bond, that is, in safe relationships without vulnerability, until he was able to trust again.

Besides infidelity, betrayal takes on a variety of shapes in divorced families with broken promises to children among the most hurtful. A father failing to keep his word to attend a child's recital or sporting event, or his not showing up for weekend visitation affects a child's ability to trust others in far-reaching ways. A young woman whose father stopped keeping his promises to be a part of her life after the divorce (she was six years old at the time) said poignantly many years later: "I thought we were buddies and he just stopped caring." The sudden loss of a loving parent in inexplicable ways damages children's self-esteem, optimism, and belief in the benevolence of others and requires remedial efforts on the part of families and others before healing can take place.

LOSS OF CONTROL

Another danger associated with romantic intimacy is loss of control of one's self, the other person, and the situation. Because romantic love intrinsically involves a lowering of defenses, vulnerability, and heightened sensitivity, people are more easily hurt, needier, more jealous, angrier, more childlike, and emotionally labile than in any other interpersonal situation. In the throes of intimacy, emotional issues that were long buried resurface and questions regarding trust, lovability, autonomy, shame, initiative, and guilt demand a new hearing.

The emotional turbulence of *love*, especially during its beginning stages when obsessiveness and ambivalence run high, is disconcerting to the person who views himself as reasonable and well-controlled. Both the obsessiveness—thinking nonstop about the other person and continuously wondering what the other person feels about the relationship—and the ambivalence—experiencing both positive and negative feelings about the other in quick succession—feel irrational and out of control. In addition, angry impulses are often close to the surface in love-smitten individuals and ready to be expressed when frustration runs high. For persons who value order and predictability, romantic love with all of its emotionality feels messy. And yet, in spite of *love's* untidiness, these same individuals—the rigid, compulsive, orderly souls—are often strongly attracted to romantic love because they seldom experience the same intensity and range of emotions in other contexts. For them, *love* is an exciting adventure by virtue of its unpredictability and volatility.

Romantic love can also feel out of control when the partner's behavior is irrational or disturbed in some way. The relationship may have started out being gratifying only to be transformed into a nightmare when the other person demands more time, energy, or feeling than one is prepared to give. Like the hero in "Fatal Attraction,"[22] the popular movie depicting the progression of a casual love affair into a torturous pursuit, one can be harassed or violated when one's desires for the relationship are different from the other person's wishes and/or motives. A common example is the situation where one person in the relationship wants only friendship while the other craves romantic and sexual intimacy. In these cases, the person who wants more from the relationship may be beset by strong yearnings and impulses that are difficult to control and can prove harassing to the other person. Unsolicited visits and unexpected phone calls or e-mails, for example, can be overwhelming to the person who only wants a casual relationship rather than an intense and unpredictable romance.

Stalking incidents often begin as an acquaintanceship, friendship, or romance before deteriorating into harassment by extreme frustration and/or rejection. One young woman of twenty-five years of age reported that she experienced months of daily stalking following her attempt to end a college romance. The young man kept following her around campus and called her every evening to plead his case about why she should continue their relationship. It was only after she made a formal complaint to the dean of the college that his behavior stopped. "Currently, beginning a relationship feels like falling into quicksand for her. She has no control over the other's behavior and also no control over the speed at which the relationship will proceed from a casual one to friendship to sex and/or love. The idea that she has some control over the speed and final destination of the relationship and that she can stop at any point along the relationship's developmental path is a novel one for her. In her past experiences with the important people in her life, intimacy was unpredictable and out of control, Piorkowski wrote."[23]

Adults who grew up in unhappy households where unpredictability was the family trademark fear loss of control in intimacy. Anxiety about a sudden quarrel erupting to spoil a family function, such as a dinner or holiday party, can mar the enjoyment of even a peaceful gathering. The experience of "waiting for the other shoe to drop," when one is not privy to the time or place of such an occurrence, creates its own brand of distress.

FEAR OF ATTACK

Fear of attack is the strongest of intimacy's anxieties for those who experienced constant criticism and/or physical abuse in their family lives. Because closeness to others was associated with unexpected and unprovoked verbal or physical abuse in their childhoods, adult children from violent families fear that intimacy will result not only in loss of control but in physical and/or psychological damage to themselves. The recurrent experience of being beaten, screamed at, called names, or berated, undermines trust in others, lowers self-esteem, and creates anxiety about being assaulted in intimacy.

Adults, who grew up in alcoholic families where the incidence of divorce is high, often distrust others because of the unpredictable behavior of the alcoholic parent. One moment the sober, alcoholic parent may have been loving and kind; the next day, the intoxicated, alcoholic parent may have been ready to lash out at the drop of a hat for any minor transgression. Amy, a professional woman in her forties, recalled in therapy an incident of being kicked repeatedly by her drunken father for slamming the door after she ran excitedly into the house. The sudden violence in response to her exuberance conveyed dramatically the disconcerting unpredictability of beloved figures. On sober days, her father was intelligent and reasonable in contrast to the bitter, abusive man he became when inebriated.

Claudia Black,[24] a well-known writer in the field of alcoholism, described the ongoing fear among family members that permeates alcoholic households. High levels of anxiety also characterize physically and sexually abusive households, the parents of which are found in large numbers in divorce courts. Children and spouses in these families are afraid to speak for fear of triggering an abusive attack. Figuratively, they walk around on eggs, slowly and deliberately, lest they become the next victims of an assault. In these families, intimacy is synonymous with terror, vigilance, violence, and accommodation to the tyranny of the abusive parent. "As an adult, then, the person who grew up in such a household fears that intimate relationships will contain these same ingredients. Having experienced angry outbursts and physical abuse as an integral part of intimacy, they expect their own adult intimate relationships to be tinged with violence. While violence may not always beget violence, at the very least it begets the fear of violence."[25]

THE RISK OF GUILT

In addition to fears about the dangers of intimacy, another subtler outcome of romantic love—namely, concerns about excessive guilt—can occur in dysfunctional, child-blaming families. In these households, the children are blamed for parents' outbursts, excesses, or errors. In Amy's alcoholic family (described in section "Fear of Attack"), no matter how irrational and unprovoked her father's angry responses were, Amy's mother blamed her or her sister for upsetting their father and often insisted that they apologize to him for even ordinary childhood mishaps, like spilling of milk, or effusive playfulness.

As a result of both parents' accusatory attitudes toward their daughters, both sisters developed an excessively self-blaming stance that shouldered undue responsibility for the behavior of family members. "No matter what goes wrong, I'm always to blame," said Amy. "If someone's depressed, I'm not trying hard enough to cheer up that person. If someone's angry, I have upset that individual in some way and need to try and undo the damage. Any emotional conflict in the family was my responsibility," she said. "I was not only my brother's keeper, but my mother['s], father['s], and sister's as well. And it continues into my own family, where I'm clearly my husband['s] and children's keepers in a big way."

Guilt can also be triggered in romantic love when one person appears to be less involved in the relationship than the partner. If one partner is "madly in love" in contrast to the other partner's more subdued kind of caring, the situation becomes rife with guilt, especially if the more involved partner regularly accuses the other of not caring enough. Whereas one partner's stronger emotional attachment may be a function of strong dependency needs or caretaking motivation, the stronger emotional involvement often ennobles that person in the eyes of family and friends. In contrast, the less overtly involved partner, often perceived as uncaring, callous, and/or emotionally cold, may feel guilty for failing to meet the reciprocal obligation of *love*, that is, loving those who love you.

In Alex and Joan's relationship, Alex appeared to have the lion's share of personality assets. He was a highly successful real estate developer who was gregarious, self-assured, quick-witted, and well liked. Joan, while equally successful professionally, was more introverted and less comfortable in social situations. As a result, she preferred to spend most of their social time in quiet pursuits with Alex alone, while the opposite was true for Alex. For Joan, Alex was everything that she desired both socially and romantically; Alex, on the other hand, had needs for more varied intellectual and emotional stimulation.

Anytime Alex would express his desire to expand their social network by including others, Joan felt inadequate and rejected. She couldn't understand why Alex didn't want to spend as much time with her as she did with him, and therefore felt that he loved her less than she loved him. Alex, sensing her greater need for him than he felt for her, felt guilty for wanting more social interaction with others, and came to believe that perhaps he loved her less than she loved him. Therefore Alex abandoned his extraverted desires for more social interaction, and as a result, he felt lonely and less fulfilled.

Sometimes guilt ensues when a person has been dishonest about his own motives, for example, he wants sex but promises love, or uses another person to enhance his self-worth. The deception may be deliberate or unintentional; however, it's ordinarily only in the latter case that guilt does occur. A person may be unaware of his own motives or experience conflicting desires and is not clear which motive is dominant in a given situation. A case in point is the man who pursues a romantic relationship with an attractive woman because of her beauty, that is, the trophy girlfriend, and then feels guilty when he discovers that he doesn't care for her as much as she cares for him. Another example is the woman who convinces herself that she's "in love" when, in effect, sexual attraction and desire are the sole motives operating in the situation. An even more common occurrence is the person who consciously seeks a permanent romantic relationship but sabotages it whenever fears of intimacy prevent its attainment.

James, a young successful lawyer of thirty-five years of age and child of divorce, found himself ending a long-term relationship for the second time in six years (with two different women) when the woman made it clear that she wanted to get married. In both instances, he was less involved in the relationship than they were, although he felt affection for both of them. After the second breakup when the young woman told him how betrayed she felt and how depressed she was, James felt remorseful about hurting someone "whose only crime was loving him." James' guilt about his behavior interfered with his ability to connect emotionally with women for several years after the second breakup.

FEARS OF REJECTION AND ABANDONMENT

Of all the fears and risks in intimacy, fear of rejection is the most common and underlies all of the other dangers. If someone disappoints, betrays, ridicules, criticizes, humiliates, and/or abuses another person, the victim typically feels rejected in addition to a myriad of other feelings. Another person's rejection may be temporary, as in momentary withdrawal, or permanent, as in desertion. Rejection can take the form of ignoring, misunderstanding, criticizing, contradicting, disbelieving, or falsely attributing malevolent motives to another's behavior; it can be directed at appearance, family/ethnic background, speech mannerisms, personality, ideas and feelings, as well as dreams, hopes, and aspirations. In short, rejection can take on a variety of shapes, can be occasional or chronic, and its seriousness can range from the trivial to the sublime.

Except for the hardened telephone solicitor or door-to-door salesman, rejection is hurtful to the vast majority of people, but particularly when it's conveyed by significant others. Because the desire to be liked, attended to, and approved of is basic to human nature, a disapproving response is invalidating and threatening to self-worth. For women especially, who have been socialized to regard approval as essential to self-esteem, rejection communicates that one has less importance or value than one would hope for. For men, who are more likely to equate competence with self-worth, rejection, while it may be less of a blow to self-esteem, still brings into question one's value as a person. One young man in describing his hesitation to approach an attractive woman to ask her for a date said, "I guess it's as simple as being afraid that she won't like me." This basic fear of being disliked can create debilitating dread and avoidance behavior in even the most academically or professionally accomplished persons.

The most extreme version of the fear of rejection is anxiety about abandonment, which has its origins in early childhood, when physical and emotional survival was clearly dependent on caretakers. In intimate adult relationships, particularly highly dependent ones, the fear of abandonment is reactivated whenever the partner is rejecting or distant and relates to concerns about emotional survival in particular. "One woman, in talking about life without her husband, asked incredulously, 'How am I going to get up in the morning without him?' While her husband actually woke her up for work every morning, she was not asking the literal question but rather wondering how she was going to structure her life without him. She was concerned about how she was going to deal with the emptiness in her life, the painful aloneness," Piorkowski wrote.[26]

For those adults whose childhoods were marred by traumatic separations or desertion, the fear of abandonment is especially intense. Adult children of divorce who had to grapple with chronic rejection in the family and literal abandonment, where one or both parents deserted the children, often struggle with intense fears of desertion, even when they're in stable relationships with loving and loyal partners. It's difficult for these adult children to believe that their adult intimate relationships could be dramatic improvements over those they witnessed earlier in their lives, when they were especially impressionable and vulnerable.

Even in low-conflict families, where the departure of a parent from the family home can occur abruptly and without warning, the loss of a parent is difficult to resolve. Without any visible explanation for the departure (no ugly fights or verbal abuse), the child is left uncertain and anxious about when another such dramatic loss will take place. Even when a departing parent becomes a regular weekend visitor, the absence of that parent from daily life (e.g. evening dinners and bedtimes) can still be experienced as a painful loss leading to fears of rejection and abandonment in adult intimacy. Parental loss through death, desertion, or permanent departure from the family home is one of the most traumatic of childhood sufferings—one that is not without consequences in adult life.

CHAPTER 5

Too Few Cultural Alternatives to Love

Contemporary culture in America appears to be as toxic to romantic love as it is to physical health. In an article, entitled "America: A Toxic Lifestyle," author Tori DeAngelis[1] points out that simply living in America may be as risky to health "as a diet of doughnuts and beer." While Americans spend more on health care than the British, they are far sicker in rates of diabetes, high blood pressure, heart disease, heart attack, stroke, lung disease, and cancer. Several researchers[2] attribute these differential health rates to longer work hours, more stress, isolation, and the overvaluation of money and material success in the United States. Focusing on the self-destructive behaviors of alienated teenagers and young adults, psychologist Madeline Levine, Ph.D.,[3] author of *The Price of Privilege: How Parental Pressure and Material Advantage Are Creating a Generation of Disconnected and Unhappy Kids*, writes about the negative culture of affluence that emphasizes "material goods over relationships and competition over cooperation."[4]

Commenting persuasively about "the interpersonal divide"—the modern divisions that separate one person from another, Michael Bugeja[5] has written: "Lacking acceptance, we feel unloved. Lacking love, we feel afraid . . . When we lose a sense of place, we also lose a sense of occasion—how to behave in real time and place in the company of others. We are forgetting how to resolve problems without creating greater ones because we are more apt to use electronic communication to mediate our disputes, instead of resolving them face-to-face. We may misinterpret motives because the messages we send and receive do not convey the subtle but vital voice tones, body movements, and other guiding interpersonal cues of physical place . . . While most pundits and educators debate the digital divide, bemoaning the underclass of people without computer access, a wider fault line has been eroding communities: the interpersonal divide."

The same factors that create stress and alienation in society give rise to the unrealistic and burdensome expectations that choke the life out of romantic relationships and lead to their demise. Among the societal factors that negatively impinge upon romantic love are geographical mobility, urban/suburban isolation, electronics overuse, overwork, limited civic, political, and religious participation, and too few friendships. In particular, the dearth of meaningful relationships at work, school, church, in extracurricular activities, or in the extended family, creates a widespread isolation that hungers for connection. Cell phones positioned on the ear like a modern-day appendage speak to the contemporary need to talk to live human beings.

With geographic mobility, that is, adults trekking across the country to live in strange cities, extended families in the form of grandparents and other relatives are no longer situated on the neighboring landscape to provide attention and care when the nuclear family fails to deliver. Likewise, close friends no longer live on the next block to provide comfort in times of stress or loss. Reduced membership in social clubs and political organizations limits the number of relationships that can provide a buffer to the hurts and disappointments of romantic love. And church/synagogue groups that once were a source of belonging and sense of community are no longer utilized to the same degree they once were. Added to this is the amount of time spent on computers, TVs, and electronic devices of all sorts, and long hours on the job, all of which provide a picture of an overworked population gaining a moment of diversion from gadgets at the expense of meaningful human contact.

In the midst of this arid desert, romance seems to be the only available oasis to satisfy the human need for relatedness. For the children of divorce, who have experienced significant disruptions in familial relationships, the cultural lack of alternate structures for emotional need gratification, specifically for the need for relatedness or connection, has resulted in romantic relationships becoming either a panacea for all human ills or a netherworld of betrayal. In the former case, romantic relationships are idealized, overvalued, and overburdened, ultimately ending in their dissolution. In the latter case, committed romantic unions (such as marriages) are avoided in favor of single, disconnected, minimally connected, and/or less tangled lives (cohabiting partners are in this last category). The most recent U.S. Census Bureau survey indicating that unmarried persons head 50.3 percent of households[6] attests to the popularity of these less involved options over marriage.

URBAN/SUBURBAN ANOMIE AND MOBILITY

Urbanization has been documented repeatedly[7] over the last century as one of the important factors that has led to the weakening of kinship/extended family ties, and increased the sense of individual isolation. "New York is a splendid desert—a domed and steepled solitude, where a stranger is lonely in the midst of a million of his race," wrote Mark Twain[8] in 1867. Over a hundred years later, Mark Twain's sentiment rings true even more. Currently, in both urban high-rises and suburban communities surrounding the big cities, neighbors seldom talk over the back fence or even nod a word of greeting to one another. Silent strangers practice their fixed gazes in checkout lines, elevators, and crowded gatherings ignoring one another. No matter the particular urban or suburban setting, the art of indifference to others has been perfected— resulting in an aura of isolation that permeates the atmosphere.

As Larry Frolick,[9] author of *Splitting Up: Divorce, Culture, and the Search for a Real Life*, wrote: "As we enter the 21st century, living in cities of five million and more, the alienation and anonymity of every individual accelerates—which puts enormous strains on long-term family commitments." The enormous strain on families, intensified by the deprivation of meaningful human connections throughout the day, creates tension-filled interactions. When daily work, volunteer, or school contacts with others are indifferent, superficial, or hostile, the craving for meaningful positive contact will fall heavily upon the family's shoulders (the romantic partner especially), who often feels burdened by such excessive demands and unequal to the task of making up for the daily diet of deprivation. The failure of the family to compensate for the isolation of modern life further adds to the sense of alienation experienced at all levels of society. The demise of the family dinner and obsessive television watching during moments of family togetherness are glaring examples of the family's failure to compensate for the lack of meaningful outside contacts during the day.

Besides the isolation, people in contemporary American society are angry. Because of stress levels and the frustration of their own legitimate emotional needs, they displace their unhappiness onto others. The phenomenon of road rage, the indifference of store clerks, and the incivility of strangers on public vehicles and thoroughfares attest to the angry mood that permeates the country. People have little time for pleasantries, courtesies, and/or random acts of kindness, and instead appear to resent the requests of others as intrusions upon their limited resources.

Civility—courtesy and politeness—is vanishing in modern America. While gentlemen doffing their hats to ladies have gone the way of Victorian spats, even "please" and "thank you" have seen a better day. As Mary Pipher[10] wrote in *The Shelter of Each Other*, "Unwritten rules of civility—for taking turns, not cutting line, holding doors open for others, and lowering our voices in theaters—organize civic life. Unfortunately, those rules of civility seem to be crumbling in America. We are becoming a nation of people who get angry when anyone gets in our way."

Along with the angry rudeness and lack of civility in the United States is the diminished quality and quantity of casual conversation. The art of chitchatting, or casual, face-to-face conversation, seems to be a dying skill relegated to a bygone time. No longer do people sit on their porches on a hot summer day calling out the local news or gossip to one another. Butchers, bakers, shoe repairmen, and taxi drivers are no longer engaged in lively exchanges with their customers about American life. People gathered together at bus stops or ticket lines in big cities seldom address one another, except for an occasional complaint about the bus service or the length of the ticket line. Even college students sitting together silently in classrooms, awaiting the start of a lecture, seem indifferent to one another—in spite of the fact that they're bound together by a common purpose and the temporal goal of attending the same class.

Part of the explanation for this social indifference and angry incivility has to do with the large percentage of population now residing in alienated metropolitan centers, and fear of strangers brought on by terrorism and mass killings at the local level. While Americans are no more moving to new locations in the last fifty years than they did earlier, they are moving in large numbers to metropolitan areas—the big cities and suburbs—from rural areas. "In the 1950s barely half of all Americans lived in metropolitan areas, whereas in the 1990s roughly four in five of us did. Throughout this era we have been moving to places that appear to be less hospitable to civic engagement. More-over, the best available research found no evidence of suburbanization abating in the 1990s."[11] Thus, Putnam attributes the decline in social connectedness over the last third of the twentieth century to the continuing eclipse of small-town America.

Contributing to the decline in social engagement of suburban America has been the increase in automobile use, which has resulted in more time spent alone in the car commuting to work and/or driving to shopping malls. For example, the evidence suggests that for every additional ten minutes spent in daily commuting, there is a 10 percent reduction in participation in community affairs, such as public meetings attended, committees chaired, petitions signed, church services attended, volunteering, etcetera.[12] Suburban life, which has grown significantly more than rural or city life in the last fifty years (it jumped from 23% in 1950 to 49% in 1996),[13] has become as synonymous with civic disengagement and alienation as that of urban America.

Especially noteworthy contributors to this country's widespread alienation are gated communities, which are rapidly growing in the Southern and Western retirement meccas of the United States. These gated communities among the affluent are innately introverted places that stand in marked contrast to the extraverted nature of traditional urban communities, which regularly spill out onto the neighborhood streets for play and social chatter. With sentinels posted at the front gates to protect the security and privacy of its residents, these gated communities appear to be self-contained fiefdoms isolated from the rest of the world. Even within these enclaves, the empty streets and poorly attended community meetings provide little evidence of social intercourse among its own residents. With all their visible barriers to social connectedness, these gated communities stand as stark monuments to the isolation and xenophobia of Americans in the twenty-first century.

Xenophobia, or fear of strangers, has become more pronounced in America since 9/11 (September 11, 2001). At that time, the American sense of security and invulnerability was destroyed by the seizure of four airplanes from major airports and the bombings of the Twin Towers in New York and the Pentagon. The most prosperous, technologically advanced nation in the world fell to its knees at the hands of a group of foreign terrorists from across the sea. The likelihood of being attacked by foreigners is no longer a remote possibility but a plausible reality right at home.

Further adding to American paranoia and insecurity was the string of mass killings in schools across the United States that began most dramatically with the Columbine High School massacre of fourteen students and a teacher (including the killers) in Littleton, Colorado on April 20, 1999. Prior to the Columbine High School shootings, however, there had been ten other school killings in recent history, dating back to 1996 in the state of Washington, but none of these had the scope of Columbine in terms of numbers killed. Following Columbine, there were another twenty-five school killings in states throughout the country, culminating in the Virginia Tech massacre in Blacksburg, Virginia that proved to be the deadliest of all (at the time of this writing). Thirty-three students and faculty were shot dead by a lone shooter who gunned down the victims as they got ready for classes in the early morning hours of April 16, 2007. Thus, it became clear that not only foreigners were likely to be the "dreaded enemy" but alienated teenagers and young adults from across the street were equally capable of murder.

The perpetrator of the Virginia Tech killings, Seung-Hui Cho, was both foreign-born and homegrown in that he was born in South Korea but lived in the United States for most of his life (from the age of eight). The issue of trust becomes further confused when the enemy does not have a clear identity. In such an atmosphere—the one permeating the United States at the present time—there is no one who can readily be trusted. Because so much distrust stands in the way of extrafamilial relationships, all these relationships, but especially emotionally laden romantic love, have a difficult time navigating through the currents and riptides that surround them.

THE IMPACT OF ELECTRONICS

In describing a modern-day family with three distressed children, Mary Pipher,[14] in *The Shelter of Each Other: Rebuilding Our Families*, wrote: "The Copelands were more prosperous and had more choices, but they were thirsty in the rain. They were stressed as individuals and as a unit. They didn't know each other very well and rarely had time together." And again later, in describing the implications of electronics on families, she wrote,[15] "Family members may be in the same house, but they are no longer truly interacting. They may be in the same room, but instead of making their own story, they are watching another family's story unfold (on television). Or even more likely, family members are separated, having private experiences with different electronic equipment."

Social critic James Howard Kunstler's[16] commentary about American family life is similar: "The American house has been TV-centered for three generations. It is the focus of family life, and the life of the house correspondingly turns inward, away from whatever occurs beyond its four walls." And then later, he writes, "The physical envelope of the house itself no longer connects their lives to the outside in any active way; rather, it seals them off from it. The outside world has become an abstraction filtered through television, just as the weather is an abstraction filtered through air conditioning."

At the present time, husbands and wives spend three or four times as much time watching television together as they spend talking to each other. However, even watching television together is becoming less common as more and more gadget interaction, whether with the iPod, a video game, or the Internet, is done entirely alone. According to one study focused on television, at least half of all Americans watch television alone. Among children aged eight to eighteen years, the figures are even more startling: less than 5 percent of their television watching is done with their parents, and more than one-third is done entirely alone.[17] The recently reported survey result that nearly 20 percent of children younger than three years of age and 43 percent of three and four years old have television sets in their bedrooms further adds to the alarm about young children and television watching.[18]

During every period of the day at least one-quarter of all adults report some television viewing, with the percentage peaking at 86 percent during prime-time hours.[19] According to one global study[20] cited by Al Gore, presidential contender in 2000, Americans currently watch television four hours and thirty-five minutes every day—ninety minutes more than the world average. With the number of hours in front of electronic gadgets increasing each year, people are doing little else besides overworking, and then collapsing in front of their television sets or computers upon arriving home. In between these television or computer hours, they are busily engaged in food preparation, laundry, cleaning up, and other chores. Time spent in meaningful conversation with others is lost amid the frantic busyness of everyday life.

Imagine two fully employed American parents coming home from a long day's work hoping for peace and quietude, only to find hungry and disgruntled children waiting to be fed, and both partners tired and distracted. After the dinner's tasks are done, the idea of pursuing a family game/project or a social activity outside the home has less appeal than the tranquilizing, undemanding lure of television or the Internet. If perchance one partner were to say to the other, "Let's skip television tonight and spend some time together as a family," the other partner, anxious about the unexpected request and the potential demand implicit in the request, would probably respond, "Not tonight, dear, I'm too tired." And the partner hungry for a more meaningful interaction would feel disappointed at the rejection, and less likely to propose alternate leisure possibilities the next time around. And so the stage is set for a continuation of family life isolated from one another and the rest of the world.

Communication via e-mail and the Internet to the exclusion of in-person contact has further eroded emotional intimacy with others. Whereas e-mails are reliable and efficient at transmitting information, they are poor vehicles for fostering emotional closeness because of their inaccuracy in conveying emotional meaning. Since facial expression and voice quality are omitted, e-mails don't readily communicate the nuances, feelings, and overall meaning of another's experience. The facts are there but not the emotional subtleties of the message.

In one classic study on communication,[21] words accounted for only 7 percent of the variance in interpreting meaning, while facial expression, voice qualities, and gestures accounted for the remainder. Human beings pay more attention to nonverbal behavior (facial expression, voice quality, gestures, posture) than words because nonverbal behavior is a more reliable, valid, and spontaneous indicator of another person's meaning than words. Words can mask, distort, or exaggerate a person's real feelings, whereas nonverbal communication stays closer to the truth, and therefore serves as a much better authenticity detector than spoken or written language.

The popularity of the Internet for a whole host of social and psychological motives has led to some disquieting results. Internet addiction, that is, being hooked on to chat rooms, interactive games, and even eBay to the point where marital, academic, and/or job-related problems are created, has become a new clinical phenomenon.[22] Lin, Wang, and Wu[23] have shown that a distinctive pattern of disinhibition on the Net, characterized by high needs for intimacy and self-disclosure along with the ambivalent attachment style, is more likely to result in Internet addiction.

In a similar attempt to distinguish between adaptive and maladaptive uses of the Internet, Weiser[24] has differentiated between those who use the Internet for social or affiliative needs and those primarily interested in acquiring goods and information. Not surprisingly, it is the social-affiliative types that are negatively affected by excessive Internet use, while the psychological well-being of the goods and information seekers is actually enhanced. In a related study on the Internet use, Moody[25] found that high levels of the Internet use were associated with high levels of emotional loneliness (feeling of emptiness and restlessness due to lack of intimate relationships), thus suggesting that the more the Internet is used to meet emotional needs rather than cognitive ones, the more likely is its negative impact.

Other interesting findings related to the Internet usage and social connections are: (1) friends met in person (at home or school) were closer emotionally than those met online;[26] (2) certain computer-mediated tools, that is, blogs, function to enhance existing relationships for bloggers who exhibit both extraversion and self-disclosure traits;[27] (3) the users of different social network sites (Facebook, MySpace, Xanga, and Friendster) tend to be more homogeneous than heterogeneous (e.g. Hispanic students are more likely to use MySpace, while Asian-American students are more likely to use Xanga and Friendster; students from highly educated homes are more attracted to Facebook than other social network sites[28]); (4) students high in social and dating anxiety were more likely to use certain online media such as Web cameras than other groups;[29] and (5) sexually permissive people and high-sensation seekers looked online for casual partners more frequently than more sexually inhibited persons, suggesting that recreation rather than compensation is the primary motivation for online partner searches.[30]

In spite of its limitations, online dating is fast becoming the primary dating service of young people. According to *US News and World Report*, forty million unique users, which represent about half the number of single adults in the United States, visited online dating sites in one month alone.[31] Because computer-based dating is based on limited channels of communication (although pictures do help), there is a widespread opportunity for disappointment and other negative outcomes. Walther[32] and other investigators have shown that communication over sparse channels can lead to idealization; if this is the case, much of the disappointment in online dating could stem from overly optimistic expectations formed on the basis of limited information.

Because of certain characteristics of personal communication on the Internet (more anonymity, greatly reduced emphasis on physical appearance, physical distance, and greater control over the time and pace of interactions), such communication is not only more limited but more artificial than face-to-face interactions. The Internet communication is also less likely to lead to positive interpersonal learning, is less emotionally satisfying, and is more dangerous because of the potentially harmful disguises worn by some users that are difficult to discern without the benefit of nonverbal behavior.

The Internet communication is less interpersonally meaningful because it represents only a partial encounter rather than a more complete immersion of one's self with another person. As for the potential danger, the likelihood of being inadvertently misled or intentionally deceived is much greater than in face-to-face interactions, in spite of the illusion of safety created by the physical distance and greater control over the extent and depth of communication. More importantly, computers do not easily transmit validation, empathy, and affection. While computers provide the opportunity for superficial contact with others, this contact, if not balanced by other meaningful, in-person relationships, can increase social isolation and loneliness, thus paving the way to depression. Just as robots are poor substitutes for human contact, so are computers poor replacements for the kinds of emotionally meaningful communication that human beings seem to crave.

OVERWORK AND OTHER PRESSURES

Another factor contributing to social and civic disengagement in the United States is overwork and related stress. People are working longer hours at a faster pace, which cuts into family, social, and leisure time. Because they're working more, they're having a hard time making a living and making a life, contends Robert Reich,[33] former U.S. secretary of labor, in his book, *The Future of Success*. Americans are twice as likely as Europeans to work fifty hours a week or more. In a similar vein, a work survey reported by the *Chicago Tribune* in 1997[34] found that just 22 percent of workers were putting in less than a forty-hour week, half were working between forty and fifty hours, and over 25 percent were working more than fifty hours—especially professionals. In another study 26.5 percent of men and 11.3 percent of women were working more than fifty hours per week in 2000 in the United States.[35] Downsizing and outsourcing have led to longer hours and more job insecurity for many Americans.

In addition, Americans added nearly a full week to their work year during the nineties, climbing to 1,978 hours on average in 2000, up thirty-six hours—almost a full workweek—from 1990. That means Americans who are employed are putting in nearly fifty weeks a year on the job, which is two weeks more than Japanese workers, about six weeks more than British workers, and about twelve weeks more than their counterparts in Germany, according to a report issued by the International Labor Organization in 2001.[36]

The overworked class of Americans tends to be college-educated persons, who are now working thirteen more hours per week than their high-school dropout brethren. As Robinson and Godbey[37] have noted, the "working class" has less work and the "leisure class" less leisure at the present time. Furthermore, dual-career families are more common—the proportion of dual-career couples has risen from 35.9 percent of married couples in 1970 to 59.6 percent in 1997[38] and are spending more time at work than they did in the past. Working time performed by both husband and wife increased from 52.5 hours per week to 62.8 hours per week during this same period. So overall, working families have less time to spend with each other and with friends than they did in earlier years.

Another factor related to overwork is financial anxiety, which correlates with a number of variables related to social engagement. People who are worried about money go to the movies less, spend less time with friends, play cards less, go to church less frequently, volunteer less, and show less interest in politics. In fact, the only leisure/social activity that increases along with financial worry is watching television. Moreover, it is not income per se that results in social hibernation but financial vulnerability, even among well-to-do couples, that dampens interest in others and the outside world. Keeping up with the Jones seems to take up a lot of energy and motivation.

In the child-centered culture of the United States, a great deal of money is spent on child improvement, that is, on sports equipment and, camps; dancing, cheerleading, and gymnastics lessons; SAT preparation classes, orthodontists, etcetera. Many of these items "are no longer luxuries of the wealthy but have become necessities that even less affluent parents seek, and through additional work, acquire for their children."[39] American youth spend inordinate amounts of money on clothing, entertainment, gadgets, hobbies, and expensive electronic equipment, all of which are status symbols in the United States.

Financial anxiety—having enough money to provide such abundance to their children—has consumed many parents, made them focus their energy on making money, and kept them away from participation in social and community activities.

The movement of women into the work force over the past fifty years has also contributed to social disengagement and increased levels of stress in the society. The fraction of women who work outside the home doubled in the United States from fewer than one in three in the fifties to nearly two in three in the nineties. The rate of maternal employment for two-parent families with school-age children is more than 75 percent with African-American and Latina mothers contributing the most to that figure.[40] The increase of women into the workforce has been occurring not only in the United States but also throughout the world. The number of women in the workforce has increased "from 26 to 38 percent in the Caribbean, from 16 to 33 percent in Central America, from 17 to 25 percent in the Middle East, from 23 to 31 percent in North Africa, from 31 to 46 percent in North America, from 27 to 43 percent in Oceania, from 31 to 41 percent in Western Europe, and from 21 to 35 percent in South America since 1960."[41]

Putnam,[42] writing about women in the United States, said "that when two women of the same age, education, financial security, and marital and parental status are compared, full-time employment appears to cut home entertaining by roughly 10 percent, club and church attendance by roughly 15 percent, informal visiting with friends by 25 percent, and volunteering by more than 50 percent." Along with the decrease in social engagement both in and outside the home is an increase in anxiety throughout the family when mothers are employed outside the home.

Whereas mothers have outside jobs for a variety of reasons, including social support, adult companionship, self-actualization, and in most cases to support the family, employed mothers are under a lot of stress. Major sources of stress include managing the household, home cleaning, and caring for sick children (350,000 children are ill daily in the United States with very few child care centers equipped to take care of sick children).[43] With the largest share of child care and housework still their responsibility (one recent study estimates that men in working families now spend an average of 10.4 hours a week on household tasks in contrast to women's expenditure of 19.4 hours[44]—a vast improvement over the 6:1 ratio from 1965[45]), employed mothers have little time for community activities or for self–care, which includes hobbies, reading, and physical fitness.

In view of the high levels of stress among working mothers, it is not surprising that employed women who report work/family conflicts are thirty times more likely to experience significant mental health problems, for instance, depression, anxiety, panic reactions, insecurity, fear of new people, and withdrawal from social situations, than women employees without such conflicts.[46] Also, physical health complaints—headaches, eating disorders, tiredness, and concentration impairment—are common among many working women who have difficulty juggling a multiplicity of roles.[47]

In a Scandinavian study investigating the manner in which husbands' work demands affected wives' lives and psychological health, Dikkers and colleagues[48] found that there was a clear interactive or crossover effect. When husbands had higher workload and more psychological health complaints, their wives experienced more of the same. The authors of the study speculated that the crossover effect may be based on time constraints—the less time and energy husbands have, the greater the corresponding demand on wives. Also, wives experience similar strain and stress as their husbands through empathic identification. Because families tend to have permeable boundaries, the stress of one member spills over onto the others elevating the overall level of family distress.

The harried, stressed, and overworked atmosphere in which they live especially affects children. Working mothers in the United States report that their children watch too much television, act out for lack of attention, eat too much junk food, have too little adult supervision, and underachieve in school.[49] Even in tightly managed households with a significant amount of adult supervision, there can be problems. In these homes, young children's lives are often overscheduled with play dates, lessons, and sport activities, resulting in free time (so important for the development of creativity and relationship skills) being at a premium. Without sufficient time to meet their emotional needs through fantasy play and to learn how to interact with peers, these children as adults, in comparison to their parents and grandparents, will have more difficulty with the unstructured world of friendships and intimate relationships.

LIMITED GROUP PARTICIPATION

In all parts of the United States, group membership of most kinds is significantly lower than it was thirty years ago, from political, civic, religious, and work-related association to volunteer participation. Volunteerism is down, bowling leagues have fallen on hard times, and civic organizations are struggling to find members. Some social and charitable organizations that provided meaningful avenues for social interaction among its members (e.g. Glenn Valley Bridge Club in Pennsylvania, the Charity League of Dallas, the Vassar Alumnae Book Fair in Washington, DC, VFW groups, among many others) have vanished from the cultural scene.

From 1970, the frequency of virtually every form of political involvement declined significantly, from the most common—petition signing—to the least common—running for office. Between 1973 and 1994, numbers attending even one public meeting on town or school affairs in the previous year decreased by 35 percent. While all socioeconomic levels reduced their civic participation to a significant degree, the decreases were greatest in absolute terms among the better educated and the younger age groups. In addition, this kind of political and civic involvement was lowest in major metropolitan areas, including suburbs,[50] where, paradoxically, it has been most needed to address the social and psychological ills of these areas.

Even popular and personally relevant civic organizations, such as the PTA, have been hit hard. One grassroots survey in the sixties found that the PTA had more members than any other secular organization. From the height of its astounding appeal at that time, however, it has declined from a high of almost fifty members per hundred families with children under eighteen to fewer than twenty members per hundred families. Moreover, "Between 1990 and 1997, the PTA lost half a million members, even though the number of families with children under eighteen grew by over two million and public school enrollment grew by over five million."[51]

Similar decreases in membership, group leadership, and participation have taken place in all sorts of organizations over the past thirty years. Unions, church groups, fraternal and veterans' organizations, civic groups, youth groups, and charities have all witnessed dwindling participation. For example, between 1973 and 1994, the number of men and women who took any leadership role in an organization was sliced by more than 50 percent. Sixteen percent of the population served as an officer or committee member of an organization during the seventies but it plummeted to 8 percent in the nineties.

As for church membership, it has fallen roughly 10 percent between the sixties and the nineties, and weekly church attendance has dropped about the same amount from a high of 46 percent in 1960 to 36 percent in 2000. Furthermore, the percentage of Americans who identify themselves as having "no religion" has risen from 2 percent in 1967 to 15.9 percent in 2006.[52] Thus, it is clear that group participation of all kinds—political, civic, and religious— has fallen during the last three or four decades of the twentieth century, and this social disengagement is most pronounced among the younger generations, including baby boomers.

As for informal social activities, such as entertaining friends at home or going to friends' homes, these activities, too, have diminished. In the mid-to late seventies, the average American entertained friends at home about fourteen to fifteen times a year, but by the late nineties that figure had fallen to eight times per year. "If the sharp, steady declines registered over the past quarter century were to continue at the same pace for the next quarter century, our centuries-old practice of entertaining friends at home might entirely disappear from American life in less than a generation," wrote Putnam.[53]

What accounts for all this reduction in group participation, including informal social contacts, and what does it all mean? Putnam[54] attributes the decline in social engagement to the following four factors: (1) pressures of time and money, (2) suburbanization, commuting, and urban sprawl, (3) effect of electronic entertainment, television above all, and (4) generational change—the slow, steady replacement of a civic/social generation with their less socially involved children and grandchildren. This last factor, generational change, is the one Putnam regards as the most important contributor to social disengagement.

Regardless of the responsible factors, the across-the-board reduction in group participation has resulted in a generation of loners hungry for social contact. In the past, group membership of some kind provided a sense of belonging, meaningful social interactions among peers, team spirit, and, in some cases, friendly competition. In addition, cohesive groups provided opportunities for altruism, interpersonal learning (learning about one's self in a peer context and how to get along with others, which is often a corrective emotional experience to pathological family experiences), catharsis, identification with others, sense of purpose, hope, and guidance.[55] Existing research evidence strongly supports the contention that the need to belong (frequent, positive, or nonaversive interactions within an ongoing relational bond) is a powerful, fundamental, and extremely pervasive motivation.[56]

In the past, people who were struggling with loneliness or a conflict-ridden relationship not only achieved a temporary respite from painful emotions by group participation, but also received additional psychological benefits as well. Friendships, laughter, and altruistic, goal-directed behavior with others went a long way in reducing loneliness, warding off depression, and in restoring/improving self-confidence.

TOO FEW FRIENDSHIPS

Along with reduced group membership of all kinds is the decrease in social support and increased loneliness that Americans experience. A number of sociologists have reported that Americans' network of confidantes, people with whom they could discuss meaningful matters, dropped from about three to two people over the last twenty years, and that the number of people saying there is no one with whom they can discuss important matters nearly tripled.[57] The modal respondent in 2005 reported having "no confidant" while the modal respondent in 1985 had three. In addition, Americans reported fewer close relationships with coworkers, extended family members, neighbors, and friends than they had earlier.

In a similar vein, psychologist Ami Rokach[58] and others found that North Americans scored higher than their Spanish counterparts on five measures of loneliness, including feelings of social inadequacy, interpersonal isolation, and self-alienation. Thus, it appears that Americans have become more isolated and lonelier than their national neighbors and Europeans, who would prefer socializing in pubs and cafes than making money.[59] Because loneliness has been negatively correlated with happiness and life satisfaction, the attitudes of the Spanish Americans and Europeans make for happier and healthier persons.

The benefits of social connectedness, whether in the form of friendships or civic involvement, have been documented repeatedly and extend to virtually all aspects of health—physical as well as psychological. From Durkheim's[60] early work on suicide and its relation to social integration, social support has been established as one of the most powerful determinants of well-being that affects every aspect of existence. "The more integrated we are with our community, the less likely we are to experience colds, heart attacks, strokes, cancer, depression, and premature death of all sorts," according to Putnam.[61] The protective benefits of social support have been confirmed for close family ties, friendships, social participation, and even casual affiliation with religious and other civic associations.

More important to the younger generation than the health benefits of social support, however, is its psychological value in warding off loneliness and depression. Striking earlier and much more pervasively with each successive generation since 1940, the rate of depression over the last two generations has increased roughly tenfold. In addition, between 1950 and 1995 the suicide rate among adolescents, aged fifteen to nineteen, has more than quadrupled, while the rate among young adults nearly tripled.

Along with these disturbing statistics of suicide are correlated findings that current teenagers spend more time alone than with family or friends, and that they have fewer, weaker, and more fluid friendships. Psychologist Martin Seligman[62] has linked these alarming rates to individualism and the failure to utilize large institutions (religion, country, family) to fall back on in times of stress. He writes: "When you fail to reach some of your personal goals, as we all must, you can turn to these large institutions for hope...But in a self standing alone without the buffer of larger beliefs, helplessness and failure can all too easily become hopelessness and despair." While it has not been confirmed unequivocally that the high rates of depression and suicide in the

United States are linked to social isolation, it does appear that young adults who are socially connected to others are less likely to be distressed, depressed, and commit suicide.

In modern America, friendships are difficult to establish and once established, difficult to maintain. Not only do friendships appear at the bottom of busy America's priority list, but also are often not geographically accessible. Graduating college seniors often return after graduation to their hometowns miles away from college friends, and upwardly mobile professionals move frequently for job promotions and new career possibilities. With all this mobility, good friends are left behind. While geographically remote friends are accessible by e-mails, they are seldom utilized or available for emotional support during times of crisis or failure. Unfortunately, the only meaningful exchanges with many of these geographically distant friends are annual holiday cards excessively filled with good cheer. And trying to forge new, meaningful friendships with acquaintances living or working next door is difficult because they, too, are overscheduled and lacking in time, energy, or motivation for new relationships.

Thus, it is glaringly apparent that today's young Americans are more socially isolated and lonelier than their grandparents and even their parents were (and are). Trying to cope with the many disappointments of adulthood, such as broken love affairs or job failures, by relying on electronics rather than people, they often become disenchanted. While some of the electronic devices, such as video games and iPods, for instance, are isolable; others, including chat rooms and cell phones, do provide some social support. However, because these modern, gadget-dependent venues specialize in rapid and truncated interactions, they are only superficially satisfying.

Lacking meaningful avenues to satisfy the human need for relatedness and connection, modern culture in America has become a barren landscape for emotional intimacy. As a result, romantic love, primed by movies, television, and romantic novels, is the new breeding ground for the hopes and dreams of a lonely populace for happiness. Overladen with expectations, romantic love, including marriage, often stumbles, leaving its users shattered. As for the adult children of divorce, who have been profoundly disappointed with their parents' version of romantic love, they become either overly optimistic or pessimistic in their own expectations of what romantic love can provide.

CHAPTER 6

Role Models of Romantic Love in Popular Culture

In her novel *Love*, Toni Morrison,[1] winner of the Nobel Prize for Literature, describes the cataclysmic experience that frequently overwhelms unsuspecting couples:

> Young people, Lord. Do they still call it infatuation? The magic ax that chops away the world in one blow, leaving only the couple standing there trembling? Whatever they call it, it leaps over anything, takes the biggest chair, the largest slice, rules the ground wherever it walks, from a mansion to a swamp, and its selfishness is its beauty. Before I was reduced to singsong, I saw all kinds of mating. Most are two-night stands trying to last a season. Some, the riptide ones, claim exclusive right to the real name, even though everybody drowns in its wake.

Wearing a variety of guises, whatever it's called (infatuation, passion, lust, or romantic love), hits hard and leaves its participants aquiver, or so a popular culture would have Americans believe.

As portrayed in the movies, TV soap operas, and romantic novels in the United States, the uncontrollable intensity of romantic love defies reason, social context, and social mores. In *Fortune's Rocks*, a romantic novel, written by a recipient of the New England Book Award for Fiction, Anita Shreve[2] describes the disastrous love affair of an adolescent girl at the turn-of-the-century with an older, accomplished physician/writer, who was the same age as that of her father. As a result of their love affair, they both suffered enormous losses—that of family, children, friends, and reputation. But as the story seems to imply, they could not help themselves—"he puts his mouth on hers. It is a kiss, but more than a kiss. Something akin to drowning perhaps...But he is lost to the most powerful sort of lust there is: that which stems from hopelessness . . . And yet she knows that she cannot stop this, that it will have its own momentum, its own beginning and its own end."

Hungrily leaping into each other's arms, today's lovers also appear to be smitten by super-potent testosterone, estrogen, oxytocin, and/or adrenaline to such an extent that respectability, restraint, and responsibility are drowned out. In the 2007 movie, *Waitress*,[3] Jenna, the heroine played by Keri Russell, literally jumps into her married gynecologist's arms for a passionate embrace. Similarly, another 2007 movie, *Georgia Rule*[4] sees Felicity Huffman so intensely attracted to her old boyfriend that she frantically begins to undress while pursuing the mating dance. Scenes of clothes being torn off in a frenzied rush to sexual and romantic ecstasy abound in today's media offerings. Cupid has been very busy in modern America with his supercharged, erotic arrows.

Even quieter sexual attraction has its intensity, which is signified in films by an intense and prolonged gaze between the couple, often enhanced by closeups. A slowly executed, sensual kiss confirms the meaning of the gaze, and usually begins the sequence of more explicit sexual behaviors. The accompanying music building to a crescendo communicates the dramatic awakening of feeling that transcends ordinary experience, and the stage is set for love, Hollywood style.

According to Raelene Wilding,[5] an Australian anthropologist, whether this intense attraction is "true" love or infatuation will depend in the movies on a distinctive narrative theme. As she and other writers have noted, the differentiating characteristic between "true" love and sexual attraction seems to be its durability in the face of hardship, such as prolonged separation, commonly called the "Romeo and Juliet" effect. If romantic feeling can survive lengthy absences, then it demonstrates its mettle as "true" love. In *Four Weddings and a Funeral*,[6] for example, Carrie and Charles acknowledge their mutual sexual attraction, but it is only after significant periods of separation that they come to believe their feelings represent "true" romantic love. Likewise, in *The Wedding Singer*[7] and *Father of the Bride*,[8] separations are the "proof of the pudding" insofar as the validity of love is concerned.

Whether it's "true" love, uncontrollable passion, or the quieter, but steady rumbling of an unnerving attraction, romantic love as a requirement for marriage is a relatively recent phenomenon. "For most of history it was inconceivable that people would choose their mates on the basis of something as fragile and irrational as love and then focus all their sexual, intimate, and altruistic desires on the resulting marriage," writes Stephanie Coontz,[9] a historian. While history is full of examples of passionate love (in fact, William Jankowiak[10] documented the existence of romantic passion in 148 out of 166 sampled cultures for an overall presence of 89%), it is only within the last hundred years that romantic love has taken hold of the Western world's hearts and minds to such a widespread degree. Jankowiak defines passionate love "as any intense attraction involving the idealization of the other within an erotic context."

Plato, for example, believed that love was a positive emotion but he was referring to the love of one man for another, which he thought led men to behave honorably.[11] The early Christians and the Victorians idealized and purified the nonsexual aspects of love while downplaying (and even excluding) its more erotic components. Along the same line, courtly love developed by aristocratic ladies and disseminated by troubadours in twelfth-century France was idealized, spiritual, intense, passionate emotionally, and yet, painful because it was unconsummated. Troubadours' proclaiming messages of undying love might be regarded as precursors to modern-day recording artists singing passionately about romantic love in all its variability, including fated, lost, and unrequited love.

Other writers have had a more cynical view of love. For Ovid,[12] love was essentially "a sexual behavior sport in which duplicity is used in order that a man might win his way into a woman's heart." Similarly, Schopenhauer[13] thought romantic love was "a trick" that nature played on humanity in order to ensure the propagation of the species. Further devaluing romantic love was the view of both Catholic and Protestant theologians in the Middle Ages, who argued that excessive married love represented the sin of idolatry. At this time, even endearing nicknames for husbands were discouraged because they were thought to undermine the husband's authority and the awe that a wife should feel for him.[14]

Other societies (Hindus, Muslims) considered romantic love worthwhile but only if it wasn't the primary reason for marrying and only if it developed after marriage. "First we'll marry, then we'll fall in love" is the Hindu formula for love and marriage. Even when married love was esteemed in a particular society, it was considered of lesser importance than commitments to parents, siblings, cousins, neighbors, or God.

In past centuries and societies, people married primarily for a whole host of other reasons (power, money, kingdoms, status, dowries, annual income, good character, religion, shared values) besides love. Even when romantic love was a part of a particular society's culture, it was not a common reason for marriage. Among the Taita of Kenya, for example, "love wives" were valued, but they did not represent the majority of wives. An eighty-year-old man recalled that his fourth wife "was the wife of my heart... I would sit with her for hours on that hill... I could look at her and she at me—no words would pass, just a smile,"[15] The status of "love wife" was a cherished one in this society, but unfortunately, one that was attainable by only a few.

How then did romantic love become such a prized treasure—such a necessity—for marriage in the modern Western world? While historians trace the notion of a love-based marriage to eighteenth-century Enlightenment, where individual rights and relationships based on reason and justice were championed, and the American and French Revolutions, where freedom became the clarion call,[16] twentieth-century America stands out as a symbol of liberty, equality, and happiness for all, including love and marriage.

Teeming with immigrants approaching its shores, suffragettes marching for the vote, flappers dancing the Charleston, Rosie the Riveters doing their jobs in steel mills, the revolt of the Hippies in the sixties, and the women's liberation movement, America exudes creativity, power, enthusiasm, innovation, technology, and the good life. Coupled with freedom, equality, and a bit of anarchy thrown in, these qualities, along with Hollywood, have spawned an image of a vibrant, sophisticated American successful in all things, including love.

While historically romantic love had been thought to be the sole province of the cultural elite, who (it was assumed) had the necessary sophistication and leisure time to cultivate an aesthetic appreciation for it, the pursuit of romantic love became everyone's quest in the twentieth century. With freedom and equality ringing throughout the land and Hollywood's assistance in providing role models for the journey, Americans of all races, creeds, and socioeconomic classes began to believe that romantic love was within arm's reach and absolutely necessary for marital happiness.

In movies, the formula for courting, romancing, and seducing was provided by a whole host of Hollywood stars, including Gregory Peck, Cary Grant, Humphrey Bogart, Clark Gable, John Wayne, Marlon Brando, and more recently, George Clooney, Hugh Grant, Denzel Washington, Brad Pitt, Tom Cruise, Richard Gere, and Matt Damon among others. Lover boys learned how to be smooth, tough, or like the boy next door, a role perfected by Tom Hanks, while lover girls tried to be assertive like Bette Davis or Vivien Leigh, sexy like Marilyn Monroe, Kathleen Turner, or Sophia Loren, coy and beautiful like Elizabeth Taylor, or the perennial girl next door, like Meg Ryan. As the writer-director, James Mangold, of the time-travel romance, *Kate and Leopold*,[17] said: "A lot of what we learn about how to woo and charm and flirt and win someone over, we learn from the movies."[18]

In Hollywood, even a hooker can find the perfect man, just as Julia Roberts did in *Pretty Woman*.[19] When she said at the end of the movie, "I want the fairy tale," she was acknowledging the essence of movies, that is, their fantastic and unrealistic quality with saccharine endings. In movies as in fairy tales, the prince or leading man appears on the scene and transforms a lackluster existence into a shining kingdom fit for a Queen. Unfortunately, the post-arrival reality for most American women—the period after women fall in love and settle into ordinary life—often resembles Cinderella's life of drudgery with her stepsisters rather than the transformed, magical existence she presumably lived after Prince Charming appeared on her doorstep.

In the twenty-first century, Hollywood seems to have lost its talent for making great love stories—magical or not. With a media metabolism pitched to high levels, Hollywood movies are less about romantic love and more about fast-paced car chases, gory murders, and eerie, frightening creatures—all designed to provide the big adrenaline rush. According to Mary McNamara,[20] a contemporary media critic, "It all comes down to simple math. Ratings, readership, Web site hits, box office returns." As a result of all this emphasis on financial return, the film studios adhere to an Attention Deficit Disorder (ADD) mentality, that is, "they pin all their hopes and dreams on the big opening weekend, not to mention publicity dollars, on enormous numbers for two or three days." If a movie or television show fails to meet these "do or die" standards, it's quickly pulled out of theatres or off the air. Love stories, realistic or not, seldom qualify for this kind of ADD, moneymaking mentality, and those that do tend to be of the fast-moving, "love at first sight," instant sex genre.

Of the top ten romantic, moneymaker movies of all times in the United States,[21] only three of them came out in the past twenty years: *Titanic*[22] (1997), *Ghost*[23] (1990), and *Pretty Woman*[24] (1990). Incidentally, the top grossing love movie of the ages was *Gone With The Wind*,[25] which first appeared on the screen in 1939. Currently, romantic stories in American movies are hard to believe—either they're too farfetched or overly trite. Richard Curtis, writer of such popular romantic movies as *Four Weddings and a Funeral*[26] and *Notting Hill*,[27] said that it's difficult to write a unique romantic story nowadays. "If you write a story about a soldier going AWOL [away or absent without leave] and kidnapping a pregnant woman, and finally shooting her in the head, it's called searingly realistic, even though it's never happened in the history of mankind," he notes.[28] "Whereas if you write about two people falling in love, which happens about a million times a day all over the world, for some reason or another, you're accused of writing something unrealistic and sentimental." So movies currently are having a hard time getting the balance right between realism and fantasy.

The modern-day American public, hooked on adrenaline stimulated by horror films, death-defying movie chases, and video games, has shifted some of its attention for romantic formulae to television soap operas and shows, such as *The Bachelor*,[29] *The Bacholorette*,[30] and wedding reality shows, such as *A*

Wedding Story[31] and *Real Weddings from the Knot*.[32] These popular television shows, filled with highly attractive men and women, instant sexual attraction, and half-hearted commitment based solely on physical appeal, have captured the imagination of America's youth. While highly engrossing to its young audiences, these shows fail to provide any solid guidelines for long-term relationship satisfaction. Instead, they appear to provide how-to-do manuals for fast thrills, short-lived relationships, and easy exits from romantic entanglements.

IDEAL WOMEN IN THE MEDIA

With their good looks enhanced by ever-flattering lighting, makeup, and hairdressers, male and female paragons of lovability in the movies tend to be uni or bidimensional, but seldom multifaceted. Meg Ryan, for example, who has played in more romantic comedies than any other star (*Joe vs. the Volcano*,[33] *When Harry Meets Sally*,[34] *Sleepless in Seattle*,[35] *French Kiss*,[36] *When a Man Loves a Woman*,[37] and *You've Got Mail*,[38] among others) is a charming, cute, and wounded "girl next door." Making her romantic victim status appealing and accessible, Meg Ryan's childlike and vulnerable persona is not threatening, in spite of her good looks, to men who want to play the strong, dominant, and protective role with women. Ryan, "the winsome blonde with the perpetually perky-but-hurt expression on her perfect face,"[39] has been an ideal movie mate for a generation of American male moviegoers.

Similarly, Jennifer Aniston has been in the role of attractive but accessible "girl next door" in major video productions, such as the popular television series, *Friends*[40] and a number of films, including the 2006 film, *The Break Up*.[41] Like Doris Day and Meg Ryan before her, Jennifer Aniston is attractive but not too beautiful, thereby making her reachable for ordinary men without grandiose aspirations. While Day and Ryan were (are) sweet and charming, Aniston's character is more sharp-witted and sassy, providing more of an intellectual and emotional challenge to her suitors.

A similar type, Drew Barrymore has more sweetness and less abrasiveness than Aniston but she, too, is the attainable "girl next door." In *Music and Lyrics*,[42] she plays the role of a plant caretaker, who stumbles upon the apartment resident and movie hero, Hugh Grant, while tending to her plant duties. According to the Hollywood formula for romantic comedies, Barrymore, an undiscovered but gifted song lyricist, and Grant, an aging music composer, work together to create an acclaimed popular song, fall in love, and live happily ever after. If over-the-hill Grant (role he played in the movie) could succeed in winning Barrymore, then the pert and perky cheerleader type, or "girl next door," could be an attainable sex partner for the millions of average men in America who go to the movies.

For more grandiose, high achieving men of a bygone era, reigning stars of exceptional beauty, such as Jean Harlow, Greta Garbo, Lauren Bacall, Gene Tierney, Elizabeth Taylor, and Marilyn Monroe, represented the gold standard for trophy women. Current variations of "the beauty" are Haile Berry, Angelina Jolie, and Catherine Zeta-Jones. Their aloofness, which most of them possessed (clear exception was Marilyn Monroe, whose vulnerability and sensuality were her major characteristics), added to their mystery and appeal. Barriers, such as aloofness or playing hard-to-get, provoke the "mystery and madness essential to romantic love" according to Helen Fisher,[43] the author of *The Anatomy of Love*.

Thus, laying claim to any of these highly coveted movie stars or any of their clones added immensely to the masculinity index of successful suitors. However, as Katz and Liu[44] warned, "The relationships portrayed by the media are a symbol of status rather than of emotional health or personal well-being." And while the admiration of other men can provide a modicum of ego-gratification to the winners of these rare gems, trophy women are not known for their long-term success as wives and mothers.

More recently, the romantic, or more accurately, erotic ideal of women in American movies and television is "hot" women—attractive women with slender and curvaceous bodies who are uninhibited sexually and enjoy the alcohol/drug-saturated nightclub scene. Their free and easy sexuality disdains convention, falling on the pornographic and/or religiously immoral side of debates regarding their behavior. Certain contemporary movie actresses (e.g. Lindsay Lohan), pop music stars (e.g. Brittany Spears) and news-prominent socialites (e.g. Paris Hilton) represent this "bad girl" or "party girl" image, which is less of a romantic ideal than an erotic fantasy for most men.

While sexually provocative and so-called "fallen" women have played significant roles in history from time immemorial, the popularity and ongoing relevance of "party girls" in contemporary American culture suggest that they are being transformed into cultural icons of desirability. Rather than being relegated to unappealing, peripheral roles as villainesses in modern-day dramas, they have moved to center stage where they play starring roles. Even Paris Hilton's most dramatic fall from grace to date, that is, her incarceration in 2007 for violating probation for a DUI (driving under the influence of alcohol or other drugs), has been the subject of more sustained media attention than that of most other contemporary stars.

During the last fifty years in America, romantic ideals have changed from the fifties "good wife," who was always sweet, gracious, passive, nondemanding, and subservient (Edith in the long-running TV series *All in the Family*[45] is a good example), to the twenty-first century's physically attractive, slender (an absolute requirement), fun-loving, sexually unrestrained, and assertive woman. From the perspective of those who view this change negatively, damsels *in* distress from the days of the silent screen have become damsels *of* distress (because they are perceived as creating upheaval along their way). However, from a positive perspective, this modern romantic ideal is seen as more confident, enlightened, and interesting than her predecessors.

IDEAL MEN IN THE MEDIA

If the ideal woman, according to popular culture, is one of three possibilities—the cute and charming "girl next door," the beautiful, sophisticated woman who turns a thousand male heads (instead of launching a thousand ships as Helen of Troy did), or an attractive, unconventional, and sexually liberated woman—what is the ideal male partner supposed to be like? According to Regina Barreca[46] who wrote *Perfect Husbands*, the male protagonist in romantic novels should be virile, masterful, attractive, tender, and sensitive. "While he need not be rich, he must be successful at whatever he does."

In the old Westerns, the ideal man, frequently played by John Wayne or Gary Cooper, was tough, adventurous, independent, fearless, and always competent. Often the strong and silent type in the movies, the ideal man could be seen riding his horse alone along deserted, craggy mountains, ever ready for any danger, human or natural, that might befall him. Never indecisive or inadequate to the task, the ideal man in the West was superman, garbed in cowboy apparel, taming the wilderness but all set to fall in love when the right woman came his way.

Other versions of the ideal man in the movies, such as the characters played by James Dean in *Rebel Without A Cause*[47] and Marlon Brando in *On the Waterfront*[48] and *Streetcar Named Desire*,[49] had the same qualities as the Western cowboy, but in addition, they were free, rebellious, and wild. Whether they're riding a motorcycle, shouting "Stella" in a muscle-enhancing t-shirt, or walking along a dangerous waterfront, women or society could not control these stereotypic "bad boys."

Clark Gable's "Frankly, my dear, I don't give a damn" as he walks out the door in *Gone With The Wind*[50] also illustrates this autonomous, independent streak that is immune to manipulation, persuasion, or coercion. The ideal man, then, is a principled, invincible man who marches to his own drummer, except perhaps for his devotion to the woman he loves.

Newer leading movie stars are softer versions of the old ideal, but they are still adventurous, resourceful, and competent. Tom Cruise, Matt Damon,

Johnny Depp, Leonardo diCaprio, and Brad Pitt have more boyish charm, playfulness, and occasionally, androgyny than their predecessors, but they are still capable of outwitting the wiliest of foes. While less formidable and more attainable than their predecessors, they are nevertheless superheroes who can outsmart their enemies by physical strength, endurance, quick reaction time, and shrewdness. In addition, aside from the fact that they can be counted on for protection and safety, they are exciting lovers. Thus, they can provide much of what is desirable in a mate, except perhaps for loyalty, reliability, responsibility, and undying devotion.

THE PROBLEM WITH MEDIA IDEALS

The problem with popular cultures' rendition of ideal mates is that they exclude many solid and valuable characteristics (and people) from their inventories. Insofar as physical appearance is concerned, for example, only individuals with above-average or exceptional good looks can qualify (and women must be thin), and certain positive (or at worst neutral) personality/character traits are ignored in favor of others less admirable. Conscientiousness, shyness, indecisiveness, loyalty, thoughtfulness, seriousness, goodness, dependability, and moral integrity tend to be excluded, while impulsiveness, daring, restlessness, wit, cleverness, and moral expediency are placed at the top of the list.

In addition, while a particular individual may have some of the desirable qualities valued by popular culture, it is unlikely that he will have most of them or that the worst of those traits will be balanced by other sterling attributes. As Barreca[51] wrote, "It is simply not reasonable to expect a husband to have the perseverance of Prince Charming and Romeo, the mysteriously silent gallantry of Heathcliff and Clint Eastwood, the sexy brashness of Rhett Butler and Dennis Quaid ... " And if he is impulsive, restless, and morally expedient, it is very unlikely that he will also be loyal, thoughtful, and dependable to counterbalance his faults.

In *Perfect Husbands*, Barreca[52] described Emma's quandary (she is the heroine in Flaubert's[53] nineteenth-century novel, *Madame Bovary*). Emma is unhappily married to Charles, who along with being devoted and very affectionate to her is steady, well-educated, and thrifty. While Emma was in love with Charles at the beginning of their relationship, she becomes increasingly dissatisfied with him and their marriage as time goes on. It appears that the more devoted to his wife Charles became, the less respect she had for him. Charles would give Emma kisses on the cheeks, arms, fingertips, and shoulders, to which she would respond indifferently with a weary half-smile. To compensate for her unhappiness in the marriage, Emma read romance novels all day long, which focused on "rowing boats in the moonlight, nightingales in the grove, gentlemen brave as lions and gentle as lambs." Similar to twenty-first-century American women who are hooked on television soap operas and romance novels, Emma is disappointed in her husband because he is not everything she imagined a husband should be. Apparently, Charles couldn't swim, fence, or fire a pistol.

While the specific failings of spouses in modern America are clearly different from those of nineteenth-century husbands, the basic reality remains the same. The more unrealistic one's expectations are for a happy relationship, the more likely it is that one will be disappointed. And if one's expectations are forged on the basis of extensive media exposure, then one is likely to be highly disappointed. As Mary-Lou Galician,[54] the author of *Sex, Love, and Romance in the Mass Media*, writes, "Higher usage of certain mass media is related to unrealistic expectations about coupleship, and these unrealistic expectations are also related to dissatisfaction in real-life romantic relationships." Segrin and Nabi[55] also found that people who watched more love-focused television, such as soap operas, had more idealistic marital views and presumably would wind up more disappointed when their own marriages failed to meet these ideals.

In one intriguing study focused on the power of the media in shaping ideals, Bachen and Illouz[56] found that images of romantic love based on powerful visual schemata influence the "facts" and forms of the depictions of love. In their study, children and adolescents, aged eight to seventeen, were asked to choose pictures that depicted couples "most in love," and secondly, a picture representing the most romantic image. What they discovered was that young people's models of romance are visually developed and particularly sensitive to the visual cues of luxury and leisure consumption so common to media such as television, movies, and advertising.

In Bachen and Illouz's study, mass media was named by the vast majority of participants as the source of love stories—94 percent said they frequently encountered love stories on television, 90 percent in movies, 83 percent in songs or music, and 73 percent in books. Being in love was not only a feeling but also a mood evoked by atmospheric cues of wealth and leisure, for instance, dining out in elegant restaurants or strolling in the moonlight along the beach. As children got older, atmospheric cues of domesticity and familiarity were added to some of the images, but the earlier cues of wealth and leisure occurring in atypical environments were still apparent. Thus, images of love and romance in American culture appear to be laden with scenes from glamorous and wealthy lifestyles. For low socioeconomic couples especially, who can ill afford such extravagance in the name of *love*, romantic ideals of luxurious dining and Caribbean cruises undoubtedly serve as a source of ongoing disappointment in their more ordinary lives.

Shapiro and Kroeger[57] found that respondents with more unrealistic beliefs about romantic love reported significantly less satisfaction with their current relationship, significantly more exposure to popular media, and significantly less exposure to television documentaries than those who endorsed more realistic views. Another study[58] with a multiethnic sample of students aged eighteen to twenty discovered that television viewing amount and viewer involvement were correlated with participants' sexual attitudes, expectations, and behavior. In particular, greater exposure and greater television involvement were associated with higher expectations of the sexual activity of one's peers, more recreational attitudes toward sex, and more extensive sexual experience. In Galician's[59] cross-generational study, generation Xers (in contrast to Baby Boomers) appeared to use more mass media in general, had more unrealistic expectations of romantic relationships, specifically in terms of expecting mind reading in partners and great sex, and also held more stereotypic views of gender roles. Men especially expected sexual fireworks in their romantic relationships, but so did the women.

MEDIA MYTH: LOVE TRANSFORMS ALL

Knocked Up,[60] a popular romantic comedy film in the United States in 2007, illustrates one of the most prevailing romantic myths in modern culture, namely, that two very dissimilar people with almost nothing in common can fall in love and live happily ever after. This myth, a version of the old adage, "Love Conquers All," supposes that *love* is such a powerful, transformative force that it can overcome all obstacles in its path. In this mythic scenario, values, interests, socioeconomic status, religion, ethnicity, and life goals don't matter, as long as there is *love*.

In the movie, *Knocked Up*, Katherine Heigl plays the role of a gorgeous, smart, sweet, rising television star, while Seth Rogen's character is of an unemployed, unpolished but good-hearted, naive, pot-using, immature young man, whose "get rich" scheme involves measuring the time lapse before nudity first appears on a particular pornographic Web site. A one-night stand between this unlikely pair (they meet each other for the first time at a bar where Katherine is celebrating her job promotion) results in an unplanned pregnancy that becomes the basis for their commitment to each other. While the movie, thankfully, doesn't depict their living together in blissful matrimony forever (in fact, the movie ends with Seth Rogen looking lovingly at his newborn daughter), the likelihood of these two ever engaging in a one-night stand, much less a committed relationship, is so small as to strain any semblance of credibility. However, for the younger generation in America, the movie, with its scatological humor, is charming and funny.

Galician,[61] in her book on romance and the media, describes the following twelve media myths that she believes contribute to romantic unhappiness: (1) your perfect partner is cosmically predestined, so nothing/nobody can ultimately separate you, (2) there is such a thing as "love at first sight," (3) your true "soul mate" should know what you're thinking or feeling (without your having to tell), (4) if your partner is truly "meant for you," sex is easy and wonderful, (5) to attract and keep a man, a woman should look like a model or a centerfold, (6) the man should not be shorter, weaker, younger, poorer, or less successful than the woman, (7) the love of a good and faithful true woman can change a man from a "beast" into a "prince," (8) bickering and fighting a lot mean that a man and a woman really love each other passionately, (9) all you really need is love, so it doesn't matter if you and your lover have very different values, (10) the right mate "completes you"—filling your needs and making your dreams come true, (11) in real life, actors are often very much like the romantic characters they portray, and (12) since mass media portrayals of romance aren't "real," they don't really affect you.

Of these media myths, three of them (#7, 9, and 10) relate directly to the belief that love has transformative powers. Based on the fairy tale, *The Beauty and the Beast*,[62] myth #7 assumes that the love of a good woman can change a man from an unprincipled lowlife into a dashing man of integrity. If he drank, gambled, or caroused around prior to falling in love, after being smitten by *love's* arrow he will give up all bad habits and become a devoted husband and father, or so the myth goes. While there is a smidgen of truth to this notion, in other words, both sexes do benefit from love's magic for a while, the rosy glow that masks a thousand failings doesn't last.

Occurring shortly after *love* hits and lasting for a year or two, this white-washing effect, or idealization, can transform the ugliest of wart-covered toads into Prince Charming and works similar magic in changing ordinary women into "belles of the ball." If during this miraculous phase, more durable love based on the real strengths of each person can begin to develop, the relationship can start to thrive. If not, when the spell wears off, disillusionment will set in and begin the long process of relationship dissolution.

Galician's media myth #9 assumes that value differences between romantic partners are unimportant because of the transformative power of love. Contradicted by a whole host of studies[63] that strongly support the premise that value similarity is a significant determinant of interpersonal attraction and relationship satisfaction, the belief that *love* will leap over and/or erase important value differences is untrue the vast majority of time. Similarities in demographics (age, race, education, religion, and social class), in physical attractiveness, in cognitive and emotional traits, and in attitudes and values clearly affect degree of liking as well as marital satisfaction. Even in interethnic relationships, similarity in age, education, values, and physical attractiveness tends to hold sway. In fantasy-ridden movies, such as *Pretty Woman*[64] and *An Officer and a Gentleman*,[65] where the romantic attraction is based almost entirely on physical appeal, the likelihood of such characters carving out an ongoing, viable relationship when they have nothing else in common is miniscule, to say the least.

In cases where opposites do attract, they may be trading one asset for another (e.g. looks or youth for money) in order to obtain a partner of similar social status or they may be operating out of the need for completion (attraction to valued characteristics in another that are lacking in one's self). In the learning channel's *A Wedding Story*[66] on TV, the answers to the question, "Why do you love him (or her)?" relate directly to the need for completion, for instance, "he brings balance to my life," or "she makes me a whole person."[67] When the need for completion is the sole reason for the attraction, disillusionment can quickly set in because the attractive qualities in a partner are not likely to change the self. In fact, the valued quality may become a source of irritation because it failed to provide any hoped-for benefits. Sociability, for example, can become irritating garrulousness for the spouse whose own shyness did not diminish by association.

MEDIA MYTHS: PREDESTINED LOVE AND "LOVE AT FIRST SIGHT"

Another of Galician's media myths (#1) deals with the role of fate or destiny in partner selection. The belief that there is only one soul mate for each person, who represents the lost missing half, is based on Plato's notion of the division of the human race into two sexes, forever longing for reunion.[68] This idealized desire for a perfect partner to complete them leads lovers to scale mountains and leap over chasms in pursuit of this Holy Grail.

One unhappily married woman, whose college romance ended traumatically when the young man left her for the priesthood, believed that she was leading "a wrong life" because she was "really meant" for the priest. Convinced that the two of them were ordained by God or fate to be together, she felt that her current life with her husband and children was inauthentic and empty. In addition, she believed that the fun-loving, curious, and passionate self she was with her boyfriend during college was directly attributable to him and now was lost forever. Although intelligent, sensitive, and poetically gifted, she initially (in psychotherapy) was unable to see that her marital unhappiness provided the fuel for her predestination theory and that her fantasies of lost, perfect love provided her some solace. Gradually, by developing her own considerable talents, she was able to give up the notion that there was only one preordained love in this world for her.

"Love at first sight" is one of those mythic beliefs (Galician's media myth #2) that has survived for generations. Folkloric stories of instant knowing, "I knew the first time I saw her that we were meant for each other," provide validation, especially when the pair has been happily married for years. To keep this myth alive, however, requires that tales of disconfirmation, that is, cases of "love at first sight" that ended disastrously, be forgotten quickly. While it is clear that the sight of an enchanted stranger across a crowded room can signal, with a fluttering heartbeat, the beginning of a supercharged affair, this intense, out of the blue emotion may be passion, infatuation, or lust, but not love. According to Sternberg's[69] definition at any rate, love requires that at least emotional closeness be added to the equation.

The surge of emotion at first glance, however, bespeaks a powerful attraction to the physical appearance or demeanor of the stranger based on strong undercurrents of association (one man recalled how enthralled he was by the first glimpse of his future wife's expansive gestures, which he associated with vitality and adventurousness). Dorothy Tennov,[70] in her book *Love and Limerence: The Experience of Being In Love*, uses the term "limerence" to refer to the strong emotional and sexual forces unleashed by sexual attraction. Often a function of idealization and/or the need for completion, limerence or infatuation represents a glimpse into a world of ecstatic possibilities, a longing for happiness unconstrained by mundane realities. Unfortunately, the chances of that glorified stranger living up to such elevated expectations are slight.

The television "reality show," *The Bachelorette*,[71] is a documentary of the mating rituals of those young people in America who believe in "love at first sight."[72] The heroine, after conversing for a few minutes with each of twenty-five competitors vying for her affection, makes a quick assessment of their romantic potential in language replete with phrases, such as "I just knew," "It was meant to be," or "My gut told me." When she finally (after seven weekly episodes) makes her decision about who will be her fiancé, an estimated twenty million American viewers are there to cheer her on (apparently twenty million people watched the engagement of Trista and Ryan, the first couple consecrated on the show). America seems to be obsessed with quick romance and the more quickly people fall in love, the better.

In the movie *Serendipity*,[73] Kate Beckinsale and John Cusack play characters that meet as customers at a New York City department store at Christmastime. Even though each has another romantic partner, they are struck by Cupid's arrow and strive to prove via contrived maneuvers that their relationship is fated by the gods. No matter how insurmountable the obstacles thrown in their paths appear to be, including wedding plans with their original partners, they defy all odds and wind up together.

Similarly, in the movie *Kate and Leopold*,[74] the main characters separated by over a century keep returning to one another via leaps off the Brooklyn Bridge until they're reunited forever in the past. Predestined love and "love at first sight" are vindicated in both these movies, providing ample support for the myth that love will prevail in spite of overwhelming circumstances against its survival.

MEDIA MYTH: SEX SHOULD SET OFF FIREWORKS

Besides the media myths related to predestination and love's transformative powers, a prevailing myth in the United States that has been given significant amounts of media attention in recent years deals with sexual perfection, that is, having great sex all the time.[75] Popular magazines, such as *Cosmopolitan*, *Maxim*, and *Playboy*, fill newsstands with "how to" articles about giving and having sexual thrills galore. As Johnson[76] wrote in an article entitled, "Promoting Easy Sex Without Genuine Intimacy," "*Cosmopolitan* and *Maxim* stress sexual perfection and prefer centerfold looks, suggesting that fantastic sex is possible (if you just know what to do), and that a woman should look like a supermodel or celebrity. The result is that the relationship—or coupleship—is grounded in an unrealistic, mythological approach to romance and love." In these magazines, sex is glorified at the expense of emotional intimacy.

In response to the statement on a mass media love quiz designed by Galician,[77] "If your partner is truly meant for you, sex is easy and wonderful," one twenty-seven-year-old woman wrote, "The mass media portrays sex as being this wonderful romantic thing that's always perfect. Nothing ever goes wrong. There's always flowers or candlelight, or both. The very first time I had sex it was nothing like on television. The whole experience was uncomfortable, scary, and not very enjoyable. And this was with someone I'd dated for four years."

In response to the same statement, a young man, twenty-five years old, wrote, "I'd been with other girls, but Liz was the first one I really cared about and imagined a future with, so with her I waited. Because I wanted everything to be 'like in the movies' the first time we had sex, I planned a very romantic evening with music and champagne, and the works. But when it came time to 'do the deed,' I froze. I was just so nervous about everything being perfect that I think I scared myself."

The responses of these two young adults are typical of the reactions of disappointed lovers whose pyrotechnic expectations about sex were shaped primarily by the media. Because sex is typically portrayed in soap operas, romance novels, and movies as romantic, intense, uncontrollable, and ecstasy-filled, the real-life fumbling, uncertainty, and mediocre pleasure that characterize many sexual experiences, especially the early ones, are sources of disappointment and self-doubt. In addition, when the experience doesn't live up to the expectation, disillusioned lovers often question the appropriateness of their partner choice and are ready to move on, even when all of the necessary ingredients to a satisfying relationship are in place.

Other unfortunate consequences of unrealistic beliefs about sex are that sexual pleasure is overvalued, that is, a frequent diet of great sex is viewed as necessary for survival and manhood (or womanhood), and lust is often confused with love. One young man, a successful lawyer, spent fifteen years of his adult life in pursuit of the perfectly proportioned, curvaceous woman, with whom he could have great sex. After many heartaches and disappointments along the way, he finally gave up his dream of sexual perfection and married a charming but average-looking woman, who had considerable talent in other areas.

Lowry, Love, and Kirby[78] conducted a content analysis of sex acts in daytime soap operas and found that 6.58 was the number of sex acts per hour with twice as many characters engaging in intercourse outside marriage as within it. Even on prime-time television shows, such as *Two and a Half Men*[79] and *Desperate Housewives*,[80] television stars hop into bed with relative strangers, and popular songs are rife with prurient lyrics and accompanying groaning in the delivery. The media's obsession with sex provides teenagers and young adults with a steady diet of fornication, adultery, sexual infidelity, and perversions. Sexual intimacy separated from emotional closeness is portrayed as the pathway to a loving relationship rather than vice versa.

Adult children of divorce, bereft of in-house role models of reasonably happy romantic relationships, are more likely to be confused about the ingredients for a successful relationship than their counterparts in healthy, intact homes. To the extent that they rely on the ever-present hum and blinding glare of television (and movies and romantic novels) for lessons on love and sex, they are more prone to adopt the popular culture's distortions of romantic love in their own search for happiness and as a result become disillusioned.

CHAPTER 7

Love by Arrangement

Writing about women in Afghanistan in his best-selling novel, *A Thousand Splendid Suns*, Khaled Hosseini[1] describes a young woman's first meeting with her prospective husband in an arranged marriage: "Mariam smelled him before she saw him. Cigarette smoke and thick, sweet cologne, not faint like Jalil's. The scent of it flooded Mariam's nostrils. Through the veil, from the corner of her eye, Mariam saw a tall man, thick-bellied and broad-shouldered, stooping in the doorway. The size of him almost made her gasp, and she had to drop her gaze, her heart hammering away.... In the mirror, Mariam had her first glimpse of Rasheed; the big, square, ruddy face; the hooked nose; the flushed cheeks that gave the impression of sly cheerfulness; the watery, bloodshot eyes; the crowded teeth, the front two pushed together like a gabled roof; the impossibly low hairline, barely two finger widths above the bushy eyebrows; the wall of thick, coarse, salt and pepper hair." And with that vivid, extremely unappealing picture in mind, one shudders at the thought of Mariam's married life with Rasheed—a marriage that did turn out to be steeped in subjugation and violence.

To the Western world schooled in individualism and free choice, the concept of love by arrangement seems like an oxymoron. From the Western perspective, arranged marriages connote loveless unions at best; dowry deaths, suicides, and domestic violence at worst. Television shows[2] in America such as *60 minutes*,[3] *20/20*,[4] and *Oprah Winfrey*[5] have portrayed the failings and often-brutal consequences of arranged marriages. In Britain, where many Asians have migrated in recent years, particularly from Pakistan, the abuses of arranged marriages, for example, bounty hunters trying to locate and return women who escaped from forced marriages, are well documented.[6] Symbolic of parental authority, group mentality, and economic bartering, arranged marriages could be regarded as cultural remnants of a primitive past. In contrast, love marriages, wherein partners freely select one another on the basis of romantic love, appear to represent democracy, freedom of choice, and individuality. In spite of all the problems of Western-style marriages, love marriages are thought to be far superior to a system that diminishes the couple to economic, familial, and political pawns.[7]

Irrespective of the negative portrayals, however, the majority of marriages in Pakistan, India, Bangladesh, Sri Lanka, and most of those in other Muslim countries are arranged, and many proponents of arranged marriage see it as advantageous in many respects. In a survey of young Indian men and women, ages fourteen to forty-two, living in India, England, and the United States, Sprecher and Chandak[8] found that the positive reasons cited for arranged marriages included family support, stability of marriage, compatibility, easier adjustment, ease of meeting partner, and happiness of parents and family. Disadvantages included limited choice, family/in-law problems, dowry treatment, and not knowing each other well. Advantages of love marriages included love, romanticism, freedom of choice, dating/sexual freedom, and getting to know each other, while the disadvantages included anguish related to sex, pregnancy, and immoral behavior, disapproval from parents and society, waste of time and money, bad reputation, and short-lived relationships. When the respondents were asked, which type of marriage they preferred, the older respondents tended to favor arranged marriages, even though they believed the couple should be consulted, while the younger ones thought that young men and women should be allowed to date and marry whomever they choose.

Regardless of the changing attitudes of young people toward marriage, the most common method of mate selection worldwide is by arrangement, usually by parents with the aid of relatives or matchmakers.[9] In collectivist, traditional, Eastern cultures, where the emphasis is on family integrity, family unity, and family loyalty, arranged marriages tend to predominate. Collectivism has been defined by Hui and Triandis[10] as "a sense of harmony, interdependence, and concern for others," which reflects the subordination of individual goals to collective goals. In individualistic, industrialized, Western nations, the focus by contrast is on personal initiative, autonomy, self-reliance, personal freedom, and independence, where the goals of the family or religious group are decidedly less important than individual goals. Here, marriages based on romantic love and individual choice prevail.[11]

In arranged marriages, women in particular tend to marry at an early age (most brides worldwide are in their mid-to-late teens[12]), and if marrying later they are still chaperoned in public. Partner matching in arranged marriages is often determined by price with the groom's family paying for the bride (bride-price or bride-wealth), which is common in Africa, or the bride's family paying a dowry to the husband, more typical of India and other Asian countries. The practice of paying to marry a woman, a more common custom worldwide than the opposite, is seen as a means of "heightening the husband's gratitude for a good wife, making him appreciate her dignity and worth."[13] In addition, bride-price or wealth is not viewed as "buying a wife" by its practitioners, but rather as compensation to the young woman's family for her domestic services, which will no longer be available once she gets married and moves away.

As for dowries, an important practice historically in Europe and some Asian countries, they have come under harsh attack in recent years because of documented abuses, such as overwhelming financial burdens on fathers and suicides of young girls trying to spare their families' economic hardship. Originally viewed as a means of exchanging wealth for higher social position, marrying a social equal, or obtaining a loyal son-in-law who will serve the family, dowries have been outlawed in some countries. In India, for example, the 1961 Dowry Prohibition Act made the giving of a dowry illegal, but the custom has persisted sub-rosa into the modern day.

The social status and reputation of the family is an extremely important factor in partner selection in arranged marriages. A further consideration in some societies is the existence of traditional marriage patterns held across generations, such as the consanguineous marriage between cousins.[14] Marriage in Iran is usually within social class and is often between parallel cousins or cross cousins. In Iraq nearly half of all Iraqis marry their first or second cousins, with the preferred union being for a daughter to wed the son of her father's brother.[15] Similar marriages arranged within extended families can be found in traditional African societies, where unions between relatives are encouraged.

This chapter focuses on marriage in several cultures and countries (India, Egypt, Sri Lanka, Turkey, and Kenya) that are markedly different from the U.S. type of marriage (arranged versus love), religious and family perspectives on marriage, and emphasis on suitability of partner choice. In the Hindu, Muslim, and African countries, marriages are tend to be arranged by parents and/or matchmakers in order to ensure "appropriate" marital choices—that is, partners of similar background, religion, and values—characteristics that have been shown to be important in marital satisfaction. In addition, in these cultures, typically, marriage is valued highly and viewed as a holy union sanctioned by God, family, and friends for the greater good of their societies. Because of this, overarching motives (religion, family allegiance) are brought into play to strengthen the marriage commitment and theoretically enhance both marital stability and satisfaction. If the positive aspects of marriage making in these cultures (e.g., enhancement of religious and family involvement, more focus on partner similarity) were woven more tightly into the fabric of American society, the marital journeys of adult children of divorce would be less hazardous.

ARRANGED MARRIAGES IN INDIA

Arranged marriages, still regarded as a central aspect of Indian society, have been part of the Indian culture since the fourth century. According to Prakasa,[16] arranged marriages serve a number of vital functions in the Indian community—they give parents control over family members, preserve and continue the ancestral lineage, strengthen the kinship group, consolidate family property, and preserve the principle of endogamy (marriage within a specified group). Arranged marriages are also believed to help maintain and enhance the social satisfaction and happiness of individuals, presumably by putting together two people and families who have a great deal in common. In keeping with the family orientation, Indian marriage is basically treated as an alliance between two families rather than a union between two individuals.[17]

The practice of arranged marriages began as a way of uniting and maintaining upper caste families and eventually spread to the lower castes where it was used for the same purpose. Because the concepts of reincarnation and karma (the beliefs that one has earned a place in the world by prior good or bad deeds in an earlier life) keep the Hindu caste system alive, people accept their station in life and therein marry within their caste. For many Hindus, especially among the 75 percent of the Indian population that resides in villages, the caste system remains strong.

Hinduism, the world's third-largest religion with approximately a billion followers, began about six thousand years ago and can be traced to the ancient Vedic civilization. A conglomerate of diverse beliefs and traditions spanning polytheistic and monotheistic systems (there is devotion to a single God while accepting the existence of other gods), Hinduism has no single founder. About 905 million of its adherents live in India with the rest of the Hindu population scattered throughout the world. In India, the second-largest country in the world with a population of over a billion, 82 percent of its inhabitants are Hindus. Countries with large Hindu populations include Bangladesh, Sri Lanka, Pakistan, Indonesia, Malaysia, Mauritius, Fiji, Guyana, and Thailand.

According to Hinduism, marriage is a sacred institution or union in which one works out his/her salvation. Unless one is married, one is considered incomplete and unholy; the Hindu man has not attained his complete self until marriage, where ideally he and his wife work together to reach God.

In Hindu philosophy, marriage is viewed as a triangle where God is at the apex and the husband and wife are at the other two corners at the base of the triangle. When they begin moving toward God together, it is believed that the distance between them will decrease until they ultimately reach God together.

Further illustrating the sacred view of marriage in the Hindu religion is the lavish marriage ceremony itself, where the bride and groom hold hands and take seven steps together around the God of fire and pledge eternal friendship to each other. The seven steps in *saptapadi* (the seven-step ritual) represent nourishment, growth, wealth, shared joys and sorrows, children, eternal unity, and lifelong friendship. Because marriage is considered the primary pathway to union with God, a great deal of importance is placed on finding the right partner. Romantic love is not considered a prerequisite for marriage; in fact, love has been considered a weak basis for marriage because it is believed to make one blind toward unsuitable qualities of a spouse.[18] In India, for example, it is assumed that love will grow after living together in marriage.

Decades ago, parents arranged marriages for their children when they were babies or very young children. Compatibility between two families was of primary concern because a young daughter had to live with her husband's extended family. They believed that if young people grew up together, they could learn over time how to understand and adjust to each other's manners. The girl did not have to leave her parents to live with her husband and in-laws until she arrived at maturity. Instead, she just visited them until the wedding, which usually occurred before puberty. Consummation of the marriage, however, normally did not occur until three years after the marriage ceremony.[19]

In a humorous portrayal of a matchmaking interview, Pulitzer Prize winner Jhumpa Lahiri,[20] author of *Interpreter of Maladies*, described it as follows: "Most likely the groom will arrive with one parent, a grandparent, and either an uncle or aunt. They will stare, ask several questions. They will examine the bottoms of your feet, the thickness of your braid. They will ask you to name the prime minister, recite poetry, feed a dozen hungry people on half a dozen eggs." And if the prospective bride passed all these tests, she was headed for a life with her husband's extended family—cooking, cleaning, child-tending, and serving tea to guests.

In the more modern age, parents are still arranging marriages with the help of kinsmen, friends, and even matchmakers, but they are not doing the arranging so early. Child marriages are now forbidden, and the legal age in India for marriage is eighteen for women and twenty-one for men. Currently, parents are trying to select mates best suited for their children by examining personal qualities, education, the social status of a prospective partner, and the horoscopes of the two, for good measure. And in more urban areas in India, they are consulting their children about marital prospects in such a manner that the final decision is shared.

Currently the use of matrimonial advertisements in newspapers is increasing and the popularity of the "semi-arranged" marriage is also growing, especially among the urban middle-class in India.[21] The semi-arranged marriage consists of prescreening young men and women, introducing suitable prospects to one another, and then allowing for a brief courtship period in which potential partners can decide whether they like each other well enough to spend the rest of their lives together. In contrast to American dating, parents and extended family members are still involved in the initial screening, the courtship is much shorter, little, or no premarital sex is involved, and there is a realistic recognition by both parties that the purpose of the courtship is marriage.[22] According to Lessinger,[23] the semi-arranged marriage "is intended to retain parental control while accommodating the youthful yearning for romantic love, which is fed by both Indian and American media."

While many young Indian men and women in modern times prefer an arranged marriage, most of them want to be consulted and have a final say about the person they will marry.[24] If they happen to fall in love, parental approval is deemed of paramount importance for a large majority of Indian youth. A young Indian woman, a college graduate with a degree in political science, was questioned by a colleague about why she was going along with an arranged marriage. "Don't you care who you marry?" "Of course, I care," she answered. "That is why I must let my parents choose a boy for me. My marriage is too important to be arranged by such an inexperienced person as myself. In such matters, it is better to have my parents' guidance."[25]

The traditional arranged marriage is getting to be an anachronism in some countries with greater numbers of young people engaging in a mixture of traditional and modern-marriage practices each year. However, the issue of how well the arranged marriage has fared in terms of divorce, marital satisfaction, and domestic violence compared to the modern love marriage is an important one. Even though the question may seem academic and irrelevant to the changing world climate, certain aspects of arranged marriages in India—namely, its emphasis upon family allegiance and similarity of background in partner selection, the importance placed upon marriage as a God-like union, and the stress upon friendship as integral to marriage—are all antidotes to marital dissolution, and as such well-worth noting.

In general, overarching motives (beyond individual satisfaction and happiness) serve to strengthen a marriage commitment and reduce the likelihood of divorce. As several studies[26,27,28] have shown, religion can serve as that overarching motive—as can family allegiance. For example, low religious participation and religious heterogeneity within the family are associated with a greater risk of divorce. With Indian marriages, both family and religious commitments underscore the marriage vows, theoretically strengthening the marriage. Regrettably, not a great deal is known about divorce in India because the Indian government does not report divorce figures to international agencies and Indian researchers do not report this data in journal articles.

What is known about marital happiness in India, unfortunately, is quite varied and dependent upon the measure being examined. On the basis of two studies published in the eighties, arranged marriages performed quite well. In Gupta and Singh's[29] study they compared love marriages in India with arranged marriages. Those who married for love were higher initially on Rubin's Love Scale than the arranged-marriage group, but by ten years plus, that is, over ten years of marriage, the arranged-marriage group surpassed the love group by far in terms of reported feelings of love. Similarly, in a study by Yelsma and Althappilly,[30] Indian couples in arranged marriages had higher marital satisfaction than American or Indian couples engaged in love marriages. Over the long haul, arranged Indian marriages apparently did better than love marriages in terms of marital satisfaction in these two studies. However, in another more recent study of Indian love and arranged marriages,[31] the only variable that was significant was sexual satisfaction, which contributed to marital adjustment. Neither type of marriage nor marital duration was related to marital adjustment.

While these studies suggest that marriages in India are faring well, the domestic violence literature presents another picture. According to reports in the Indian newspapers and scholarly publications, approximately 40 percent of married Indian women face physical abuse by their husbands,[32] a figure that is higher than the one-third estimate for both the United States and worldwide. Furthermore, the rate is actually even higher among low-caste women (57%) in comparison to the reported rate of 17 percent among high-caste women.[33] Abusive relationships were also reported more frequently among illiterate men and women than among those with secondary schooling or more, which suggests that an uneducated patriarchal mentality contributes dramatically to domestic violence in India and elsewhere.

ARRANGED MARRIAGES IN MUSLIM COUNTRIES

Islam, the second-largest religion in the world after Christianity, has about 0.9 to 1.4 billion followers, 85 percent of whom are Sunnis and 15 percent are Shi'as. Originating with the teachings of Muhammad, a seventh-century Arab religious figure, who was not regarded as divine but as a prophet, Islam is the predominant religion throughout the Middle East as well as in parts of Africa and Asia. Muhammad is viewed as the restorer of the original monotheistic faith of Abraham, Moses, Jesus, and other prophets, whose teachings, it is believed, were corrupted by followers. Besides Africa and Asia, large Muslim communities are found in Western Europe, the Balkan Peninsula, and Russia. Often the state religion in many countries, Islam is a sociopolitical system that regulates all aspects of political, religious, and social life. Among the *Five Pillars of Islam* practiced by Muslims throughout the world are the five prayers a day facing Mecca, fasting during the month of Ramadan, and the Hajj or the pilgrimage to Makkah (Mecca) at least once in a lifetime.

Marriage in Islam is regarded as a religious duty wherein one preserves one's faith and safeguards one's journey toward higher levels of spirituality. In some cases, marriage is obligatory, that is, when a person is so tormented by sexual desire that they fear falling into the sin of fornication. In other cases marriage can be forbidden, for example, when a person cannot fulfill spousal duties, either sexual or economic. And while marriage is intended to fulfill multiple purposes, which include spiritual tranquility and peace, along with cooperation and partnership in fulfilling the divine mandate, its primary goal is to provide a safe haven for the fulfillment of sexual needs. Thus, marriage is seen as a legitimate means of satisfying physical needs, obtaining pleasure, and reducing the temptation to engage in sinful, carnal desires outside the marriage.

In contrast to Hindu marriage ceremonies that are replete with colorful garb, incense, music, and rituals, Islamic weddings are simple. Since the marriage is accomplished by the signing of a civil contract in a home or judge's office, and not necessarily in a mosque, the wedding ceremony itself is arbitrary, but there is often a marriage celebration or reception given by the family. In these instances, the receptions, where the bride may wear a Western-style gown, are usually held separately for men and women. More elaborate wedding festivities, including a procession of guests with bridal gifts and/or the groom riding a horse through the streets in celebration, take place in some parts of the Islamic world.[34]

Under strict Islamic law, purity and chastity prior to marriage are not only encouraged but also demanded. Muslims are not permitted to touch, have social conversation, engage in personal communication via the Internet, or date members of the opposite sex. Because of these restrictions, Muslims are encouraged to marry early, and to do so with the assistance of family, a service, or a matchmaker, who is responsible for investigating the backgrounds and conducting marriage interviews. Arranged marriages are definitely preferred by Muslim families, but forced marriages, in which there is family coercion and lack of consent by one partner, are considered contrary to the teachings of Muhammad. Ideally, insofar as the Koran is concerned, marriage prospects should be selected on the basis of their good character and spiritual maturity, but in reality, wealth, physical appearance, social standing, and profession have become important factors in determining the suitability of a prospect.

Historically, women protected their bodies by wearing a body-covering robe and veil, or purdah, as a means of maintaining moral standards, that is, reducing temptation, both for themselves as well as men. However, as a result of higher education, Western influence, and the fact that professional middle- and upper-class women are increasingly in the work force, certain countries have relaxed these standards. Egypt, for example, gave up the purdah years ago.

While the term "dating" has been considered a euphemism among Muslims for premarital sex, a more acceptable version of "dating" for American Muslims made its appearance in the United States in 2000. At a "Matrimonial Banquet,"[35] Muslim young men and women (with the help of parents) can meet each other and later pursue promising relationships via e-mails and phones (clearly forbidden by Muslim parents in the past). At these banquets, which bear an uncanny resemblance to speed-dating events held at bars throughout the United States, the women are seated at tables, where young men stop by to chat for "seven minutes" (it is not clear how the time of seven minutes was arrived at) before heading for another table. At the end of the event, appealing prospects are pursued at a social hour, where the organizers of the event maintain that a number of successful marriages were initiated.

ARRANGED MARRIAGES IN SRI LANKA

As "matrimonial banquets" in the United States illustrate, Muslim marriage practices do vary by country, and in certain areas the distinction between arranged and love marriages gets blurred. In Sri Lanka, for example, DeMunck[36] studied the marriage practices of Muslims living in the remote, rural village of Kutali. Studying village life over a thirty-month period, he found that ten of the eighteen couples married during that period said they married "for love," even though the marriages were arranged to cross cousins and solidified with dowries. Cross-cousin marriages, which involve the offspring of a parent's cross-sex siblings, tend to be preferred in Southeast Asia, where sexual attraction is fostered by some socialization practices. Among the practices DeMunck observed in Kutali are, (1) bathing at public wells or in the river (nude bathing is not acceptable but flirting is appropriate here), (2) frequent visiting among cross cousins (brother–sister love is idealized in South Asia and is regarded as the strongest and most enduring affective bond), and (3) circumcision rites for males, following which female cousins come to visit, bearing gifts of candy-like treats to sweeten the period of convalescence.

While flirtation between cross cousins is encouraged, strong sanctions against the expression of sexuality prior to marriage serve to increase sexual desire. Once sexual desire is focused on a specific individual, however, the word gets out and parents work hard to arrange such a marriage, provided the dowry is right. Thus, the ideal marriage in this Muslim village is both arranged and for love. As DeMunck writes, "Kutali villagers do marry for love and for economic reasons. Economic reasons and parental authority are foregrounded in the arranged marriage-dowry complex, while love is seen as a 'silent partner.'" Further, he adds that cultural institutions and socialization practices also affect marriages in the West, for example, upper-middle- and upper-class families in the United States are more likely to encourage their children to attend private universities where they will meet and probably marry someone like them, but "in the West, the arranged aspects of marriage act as silent partners, while in South Asia love is the silent partner."

ARRANGED MARRIAGES IN TURKEY

Just as Istanbul straddles the East and West by its location (it sits on two sides of the Bosphorus Sea separating Asia from Europe), so does Turkey's culture regarding marriage show signs of both Eastern and Western traditions.[37] Turkey is regarded as "a traditional and patriarchal culture in the process of modernization," but there continues to be a heavy emphasis on collectivistic values regarding the importance of the family and on religious values with Islam as the state religion influencing all aspects of daily life. About half of the marriages in Turkey are arranged with families initiating the marriage and guiding the arrangements, while the other half are more western in style. Even when a man and woman decide to marry independently, the families play more significant roles in wedding and marriage arrangements than they often do in the West.

In the case of a traditional or arranged marriage, the groom's parents mobilize their social network in search of a suitable bride. Consistent with their value system , good family background, similarity with respect to education, monetary means, and social status, good character, spousal harmony (love, respect, and support), and ability to adapt to the family, are considered desirable characteristics in a mate. Brides are expected to be modest and obedient, and to come under the authority of their mothers-in-law once married. However, according to Jenny White,[38] "resourceful women can influence whom they marry, under what circumstances, and how they behave after marriage." For example, a young woman can make herself attractive to impress mothers looking for brides, or if she is industrious can have a substantial trousseau to bring into her marriage, which increases her appeal among matchmakers.

After screening of prospects, which includes matchmaking interviews with the women's families, the groom's mother chooses a prospective bride, discusses her choice with her husband, and if he agrees, informs her son about the family choice. Hortascu[39] writes: "Depending on the degree of traditionalism in the family, the couple may or may not be introduced and may or may not have a few 'dates' alone or in the presence of family and/or friends." While the son's opinion is usually considered in selecting a mate, he is more likely than not to go along with his family's decision.

In a modern version of the arranged marriage that is becoming more common in Turkey, the prospective spouses are introduced by their families and then are left to make their own decisions after a few dates. Love marriages are also on the rise, especially among the young, urban, and educated sectors. Even in love marriages, however, there is a high degree of family direction and involvement in wedding arrangements.

ARRANGED MARRIAGES IN EGYPT

In Egypt, which is a modern Muslim country by many standards, a surprising number of marriages, even among middle-class Egyptians, continue to be arranged or at least orchestrated by parents and relatives. Families take an intense interest in their children's marriages because marriage continues to be viewed as a union between two families. Therefore, it has been extremely important that both families have as much knowledge about the other family as possible in order to prevent "unsuitable" choices, that is, partners from families marked by divorce, insanity, or lower social status.

Suitability for marriage is defined as equivalence in lineage, religiousness, profession, and social status, and in being free of defects that would warrant annulling the marriage contract. As for social status, Bahira Sherif-Trask[40] writes, "this preoccupation with social status carries great importance at the time of courtship, for if this issue is ignored, a marriage may be marked by difficulty or even failure." Unwittingly (or deliberately), the extended family may contribute to marital failure by repeatedly ignoring or criticizing a daughter or son in-law of lower standing, which clearly adds to the turmoil surrounding an "unsuitable" marriage.

Currently, however, level of education and employment opportunities may outweigh other factors in determining the rank of an individual for marriage in Egypt. Women from middle-class families, who achieve higher professional levels than their parents (e.g., doctors), can marry men from the lower class, provided these men have equivalent social status—the same educational level or work experience abroad—which is equated with financial success, increased sophistication, and ultimately higher status in Egypt.

In contrast to Western values, upper- or middle-class Egyptian men do not necessarily view attractiveness as an important marriage criterion for a wife; rather they tend to fear beautiful women for their potential in attracting other men and their perceived extravagance with money. Beauty is seen as an important feature of film and television stars, belly dancers, and women with whom to have affairs, but for wives, mothering skills and good morals are the important criteria. Marriage choice in most Muslim countries is determined more by one's values regarding family life and suitability in terms of social status rather than physical attractiveness.

Another difference with Western practices is the length of Egyptian courtships; the average time between meeting the prospective spouse and marriage is more than three years. During this time, individuals meet with their prospective spouses alone or in the presence of family and friends. Couples in arranged marriages tend to interact with their prospective partners more frequently in the presence of relatives than alone or with friends. In addition, they tend to report lower levels of reciprocal self-revelation and lower emotional involvement with their partners and greater emotional closeness to their families of origin than those in modern marriages.[41]

ARRANGED MARRIAGES IN KENYA

Kenya, an African nation that is the size of Texas or France with a population of 30 million, is predominantly Christian (70%) with indigenous religions practiced by another 23 percent of the population. While Kenya is a nation of striking contrasts in terms of marital practices, strong clan and extended family ties characterize even the most modern marriages. From an East African perspective, marriage establishes and reinforces family alliances and connects all generations of a community. In addition, "marriage is a symbol of status and an avenue through which individuals gain further acceptance and respect within the community."[42]

The most traditional marriages occur among rural tribes, such as the Maasai—known as warriors, shepherds, and lion hunters—while the Kamba clan, a more modern, urban, and educated group of farmers and herders, has adopted some Western values regarding courtship and marriage. Among the Maasai, for example, polygamy, the practice of having multiple wives, continues although to a lesser extent than in previous years. According to

1998 figures, 16 percent of married Kenyan women were in polygamous marriages in contrast to 30 percent in 1977.[43] By tradition, having multiple wives was a sign of wealth, evidence of higher social status, and a guaranteed means of having many children, both to increase the workforce and to provide support during old age.

Traditionally, the process of selecting a spouse in Kenya was either (a) totally arranged with the father of the groom initiating the process, (b) semi-arranged—the father of the groom would select a prospective bride, but the final choice was dependent upon the son's approval, or (c) self selected by the son with the family conducting the negotiations. In the latter case, the man would declare his interest through gifts of livestock but if his offer was rejected, the livestock had to be returned—similar to the Western practice of giving and returning an engagement ring if the marriage is called off.

In contemporary Kenya, especially among the more educated groups such as the Kamba, mate selection is based more frequently on individual choice and romantic love. However, even in these modern marriages, young people value their parents' consent and advice on marriage before proceeding. Once parental approval has been given, traditional courtship and marriage rituals, including the negotiation of bride-wealth, take place. Interestingly, bride-wealth is considered a communal responsibility rather than an individual one. In cases where the father of the groom is unable to pay the amount of money required by the bride's family, the clan takes it upon itself to raise the money and provide for its less solvent member.

Divorce has been rare in Kenya because marriage historically is regarded as a union of families or clans and if the marriage fails, a great deal is at stake (e.g. property, livestock). To keep the marriage intact, a council of elders is summoned in rural communities to negotiate differences when a couple faces problems. In some cases separation is recommended as a stopgap measure, but if the reconciliation efforts are not effective then divorce is considered as a last resort. In traditional marriages, a man divorces his wife, if she is a " habitual adulterer, a witch or had bad character," but the opposite—the wife divorcing him—is not allowed. Divorce is said to have taken place when the bride-wealth paid at the time of the marriage contract is returned to the groom's family. The returned bride-wealth is referred to as "the goats of rejection," symbolizing the husband's rejection of his wife.

SUMMARY

Depending upon the criteria used, arranged marriages have fared well, and in a few instances better (e.g. marital stability) than love marriages. Insofar as divorce is concerned, for example, the rate of divorce in Muslim countries, where most of the arranged marriages occur, tends to be about one-fourth that of the United States. The United States rate is significantly higher according to both 2002 and 2006 compiled statistics (in 2002, it was 4.1 per 1000 population while the recent figure is 3.6),[44] than that of Egypt (1.18), Iran (0.69), Sri Lanka (0.15), Turkey (0.5), and UAR (0.87).[45] Divorce figures are not available for India and Kenya. It should be emphasized, however, that divorce in these Muslim countries has not been as easy to obtain, especially by women, as it has been in the United States. In addition, the Indian, Muslim, and African cultures, where the majority of arranged marriages are found, have been far less accepting the divorce than Western culture.

The results of the few marital-satisfaction studies comparing arranged marriages with love marriages are mixed. While the findings of the two Indian studies already cited[46] are in favor of arranged marriages, two others with other populations provide support for free choice and romantic love. An older study by Blood[47] questioned Japanese men and women about their marital satisfaction in love and arranged marriages. He found that men were equally happy in either form but women who were married longer and in arranged marriages were less happy than women in love marriages. Similarly, Xu and Whyte,[48] in a study of Chinese women found that women were happiest when allowed to choose their own partners, and that more arranged than love marriages ended in divorce.

As for domestic violence as an indicator of marital stability, the data from different countries are not comparable because of different measures, varied sampling techniques, and inconsistent recording strategies. In addition, it is only since the mid-nineties that some third world countries began to be cognizant of domestic violence as a serious social, ethical, and health problem and started documenting such abuses. In spite of such limited data, however, a few tentative conclusions can be drawn.

While the estimates of domestic violence range from 20 to 50 percent in different countries with the figure of 33 1/3 percent being the worldwide average,[49]—at least one in every three women around the world is beaten, coerced into sex, or otherwise abused during her lifetime (the U.S. percentage is 31%), certain countries appear to have higher than average incident reports. For example,[50] India (45%), Japan (59%), Kenya (42%), Korea (38%), Nicaragua (52%), and Uganda (41%) lead the nations when it comes to domestic violence. The mixture of Eastern, African, industrialized, and Central American nations among the leading countries suggests that the incidence of domestic violence has more to do with educational level, economic hardship, and cultural patriarchy than other factors. In Syria, for example, a study of domestic violence[51] found that violence against women was more prevalent in the countryside than in cities, in homes with less educated husbands, with women married at very young ages, and/or where there was significant economic hardship. The overall rate of domestic violence in Syria was reported to be 25 percent.

In general, the kind of marriage—arranged versus love marriage—does not appear to be causally related to domestic violence, but when violence does occur in Eastern and African countries, it is more likely to be a part of a forced marriage than one that is merely arranged. In a forced marriage, total disregard of one or both participants' wishes pervades the marital climate from the beginning, and sets the stage for domestic violence later on. Fortunately, such marriages are dwindling worldwide, especially among the more educated classes, and are being replaced by a more modern version—the semi-arranged marriage—where the family does some of the matchmaking, but gives the final choice of partner to the prospective bride and groom.

Semi-arranged marriages have some advantages over the kind of love marriage that is based exclusively on strong romantic and sexual feelings without regard to compatibility or shared values. In semi-arranged marriages, the emphasis on "suitability" or similarity of background, educational level, social status, values, and religion, all of which contribute to marital stability, creates a strong foundation to the marriage. In addition, family allegiance and parental approval are important considerations in these marriages and influence the marriage commitment. With strong overarching motives, that is, motives central to personality that affect broad areas of life, the marriage commitment tends to be strengthened.

In contrast, children from divorced families have fewer anchors to assist them in weathering the emotional storms of marriage. While they may have a strong religious commitment, it is much less likely that they will have a strong sense of family loyalty. Because their nuclear family was splintered by divorce, the concept of family allegiance may have little relevance to them. In addition, parental conflict may make it difficult for them to decide which parent's characteristics and values to emulate[52] and how to choose appropriate or suitable partners. In fact, because of significant family turmoil, they may select a partner with traits opposite to the family's characteristics as a hoped-for means of avoiding conflict in their own marriages. Unfortunately, these opposite choices also can lead to disappointments. For example, passive, easy-going partners, chosen to minimize angry impasses in their own marital relationships, often create their own brand of unhappiness when they turn out to be nonassertive and indecisive as well.

While there are other overarching motives besides religion and family loyalty (e.g., love of children, patriotism, honor, friendship) to strengthen marriage commitments, adult children of divorce lacking healthy parental role models and a stable family system, often look to their peer group and popular (or national) culture to guide them in their efforts to sustain a marriage. When the culture is flawed and its heroes are made of clay, adult children of divorce are left confused and ready to consider the divorce option themselves whenever marital dissatisfaction appears on the scene.

CHAPTER 8

Love Marriages Around the World

Although *love* is supposed to make the world go around, in modern times it is faltering and not doing its job. Around the world, marital love especially seems to be in short supply. Marriages are down, divorces and domestic violence are up, and the single life is gaining prominence as the dominant lifestyle in a number of countries. In the United States, for example, the percentage of households headed by single persons (whether never-married, divorced, or widowed) passed the 50 percent mark in 2005.[1]

What is happening with marriages around the globe? Statistics regarding marriage, divorce, domestic violence, and/or marital satisfaction tell part of the story, but a comprehensive answer to that question requires an understanding of the social and political climate in which a marriage occurs, that is, the cultural or national context at the very least. Widespread catastrophic events—wars, tsunamis, terrorist attacks—and far-reaching social or political movements, including the women's movement and radical shifts in governance, such as changes from communism to a free-market economy, clearly affect marital quality in a variety of ways.

Marriage, from the ecological perspective of Bronfenbrenner,[2] exists within three distinct and yet overlapping circles or spheres of influence. These spheres range from the immediate circle of the marital couple itself, which consists of their internal dynamics and communication patterns, to the societal influences sphere, which includes the values, norms, and expectations of the culture-at-large. In between these two circles is the immediate social sphere of the couple, comprising family and friends who have the potential to influence the couple. Riding on a sea of differing waves of influence, marriages can be buffeted about or facilitated, depending upon their own, sometimes very unique, spheres of influence.

Some of the countries highlighted in this chapter have undergone momentous political and cultural changes in recent years (especially Russia), and this social upheaval is accompanied by high divorce and domestic violence rates. At the opposite extreme are countries experiencing economic prosperity and social tranquility, for example, China, where the low divorce rate mirrors the country's overall stability. The role of cultural factors in marriage is further explored in countries like Japan, Italy, Spain, and the Netherlands, where different degrees of social change, diverse values, and divorce intermix.

When the cultural ambience of a country is toxic to healthy lifestyles and marriage, as is true in the United States, there is less opportunity for adult children of divorce to find cultural and social antidotes to their family's dysfunctional brew. Not only are the cultural icons in the United States lacking in emotional substance, but also the concept of romantic love is highly confusing to most young people in the United States. Emotionally charged, ecstatic views of love found in American culture are difficult to reconcile with the grim realities of domestic violence and divorce.

In a study of the role of culture in romantic love, Swidler[3] found that most of the middle-aged Americans whom she interviewed debunked movie or mythic love and instead subscribed to a "prosaic-realistic" perspective, which is decidedly less idealistic and more reasonable than mythic love. From this perspective, real love is believed to grow more slowly and more uncertainly than mythic love, and is based more strongly on compatibility and other practical traits than on glamorous or heroic qualities. This more realistic view, which is prevalent in many countries with lower divorce rates than the United States, tends to replace the mythic perspective in the minds of most Americans over time, but young people—especially those from dysfunctional families—are most susceptible to the damage wrought by the overly romantic perspective.

Furthermore, the United States is regarded as "the most violent industrialized country in the world."[4] In the United States, every day four women are murdered by a male partner, and every year more than a million women visit doctors and emergency rooms after having suffered physical violence at the hands of a partner. Of the large industrialized countries, only Russia surpasses the United States in spousal homicide[5] (1.7 versus 1.0 per 100,000)—a contest that no country really wants to win.

MARRIAGES IN RUSSIA

In the post-communist era Russia has been smitten, not by love, but by upheavals at all levels. In this passionate and poetic country that has generated romantic literature of epic proportions, Dr. Zhivago is not seen anymore trudging through the snow-encrusted countryside in search of Lara; instead the image of the starry-eyed lover on an arduous journey has been replaced by a demoralized spouse heading for the divorce courts. With Russia leading major countries with its divorce rate[6] (5.3 per 1000), a disillusioned reality has supplanted the grand, romantic visions of an earlier time. In 1970, for example, approximately 30 percent of Russian marriages ended in divorce, but by 1995 the rate has risen to more than 60 percent.[7]

Among the various factors that have contributed to discontent in Russia are (1) the steep decline in income and living standards across the nation during the nineties, which apparently has been reversed since Putin took office in 1999, (2) the transition to a market economy, which has created widespread occupational changes, increased geographical mobility for individuals and families, and as a result, added significant conflict to the family unit, and (3) the housing shortage. In addition, the overall health of the Russian population has deteriorated due to the weakening of the public health system, the population has declined as a result of falling birth rates and increased mortality rates, and extreme poverty characterizes approximately one third of the population.[8]

In the midst of all this social turmoil, Russian marriages have been significantly affected. Besides the social factors already mentioned, widespread alcohol abuse (alcohol consumption has risen six-fold since 1988),[9] unemployment, liberal divorce laws, and gender-role conflict have had a strong impact upon marital dissolution. The latter factor, that is, disparate values about gender roles, is an important variable that contributes to household labor conflict, especially for women. In a study of couples in Metropolitan Moscow,[10] Cubbins and Vannoy found that wives experience more marital unhappiness the more household work they do relative to their husbands—a finding similar to the conclusions drawn from research on U.S. couples.[11] In addition, the less satisfied Russian wives are with the division of labor, the more likely they are to think about divorce.

Family changes in Russia have been moving to a more egalitarian model since perestroika although there is still a preference for some aspects of the patriarchal model. In a study of Russian marriages in the nineties, Vannoy and others[12] conclude that a profound contradiction exists between the predominant ideology about gender roles and the reality of these roles. Most couples prefer that men be the sole breadwinners, even though 90 percent of the women are employed and have been for most of the twentieth century. As Vannoy and colleagues have noted:[13] "Present public opinion, in fact, is hostile to the idea that a woman cannot find total satisfaction and self-realization within the family." In the family, a wife is expected to be both the manager of money as well as the guardian of the emotional and social well-being of family members while the husband makes all the money.

This disparity between reality and ideology was a frequent source of family conflict in Russia in the nineties because the faltering economy and lack of employment opportunities made it especially difficult for men to maintain their preferred role as the main provider. Also, as a result of Western influence, the ideological winds regarding the family unit have been shifting. The child-focused family structure that replaced the patriarchal family after the Second World War—basically a traditional model in terms of roles and communication patterns with many partners staying together for the sake of the children—has been competing with the newer, spouse-focused family. Similar to the modern Western family with its emphasis on gender equality and spousal happiness, the spouse-focused family has become a viable alternative to the traditional model since the break up of the Soviet Union.

Accompanying the ideological heterogeneity regarding family life is greater interspousal conflict as each spouse, having incorporated the changing family climate to a different degree, brings his or her own perspective to the family scene. Differences in husbands and wives' views about gender roles do increase the level of tension experienced in marriages.[14] When added to the stress created by extensive, and often chaotic, social, and political changes, as have occurred in Russia, gender-role conflict can produce an overwhelming strain upon families. Olson & Matskovsky,[15] writing about the changes in family life in Soviet and American societies in recent years, said: "Whereas the nature of social change in the United States might best be described as evolutionary, social changes in the former USSR have been truly revolutionary."

Further adding to the revolutionary strain upon marriage in Russia is domestic violence. Domestic violence in Russia at the present time appears to be a classic illustration of anomie, a condition of social chaos and normlessness brought about by rapid social changes with accompanying disruption of the social infrastructure. In a comparison of the conditions in American society associated with violence and the prevailing social conditions in Russia, Voight and Thornton[16] conclude that Russia, like the United States, is a violent society due to the following characteristics: uneven distribution of wealth, lack of meaningful employment for a large portion of the population, sexist and racist attitudes, competition rather than cooperation as the dominant work motivation, the denial of basic benefits to the unemployed, disregard of the consequences of relocation, and victimization of certain groups of people.[17]

In addition, domestic violence in Russia appears to be a case of powerful men abusing powerless women, that is, women who lack tangible resources such as education, occupational status, and income. In the 1999 study by Vannoy and colleagues[18] of approximately 1000 couples from Moscow and two other smaller cities, they found that women with less education, lower occupational status, and less income were more likely to be the victims of abuse. In addition, husbands who had less education and lower occupational status were more likely to engage in verbal abuse, but employed husbands were more likely to be physical abusers. Whereas about one-fourth of the wives suffered physical violence from their husbands (one-third of the divorced women reported abuse from former husbands), it was surprisingly the women, especially in the youngest age cohort (eighteen to twenty-nine), who were more likely to initiate both verbal and physical abuse. The more destructive acts of violence, however, were clearly performed by men, most frequently while under the influence of alcohol. The authors of the study conclude that "violent behavior in marriages is a part of the patriarchal legacy in Russian society, as in many other parts of the world."

In this large-scale study of Russian couples, marital quality was not related to "the relative socioeconomic attainments of spouses as individuals or the overall socioeconomic attainments of families in general" as it is in the United States. Education was found to be more important in influencing marital quality with educated women being the most satisfied. In addition, emotional sensitivity turned out to be one of the most important predictors of satisfaction for both spouses, while assertiveness, independence, and risk-taking were considered positive traits for men but not for women. In other words, marital quality was enhanced when men were forceful and dominant but not when women were so described. Thus, it appears that Russians prefer a patriarchal family structure most of the time, but in addition want their husbands to be emotionally sensitive and involved in household labor and childcare to some degree—all of which suggest contradictory beliefs and values in the process of change.

Other findings that shed light on the high divorce rate in Russia relate to children, both before and after they appear on the family scene. Premarital conception does increase the risk of divorce,[19] and the surge in births outside of marriage[20] (from 11% in 1980 to 20% in 1994) has played a role in this outcome. Couples who have a child prior to marriage often feel compelled to marry—motivation that puts the relationship on shaky ground.

In addition, having children and/or teenagers in the home decreases marital quality compared to childless homes or empty nests.[21] Unfortunately, it is at a time when young children are still in the home that most of the divorces occur (the average duration of marriages in Russia ending in divorce is 5.0 years).[22] Once children leave the home, couples who are still together frequently report an increase in marital satisfaction, but often lead separate lives, deriving their gratification from individual pursuits or external relationships, not necessarily from interactions with one another.[23] Thus, it appears that when couples are struggling to survive economically, children create additional hardships that undermine already burdened unions.

The political, occupational, and economic instability in Russia during the nineties has resulted in social crises affecting all aspects of family life, but marriage in particular. The number of divorces almost quadrupled between 1960 and 1995,[24] and the number of remarriages has also seen a dramatic increase with their proportion (over total number of marriages) rising almost threefold during a comparable period. In a country undergoing rapid social change, marriages appear particularly fragile.

In addition, the overall lack of religious affiliation in Russia (religious participation often strengthens marital commitment) has further left the institution of marriage adrift. In one study,[25] 36 to 82 percent of respondents reported "no religious affiliation," depending upon their sex and residence. Another estimate[26] places the "unaffiliated" in Russia at about 65 percent, which suggests that about two-thirds of the population is not connected to any religious institution.

In a society in the midst of upheaval and change, where the government and/or religion provide very little direction, couples are left to their own devices, that is, to the variable winds of feelings and preferences, to determine their marital fate. Because of so much instability in Russia at the beginning of the twenty-first century, the future of marriage in this country is shrouded in uncertainty.

MARRIAGES IN CHINA

In contrast to the recent turbulence of Russia, China, having undergone several major political upheavals in the twentieth century, is now in a period of consolidation, economic growth, and relative quiescence insofar as social change is concerned. Prior to 1949, when the Peoples Republic of China was formed, China operated as a feudal society in many respects with arranged marriage being the primary means of mate selection. Marriages were arranged through the help of a professional matchmaker, who was consulted when children were young, or even before they were born.[27] This manner of initiating marriages existed for thousands of years in China, but arranged marriages were abolished in 1950 with the passage of the Marriage Law.

In addition to abolishing arranged marriages, the government worked hard to promote love and mutual companionship as the basis for mate selection and encouraged women to join the labor force as part of the emphasis on gender equality. Although arranged marriages have continued to be practiced in some remote rural areas, even in these cases, the young adults' preferences are taken into account. In the era of strong communist control, mate selection was greatly affected by the political and social background of individuals. In one study of young people between 1967 and 1976,[28] 54.1 percent of the respondents ranked family political background and personal political status as the third most important criterion for choosing a mate, after health and reliability.

Since 1978, China, the world's largest country with a population of 1.2 billion, has become a modern industrial society. When the state-controlled economic system gave way to a free market economy, "wealth replaced political status as the primary yardstick for success."[29] The revised Marriage Law in 1980 explicitly stated that marriage should be based on mutual affection, and that divorce could be granted when there was complete alienation of affection. Divorce has become more acceptable in recent years, although it still is rather infrequent compared to other large industrial nations. The divorce rate in China is 0.95 per 1000 population,[30] a surprisingly low figure—about one-fourth that of the United States.

With the emergence of China as a world economic and political player in the latter part of the twentieth and early twenty-first centuries, the sexual and marital practices of China have become more similar to that of Europe and the United States. A 1990 national survey involving more than 20,000 respondents in fifteen provinces revealed that 30 percent of Chinese youth engaged in premarital sex and that 86 percent approved of premarital sexual behavior.[31] In modern China women select spouses on the basis of wealth, advanced academic degrees, and body height, whereas men choose romantic partners on the basis of beauty, health, gentleness, chastity, and youthfulness.[32] In addition, besides social status, reputation, and wealth, Chinese women want emotional compatibility, sexual enjoyment, and freedom to act independently in their marriages—desirable qualities in most parts of the world.

In spite of some attitudes toward love and marriage that are similar to Western mores, the restrained manner of the Chinese permeates their courtship and marriage practices. Their conservatism and greater sensitivity to the pragmatic aspects of a relationship, for example, result in their being less vulnerable to impulsive and maladaptive choices. "The notion of a love that sweeps all before it—social condemnation, parental disapproval, economic concerns, flawed reputation of the beloved—is not typical for these young Chinese, nor is it glorified," wrote Robert Moore, a Chinese scholar.[33]

Instead, cautiousness, secrecy, and subtlety characterize the courtship of young people in China. In contrast to the bold flirtatiousness of their American counterparts, the dating behavior of the Chinese is shy and measured. As a couple develops their affair, they reveal their affection for each other in carefully calibrated increments, with actions speaking much louder than words. If negative character traits, such as laziness or frivolousness, manifest themselves early on during the dating period, affairs are ended abruptly. Feelings appear to play a secondary role to rational considerations in mate selection, and parental approval of spousal choice is more important in modern China than in the United States.

Among the Chinese, seriousness of purpose is a highly valued character trait that stands head and shoulders above other qualities. To appear lacking in purpose, or *qingfu*, a Chinese term that literally means "light and floating," is seen as adrift, undisciplined, and weak in character. The term *qingfu*, often translated as "frivolous," is used in a derogatory manner by the Chinese to apply to romantic and sexual behavior that is not strict and conservative. Having too many romantic partners, being ostentatiously affectionate in public, and flirting openly with a potential partner, are all regarded as *qingfu*, a social stigma with damaging consequences to one's reputation.[34]

Marriage is considered an important social/cultural event in China and in Chinese communities around the world, and seems to be strengthened by a number of social and philosophical factors. Barriers to divorce include rejection by relatives and loss of face.[35] In addition, the concept of *yuan*, the Buddhist belief (akin to karma) that personal relationships are predestined to success or failure, has been regarded as the cement or glue in marriage. Finding one's true love—a love determined by fate—ensures happiness in marriage—a belief even modern university students appear to endorse. In a study comparing Chinese with British students, the former subscribed to the concept of *yuan* to a greater degree than the latter, but the British also scored high, thus coming across as surprisingly fatalistic about love and romance.[36]

One of the few studies on Chinese marriages compared arranged marriages with those freely chosen on the basis of love among women married between 1933 and 1987 (see Chapter 7 for detailed discussion of arranged marriages). In this large-scale study of 586 Chinese women,[37] it was clear that women were happiest when allowed to choose their own mates, and that more arranged than love marriages ended in divorce.

Whereas China's low divorce rate may be a function of strict divorce laws and the social stigma of divorce, the cohesive factors, or overarching motives, that are operating to maintain marriages are not readily apparent. Nor is it clear how happy these intact marriages are. The All-China Women's Federation study,[38] which places the share of Chinese families affected by domestic violence at 30 percent, suggests that China is experiencing the same rate of domestic violence as that of other countries. China does not officially collect data on domestic violence, however, so it has been the self-appointed responsibility of groups dedicated to women's rights to provide some data on this problem.

As for cultural factors providing some degree of marital stability, neither formal religion nor patriotism seems to serve in that capacity. It has been estimated that a very small share (less than 10%) of the population have formal connections with religion, and the majority of those who do are Buddhists.[39] In addition, family allegiance, while much stronger than in the United States, seems to be diminishing as more and more young people select their own mates in school and work settings, and live apart from their families.[40] What may, however, provide at least a partial explanation for China's marital longevity lies in the Chinese temperament. The personality or character traits that are valued in China, such as seriousness of purpose, restraint, and reliability, are regarded (in most cultures) as indicators of maturity and stability, and as such, are powerful antidotes to rash and imprudent marital decisions of all kinds.

MARRIAGES IN JAPAN

Unlike China, Japan—its neighbor in the Far East—is in the midst of a profound crisis affecting family life. In the context of the economic slowdown of the 1990s, the marriage rate has fallen, the divorce rate has risen, the number of young men and women choosing to stay single has increased, and the fertility rate has fallen to a level well below replacement (the level of 1.29 in 2004 was significantly below the maintenance level of 2.1). Accompanying these troubling statistics is the aging nature of Japan's population. In 1950, the proportion of the population aged sixty-five and over represented only 5 percent of the country; by 2005 it had risen to 20 percent.[41]

The main factors responsible for the low fertility rate are the improved employment opportunities for women, the rapid growth in the educational attainment of women, difficulty in raising children, especially by working mothers, and the rising average age of first marriage. In 1970, the average woman earned only 62 percent of what her male counterpart earned, but that percentage climbed to 83 percent by 1999. In addition, the percentage of managerial posts held by women tripled between 1982 and 2003. Job prospects have improved for women, although the recession of the nineties saw a sharp downturn in the overall job market for university graduates; many young people were unable to find long-term positions in firms and had to work at tangential employment or move to distant locations to support their families.

For those educated Japanese women who want to work and raise a family, childcare facilities have not kept pace with the demand. Childcare facilities are perceived to be inadequate or overly expensive, making it difficult for working mothers to manage both financially and emotionally. Also, rising aspirations for material wealth and the cost of marriage have delayed marriage, which has led to the drop in the number of children born (out of wedlock births are very low in Japan, i.e., 1.9 percent of all births compared to 34 percent in the United States). The average age of first marriage in Japan is 29.6 for men and 27.8 for women.[42]

Another factor contributing to the unattractiveness of marriage for Japanese women is the unequal distribution of household labor. Men, who have long assumed the primary responsibility for earning money in the family, continue to spend long hours at work—either handling work responsibilities or socializing with colleagues—which leaves relatively little time for the family. According to one survey,[43] men spend on average as little as five minutes per day on housework, compared to three to four hours for full-time working women, and less than half an hour daily on childcare, compared to over four hours for women—an inequitable situation likely to create conflict and resentment.

One study[44] did find that Japanese women do feel deprived when it comes to household work allocation, but this same investigation reported that the amount of household work performed by Japanese men is negatively related to their marital satisfaction. In other words, inequitable distribution of household tasks affects Japanese women negatively, but when men participate in a more democratic arrangement, the men are likely to be the unhappy ones—a no-win situation by any standard. In addition, the absence of men at home leads to stress and mental health problems, as women feel increasingly isolated in their suburban neighborhoods.

As a result of women's negative perceptions of marriage, their expectations of prospective marriage partners have gone up. As Carroll[45] has described, women in Japan today expect not only three "highs" (high income, high level of education, and tall height), but also three "goods" (good-looking, good natured, and good background). Higher expectations of marriage are thought to delay matrimony as greater numbers of women with specific requirements are unwilling to settle for less.

The patrilineal system in Japan, where the oldest son takes over as head of the family clan and has responsibility for taking care of family duties, has also contributed additional stumbling blocks to marriage. In cases where there is no son, a son-in-law may be adopted into the family to fulfill this role. However, if he is a first son, he already has responsibilities to his own family, and cannot easily take on this new assignment. Thus, some of the women who have no brothers may feel restricted to finding a spouse who is a second or third-born son, and therefore available to act according to patrilineal prescriptions.[46]

Whereas Japan has long been regarded as a collectivist society, wherein the individual subordinates personal goals to that of the group or family, modern

Japan is a curious mixture of group orientation with that of individualistic pursuit. "Visitors to Japan report that individualistic and collectivistic beliefs, attitudes, and customs seem to coexist—a situation that, to outsiders, appears to be full of inconsistencies and contradictions," wrote Murray and Kimura.[47] Pragmatism and accommodation to the other in order to maintain harmony remain as hallmarks of the Japanese style, but individual happiness and personal freedom are also valued.

Arranged marriages are still around, but they account for only 10 to 15 percent of new marriages, and have moved away from the traditional idea of uniting two families to assisting two people find each other. These arranged marriages range from semi-coercion or persuasion to simple introductions of eligible men and women to each other. College students who are in favor of arranged marriages feel that love marriages are not trustworthy, and that they have a better chance of meeting suitable partners through a *nakodo*, or matchmaker.

Romantic love, if experienced, is thought to be a component of new love and not a necessary ingredient of ongoing relationships. Once a commitment is made, there is "more emphasis on the aspects of a relationship that provide assurance, including loyalty, compassion, mind reading, and the support of the couple's social network, with little discussion of the relationship."[48] The Japanese believe that words cannot adequately explain many matters, such as love and commitment, and that the essential matter is shared understanding. In contrast to Western culture with its focus on passion as a sustaining ingredient in romantic relationships, the Japanese are convinced that a deeper, more companionable love will develop after marriage, not as a function of discussion and verbal communication, but as a result of respect and shared understanding.

Historically, Japan's marriages were viewed as stable and long lasting. Its divorce rate had been regarded as low,[49] but in the four years from 1998 to 2002, the rate has risen from 1.92 to 2.27 per thousand,[50] a rate comparable to that of most European nations. In addition, some of the indicators of domestic violence in Japan are alarming. In a 1993 survey, 59 percent of women surveyed reported being physically abused by their partners.[51] While there have been some methodological questions about this report, for example, the proportion of divorced women in the sample of respondents, the report and pressure from women's groups led to the Japanese government beginning to collect statistics on domestic violence in 1998.

Although it has been estimated that less than 1 percent of women who experience domestic violence in Japan contact the police,[52] there has been a dramatic increase in the number of reported cases of domestic violence each year since 1998. For example, there was a 63 percent jump in reported cases from March 2002 till March 2007.[53] A survey of 2,888 respondents published by the Cabinet Office of Japan (Gender Equality Bureau) in 2006 puts the number of victims of domestic violence, mental harassment/terror and/or sexual coercion at 33 percent[54]—a rate comparable to the international average.

A 1999 case that highlighted the issue of domestic violence in Japan was the arrest of a Japanese Counsel, for domestic violence in Vancouver, who allegedly said that hitting one's wife was acceptable under Japanese cultural practices.[55] In the midst of the international focus on this case, a number of explanations were provided for what was regarded as a new problem in modern Japan. The patriarchal structure of Japanese society, wherein women become members (and traditionally were regarded as possessions) of the husband's family once they marry, has been the factor most frequently cited. Among the other culprits was the stressful nature of Japanese society, especially for powerful men (most likely to be the abusers), and small family size, likely to produce men who are excessively attached to their mothers and overly demanding of their wives.[56] Sexless marriages to women perceived as maternal figures, which has been mentioned as a problem responsible for the low birth rate in Japan,[57] can also be regarded as a contributing factor to domestic violence.

Japan appears to be in the midst of a family crisis that clearly has implications for marriage and divorce. Although Japan's divorce rate is not as high as that of Russia and the United States, it is getting closer to the Western average. In one study[58] comparing Japanese marriages with American unions, it was found that the Americans were generally more satisfied with their marriages than the Japanese, and regarded marital companionship as more important than income in affecting their marital satisfaction. In contrast, the reverse was true for the Japanese, who appear to be more concerned about socioeconomic features than the emotional or interactive aspects of marriage.

Domestic violence appears to be increasing in Japan, both as a function of the patriarchal nature of Japanese society and modern-day, stress-producing values. Religion, a combination of Buddhist, Shinto, and Confucian philosophies, is having a hard time combating the materialistic mindset of an affluent and yet, beleaguered society. In short, Japan, like Russia, is witnessing upheavals at all levels that are bound to affect family life in unforeseen and unpredictable ways.

MARRIAGES IN ITALY AND SPAIN

Although the divorce rates in Europe are increasing along with decreasing marriage rates and increasing rates of cohabitation, divorce is generally rarer and less readily available in Europe than in the United States. In addition, a number of European countries have long waiting periods (over three years) between the filing and granting of a divorce and mandatory counseling requirements aimed at reconciliation, both of which are correlated with below-average divorce rates.[59] In a recent study of divorce practices and rates, Crouch and colleagues found that all of the nations with the lowest divorce rates have either mandatory counseling or a three or more years waiting period between the filing and granting of divorce; within the United States, these same correlations generally hold true for individual states.

Italy and Spain are among the eight nations with the lowest divorce rates (Italy: 0.6 per 1000; Spain: 0.94 per 1000) that have either a mandatory counseling requirement or a long waiting period (the other six are Ireland, Greece, Poland, Bulgaria, Portugal, and France in increasing order of divorce rates). In addition, Italy, like Japan, has low fertility rates, low birth rates outside marriage, and a large aging population (the two countries lead the world in percentage of population over sixty-five). In both the countries, children tend to live at home with their families until marriage, and thus there are low cohabitation rates in these two nations. The industrial structure in both the countries is similar with many small firms and family-run enterprises, which resulted in periods of rapid economic growth in the fifties and sixties.[60]

Unlike Japan, however, Italy has low rate of female employment, where it holds the distinction of having the lowest rank among nations[61] followed by Greece and Spain. The combination of very low fertility rate and equally low rate of female employment in these three Mediterranean countries has baffled demographers looking for explanations. However, sociologists have come to the rescue with their concept of the "long family." The "long family" refers to the tendency for children to remain with their parents well into adult life, thereby postponing many of the developmental tasks of adulthood, including self-supporting employment, marriage, and having children.[62]

Of the fifteen-member European Union, Italy has the highest share of young people, aged twenty to twenty-nine, living with their parents. Surveys[63] show that 81.9 percent of young Italians in their twenties live with their parents compared to less than half in countries such as the United Kingdom (42.7%), the Netherlands (36.2%), and Denmark (29%). As children get into the thirties, the gap among countries widens further with Italy's percentage at 45.6 percent substantially greater than Denmark's low of 2.8 percent. Spain is right along side Italy with its share of 80.5 percent for the twenty to twenty-nine age group and 46.4 percent for the young thirty-year-old age group (aged thirty to thirty-four).

What is further disquieting about Italy's percentages is that the overwhelming majority of adult children who resided with their parents never married, and that a larger percentage of these young adults were unemployed (even though better educated) than the adults who did not live with their parents. Although living at home is economically beneficial when there is a tight housing market, especially for young adults furthering their education, or for those having difficulty securing employment commensurate with their level of schooling, the "long family" in Italy also serves to foster dependency and developmental delays in assuming the tasks of adulthood.

The negative effects of the "long family" in Italy can be viewed, at least in part, as a function of the rigidity of gender and parental roles in relation to household duties. In Italy's more traditional culture, a mother's cooking, cleaning, and household services can be seen as an inducement for young adults to continue living at home. In a telephonic survey conducted on a large sample of twenty to thirty-four-year-old Italians, the following disadvantages of leaving home were cited most frequently: economic disadvantages (53%), housework (45%), cooking (29%), and ironing/cleaning (16%).[64] Since men are over-represented in the group of young adults residing at home, it is safe to assume that the avoidance of household duties is a strong motivation for young men to continue living with their stay-at-home mothers, for whom the performance of household tasks is seen as part and parcel of their identities.

Like Italy, Spain—another Catholic country—has witnessed an increase in the age of first marriages, a decrease in the number of marriages, a low divorce rate, and a low cohabitation rate influenced by the tight housing market and limited employment opportunities for young adults. Here, too, the concept of the "long family" can be used to explain the high percentage of young adults still residing with their parents well into their thirties, but, the *noviazgos*,[65] committed love relationships where exclusivity and fidelity are expected of each partner, differentiate Spain from its comparable sister countries (Italy, Greece).

The *noviazgo*, similar to an engagement in the Western world but without a decision to marry, is a long-term romantic relationship, whose average length is approximately forty-three months. As such, they are serious love relationships requiring time, energy, and interpersonal skill to maintain, but without the living-together component characteristic of other European countries. According to a survey[66] in Spain among couples that were or had been in *noviazgos*, 67.6 percent reported being in committed relationships for at least three years with only 29.4 percent having experienced shorter-term relationships of less than a year. The focus in Spain on serious love relationships apart from marriage has led to a higher marriage rate than in Italy (5.1 versus 4.5 per 1000 population).[67]

In Spain, there has been a growing change in attitude among men and women regarding the importance of women getting an education and working outside the home, but this more modern mindset has not always been reflected in practice. In one 1997 study,[68] fully 75 percent of the men and women, aged fifteen to twenty-nine, supported a family model where both husband and wife work outside the home and share domestic responsibilities. This finding was in dramatic contrast to a similar survey in 1975 where 81 percent of men and 83 percent of women agreed that household chores were a woman's work.[69] In addition, the percentage of women who identified themselves as housewives dropped from 54 to 32 percent in the twenty years between 1978 and 1998.

However, in studies examining the number of hours Spanish men and women actually spent performing household tasks, the findings are different from expressed egalitarian attitudes regarding the division of household work. Even though the number of hours spent by Spanish men in domestic activities has increased over time, they are still spending significantly fewer hours doing chores than women (three-plus hours versus seven-plus hours per day).[70] Machismo–a traditional attitude in countries like Spain–dies very slowly, and typically only when there is no other choice given the interpersonal and social reality of working wives.

Spain appears to be a country in transition—moving more quickly than its neighbors into the twenty-first century but still wedded to its traditions. It embraces modern concepts of personal freedom, individualism, and the pursuit of happiness while struggling to maintain religious and cultural values regarding the importance of family life. Both Spain and Italy are heavily Catholic with over 90 percent of the population in each country identifying themselves as such.[71] As Reyes[72] has noted about Spain, "these changes have produced a society that appears to be in conflict with itself, that is, a society that is divided between the pursuit of individual or personal liberties and the maintenance of cultural traditions that have centered on family obligations and conservative religious values for many centuries."

MARRIAGES IN THE NETHERLANDS

The Netherlands, with a population of 16.3 million is an ultra-modern, liberal country with great diversity of lifestyle, and its divorce rate at 2.05 per 1000[73] is low average among nations. Its divorce rate is lower than divorce rates in other countries in Northwestern Europe, such as Denmark and Sweden, but higher than rates in Southern European countries. The normative model of marriage at the beginning of the twentieth century in the Netherlands has been replaced in the twenty-first century by diversification of living arrangements[74] with legal validation accompanying most of the lifestyle choices. For example, the requirement of marriage to define a family or household has been dropped; in 1996, a family was defined as a household in which one or more people have responsibility for children. In this pluralistic culture, cohabitation, marriage with children, marriage without children, single parenting, and living alone are all viable and acceptable options.

Van Praag and Niphuis-Nell[75] made a comparison between first-time home leavers (first point at which a son or daughter leaves his or her parental home to reside in a different home) for the period 1986–1990 with those of 1961– 1965. In the earlier period, 15 percent lived alone, 78 percent were married, and 2 percent cohabited in comparison to 36 percent living alone, 30 percent cohabiting, and 27 percent married in the more recent group. In more modern times, the majority of young people are opting either to stay single or cohabit than get married, choices validated by the legal system in the Netherlands, where registered partnerships and cohabitation contracts exist alongside marriage. According to van Dulmen,[76] "Marriage is no longer seen as a logical next step in the process of relationship development. Rather, couples have various options as to how to legally bind their relationships."

The diversity of lifestyle choice in the Netherlands is accompanied by varied religious preferences, cultural backgrounds, and beliefs. Most Dutch (60%) are not affiliated with a church; of those who are, 22 percent are Roman Catholic followed by the different Protestant groups.[77] Because the non affiliation and the Catholic/Protestant groups are more likely to be tolerant of premarital sex—a belief fundamental to cohabitation and other nonmarital living choices—than more conservative religions, such as Dutch Reformed, Jews, Muslims, and Hindus,[78] nontraditional lifestyle choices will continue to increase in popularity in the Netherlands.

How stable are these nontraditional unions compared to marriage? The evidence from all countries, including the Netherlands,[79] is fairly strong that the rate of dissolution of nonmarital relationships is much higher than the rate among married couples. In a survey of twenty-five to twenty-nine-year-old women in the Netherlands, 10 percent of marriages and 24 percent of nonmarital relationships ended within nine years from the start of the association.[80] Also, partners who live together before marriage are three times as likely to get divorced as those who don't. However, the fact of cohabitation may not be the critical factor determining divorce; rather, it may be that those who do not cohabit have strong religious views against both cohabitation and divorce,[81] a hypothesis supported by the low rates of both among non-Dutch residents of the Netherlands.

Another possible explanation for the poorer marital success rate of cohabitants relative to noncohabitants has to do with the quality of commitment. For those individuals who regard cohabitation as a trial run, that is, as an opportunity to determine whether the relationship is viable or not, their commitment to the relationship is often exploratory and tentative. Then when faced with serious obstacles, their motivation to end the relationship can be stronger than their desire to maintain it. In contrast, the more strongly committed individuals tend to view a marriage or relationship promise as a sacred vow rather than an insubstantial agreement, and work hard to improve the relationship in spite of problems.

In a study of marital status and happiness among seventeen nations, Stack and Eshleman,[82] in 1998 found that being married was three to four times more closely tied to happiness than was cohabitation, and that marriage increased happiness equally among men and women. Two factors that appeared to be responsible for this correlation were improved financial status and better health. Greater emotional support appeared to be a benefit of both marriage and cohabitation, but marriage provided additional security, both financially and physically.

Domestic violence in the Netherlands appears to be on par with that of other European countries. A large-scale study conducted in 1997[83] by the Ministry of Justice concluded that 27 percent of the respondents had been victims of domestic violence with 21 percent of them suffering for more than five years. Furthermore, roughly the same number of males as females were victims, but the violence against women was more serious and often took the form of sexual abuse. Not surprisingly, 80 percent of the offenders were men.

In contrast to other more traditional countries, the Netherlands is fast becoming a secular, modern society with many lifestyle choices other than marriage. Since the sixties when the "pillars," that is, primary social/cultural organizations, were dismantled, the Netherlands has become a melting pot of nationalities and cultures. The four main pillars, each representing a major group of people with its own political party, newspaper, TV/radio station, and youth organization, were the Catholic, the Protestant, the Liberal, and the Socialist. When the pillars were the main social features of Dutch society, marital values tended to follow the religious and/or cultural features of each pillar.

Currently, Dutch society is becoming even more diverse than it had been as a result of increasing numbers of immigrants from former Dutch colonies, such as the Netherlands Antilles and Suriname, as well as from African, Asian, and former Eastern European countries. The influx of settlers from countries with traditional values has tempered the modern, liberal thrust of the Netherlands and slowed down the divorce rate relative to other European countries. The blend of traditional and modern values in the Netherlands has resulted in a progressive society, but without the materialistic flavor that characterizes the United States.

Overarching motives that can stabilize marriage are evident in countries with strong religious overtones (Muslim nations, Italy, and Spain), with traditional family values (China and parts of the Netherlands), and/or with cultural values emphasizing discipline, hard work, and seriousness of purpose (China). In contrast, Russia and Japan, both in the midst of some degree of social upheaval, are manifesting characteristics, such as materialism, hedonism, and a degree of lawlessness, that leave its residents floundering and in search of meaningful values. When this occurs, marriages are often undermined as each member of the union becomes obsessed with the struggle to find meaning and sustenance, leaving little time or energy for the marital relationship. Thus, the national culture of a country with its unique values, expectations, and degree of social unrest either facilitates or hinders its own love-seekers, most of whom are striving to build solid and satisfying marriages that last forever.

CHAPTER 9

Lost in the Land of Married Love

Without a map to pave the way, adult children of divorce are left to their own devices to figure out their marital journeys. Because their model of marriage derived from observations of their parents' marriage is filled with warnings and danger signs, they do not know where the navigable waterways and well-paved highways are. In addition, they don't know where the rest stops are and how frequently a respite is in order. Unless they have been exposed consistently to other marriages that are happy, all they know experientially is that marriage is a hazardous journey likely to lead to disaster and termination.

Adult children of divorce don't realize that romantic love does decrease after a time and with it goes marital satisfaction, which drops dramatically after the first year of marriage and then again after the second year.[1] Recent survey research of 9,637 households in the United States[2] essentially supports this finding by noting that the marital happiness of couples married between four and six years was significantly lower than that of the more recently married group (one to three years).

What makes the finding of decreased marital happiness over time understandable is that the ingredients that fuel romantic passion—fantasy, novelty, and arousal—dissipate naturally after lovers begin to know one another. For example, after just two years of marriage, spouses express affection for each other only half as often as they did when they were newlyweds.[3] Moreover, worldwide, divorces occur more frequently in the fourth year of marriage than at any other time.[4]

"To the extent that romance is enhanced by idealized glorification of one's partner, we should expect it to decline when people begin living together and reality slowly intrudes,"[5] wrote Sharon Brehm in her book on *Intimate*

Relationships. While romantic passion does fade as reality-based knowledge takes over, in happily married couples passion is replaced by a quieter and deeper love without "the bells and whistles." Termed companionate love by Sternberg,[6] this decidedly more durable love is based on friendship, affection, shared emotional intimacy, and commitment.

People who have been happily married for decades tend to express a lot of companionate love for their spouses,[7] which makes for a different kind of relationship than the kind that sparked its beginning. In a study[8] in India in which arranged marriages were compared with love marriages, the arranged-marriage couples started out feeling less love for their spouses than those in the love-marriage group, but by the tenth year of marriage they were feeling significantly more loving than the love group. While the finding that arranged marriages are superior to love marriages over the long haul has not been replicated in other studies, a number of studies on arranged marriages[9] have shown that a quieter, less romantic love often develops over time. Companionate love tends to develop more slowly than romantic love, but it is more stable and lasts longer.[10]

Adult children of divorce don't realize that successful marriages are based on two kinds of love, not one, and that the transition from one to the other is often perilous because of the disappointment that frequently accompanies the transition. In a scene in one of Madeleine L'Engle's novels,[11] a younger woman approaches her older friend in distress. Sobbing, she says, "I think that my marriage is dying." The older woman responds wisely: "My marriage died seven times. The question is not whether your marriage is dying or has died, the question is whether there is a chance for your marriage to resurrect and your willingness to participate in the resurrection." In other words, marital satisfaction even in the happiest of couples changes over time, and the rewards as well as costs of the relationship vary as a function of a whole host of variables, including children, job changes, geographical moves, and each partner's satisfaction in his/her individual life.

Besides being unaware of the fact that marital satisfaction in even very successful marriages fluctuates a good deal over time, what other aspects of marital reality are adult children of divorce not privy to? Research from studies of happy couples provides some interesting answers, some of which are intuitively obvious while others are not. For example, the fact that communication skills emerge as one of the primary indicators of marital success is no surprise. Likewise, the importance of similarity of values/interests has been known for some time, but the specifics of both these factors are not readily apparent, not even to happy couples who learned them through observational learning in their own families or stumbled upon them by accident and then had the good fortune to marry a responsive and emotionally healthy partner.

SENSITIVE, LOVING COMMUNICATION: CHICKEN OR EGG?

Happy couples, who are generally satisfied with the emotional and social aspects of their relationship, talk a lot to each other. They talk more frequently, directly, and positively than distressed couples about a broad range of topics, including work, school, home maintenance, family members, conversations with others, food, travel, and politics. They also share their feelings and can discuss deeply personal material with one another. Studies have shown that the more spouses self disclose, the more happily married they tend to be.[12]

And while happy couples are comfortable bringing up conflictual matters, they are actually not in conflict frequently. Rather they are more likely to agree, approve, and laugh together so that talking itself is a pleasurable activity. Even their enjoyment of mutual leisure-time pursuits is enhanced by communication during the activity. In contrast, unhappy couples fight a good deal and create many problems for their children; parental marital discord or conflict is correlated with a multitude of negative outcomes irregardless of whether parents divorced or stayed together disharmoniously. Higher levels of parental marital discord have been associated with their children's insecure romantic attachment styles, anxiety about personal relationships, fear of intimacy, less emotional closeness, and less satisfaction in romantic relationships, including marriage, and more cynical attitudes (less benevolence) about marriage and the world.[13] As for children of divorce, they report more parental conflict, more triangulation, less respect and communication between parents, less involvement, and poorer parenting behaviors from fathers than children from intact families.[14]

Does the marital satisfaction of happy couples cause their positive communication or vice versa? Some research suggests that both are true. Across a number of countries, that is, Brazil, Italy, Taiwan, and the United States, constructive communication was positively associated with relationship satisfaction,[15] whereas the demand/withdrawal pattern, where typically the wife demands and the husband withdraws, was negatively associated with it. Relationship satisfaction can determine how hard people work to communicate well, that is, if they're happy with the relationship, they're more likely to be attentive and try hard to understand each other, and vice versa. Rose-colored glasses, or their opposite, dark tinted ones, clearly influence what is being seen. But it's also true that people unknowingly resort to poor communication strategies, because they don't know any better and haven't learned how harmful their communication approaches can be.[16]

Research[17] has shown that dissatisfied couples are more likely to engage in negative-affect reciprocity, that is, when one partner is critical and contemptuous, the other is likely to follow suit; once these patterns start, they are more likely to get locked into these vicious cycles than happy couples. In addition, unhappy couples are more likely to misinterpret communications from spouses[18] (even though they do a better job with strangers), be insensitive to nonverbal cues, and to attribute selfish and negative intentions to their partner's behavior (e.g. he's just trying to hurt me) rather than the more benign attributions (e.g. he had a bad day) made by happy spouses.[19]

There has been growing evidence in recent years that the ways in which couples perceive, interpret, and evaluate each other and relationship events have a significant impact on the quality of their relationships.[20] Unhappy couples are more negative in general, fail to live by the 5:1 rule[21] (five positive interactions for every negative), and tend to engage in especially destructive patterns, such as stonewalling, defensiveness, contempt, and criticism. Cross-cultural studies have been consistent in finding that the marital communication of distressed couples is highly negative and quickly leads to escalation in a disagreement. In comparing Australian couples with German ones, Halford and colleagues[22] found this consistency but also discovered that the German couples had higher rates of criticism and refusals than their Australian counterparts.

In an interesting study by Gottman and Levenson,[23] researchers coded the interactions of couples during an argument. Spouses were given points for attempts at warmth, collaboration, or compromise, and minus points for displays of anger, defensiveness, criticism, or contempt. Not surprisingly, the couples with the highest points were more satisfied with their marriages than the other couples. More interestingly, however, was the finding that more than half of the lowest scoring couples (56%) were divorced or separated four years later, whereas just under a quarter (24%) of the highest group had split up. The couples' behavior during an argument was predictive of both marital satisfaction and the dissolution of the relationship.

To address negative behaviors during conflict and other dysfunctional communication patterns, communication skills training courses have become a staple offering around the country for many groups, including premarital, predivorce, and distressed couples of all kinds. In these courses, which unfortunately are all too short to make up for years of maladaptive learning, the emphasis is on learning a smattering of active or empathic listening, on utilizing "I" messages to convey desires, hopes, and needs, and on developing some conflict-resolution strategies.

While communication skills training courses have been shown to be modestly successful, they can't possibly cover all the nuances of communication, which run the gamut from admiring complimentary messages to contemptuous and deafening silence. Nor can these courses provide detailed answers to all the individual questions that may arise, such as when to confront a part-ner's disturbing behavior or how to bridge a tension-filled distance without creating chaos. Not surprisingly, one of the most successful of these programs, the Premarital Relationship Enhancement Program (PREP) is geared to pre-marital couples, where optimism is naturally high and disillusionment low. In one study,[24] the PREP participants fared significantly better than controls in terms of staying married, constructiveness of communication, avoiding phys-ical violence, and marital satisfaction.

Adult children of divorce who have grown up in high conflict homes are often understandably anxious about many relationship issues, including how to raise delicate topics with their spouses. In their families-of-origin, they seldom observed emotionally laden issues, such as the spouse's excessive drinking, gambling, or failure to complete household tasks, being addressed without physical and/or verbal fight eruptions. Because they don't want to disturb the status quo and initiate warfare in their own families, they are often silent about serious issues to such an extent that they wind up depressed. This "silencing of the self" to avoid conflict can lead to significant withdrawal from the marital relationship and general unhappiness.

Even in divorced families with low conflict, the adult children are often at a loss as to what should be confronted or avoided in their own romantic relationships. Because it wasn't clear in many instances what contributed to their parent's divorce, they wind up uncertain as to how to proceed in handling their own disappointments and problems with their partners. The absence of clear-cut signs of dissatisfaction in their parents' relationship left them bewildered about what constitutes a satisfying marital relationship and how to achieve one.

Amato and DeBoer's[25] study, which found that the likelihood of divorce was greatest in young adults from divorced families with low conflict than in other groups, provides support for the hypothesis that divorce is especially confusing when there are no warning signs of its impending arrival. Further supporting this proposition is research by Duran-Aydintug,[26] which showed that young adults with less information about the reasons for a parental divorce reported more problems in dealing with the divorce. Less information about the parental divorce was also associated with more difficulty in assessing the quality and strength of their own romantic relationships.[27]

In general, adult children of divorce have poorer communication skills, more negative interpersonal behavior related to anger, higher rates of conflict, and more withdrawal in their romantic relationships than other groups.[28] All of these factors do not bode well for marital success unless there have been remedial efforts of some kind or positive romantic experiences along the way.

EXPECTATIONS, PERSPECTIVE, AND COMMITMENT

It is well known that people often get what they expect in relationships and that they tend to create the kind of relationships they expect (e.g. self-fulfilling prophecies). In two interesting studies[29] in support of this hypothesis, the experimenters gave the subjects erroneous information about whether the people they were talking to on the phone were attractive or homely (first study), or whether they were liked or not (second study).

In both studies, the subjects behaved in ways that were consistent with the information given, and the people they talked to responded accordingly. For example, male subjects who thought they were talking to attractive women were warm, sociable, outgoing, bold, and socially adept, to which the women responded in like manner. In contrast, the unfortunate women who had been erroneously labeled "homely" were exposed to dull, aloof conversations that failed to energize them and instead triggered equally lackluster behavior on their parts. In essence, people tend to live up to the expectations placed on them in never-ending cycles that are difficult to break.

The relationship between expectation and marital satisfaction has been established in a whole host of studies dating back to the seventies.[30] To the extent that one's beliefs about marriage (or anything else for that matter) are realistic, the more likely it is that one will be satisfied. Epstein and others[31] have identified five major types of cognition that influence partners' emotional and behavioral responses to each other: (a) selective perceptions, or what is attended to, (b) attributions, inferences made about the causes of certain events, (c) expectancies or predictions about future events, (d) assumptions, basic beliefs about the characteristics of the relationship and each other, and (e) standards involving beliefs about what characteristics each partner and the relationship should have.

These five forms of cognition have shown to affect marital satisfaction and communication with the most research attention given to attributions and standards. Epstein and others[32] have shown that two factors—adherence to standards and couple consensus on standards—were associated with level of marital adjustment for both Chinese and American couples. Similarly, in an earlier study, Fletcher[33] found that the higher the consistency between ideals and related assessments of the current partner and their relationship, the greater the degree of couple satisfaction.

In addition, Eidelson & Epstein[34] have demonstrated that marital satisfaction is negatively correlated with scores on their questionnaire—the Relationship Beliefs Inventory (RBI)—that was designed to assess unrealistic expectations. Three of the scales, that is, the mind reading scale—the expectation

that partners should know what is needed or felt without being told, the dis-agreement scale—the belief that conflict is destructive, and the unchanging partners scale—the belief that partners cannot change, proved to be particu-larly sensitive to marital unhappiness. Other unrealistic expectation scales in their questionnaire and other surveys relate to sexual perfectionism, stereo-typical role behaviors, predestined love, and total absorption in the other, that is, never wanting to be apart.

While a number of studies based on interview data have shown that the beliefs about marriage of adult children of divorce are not idealistic,[35] the fact that adult children of divorce, especially those from high-conflict fami-lies, have lowered marital satisfaction[36] suggests that their marital expectations often serve as self-fulfilling prophecies. Incidentally, one study[37] has shown higher levels of dysfunctional beliefs about romantic love in couples in *fault* as opposed to *no-fault* divorces. Another study[38] has demonstrated higher re-lationship ideals in children of divorce, specifically around affection, passion, and independence. Thus, the research evidence regarding ideals is mixed and may point to conflict between ideals and expectations in these adults. Based on their family-of-origin experiences, however, it appears that children of divorce generally have less favorable expectations about the success of their future marriages than those from intact families[39] and less overall trust when it comes to intimate relationships.[40]

Some of the marital expectations of children of divorce undoubtedly relate to perceived signs of marital dysfunction in their original families, which then serve as warning signs of impending trouble in their own marriages. A neg-ative model representing the parental qualities that were problematic, or the negative parent in his or her entirety, is often erected and serves this alarm function. In trying to avoid any resemblance to the offending parent, these adults frequently veer so far off the threatening course in their choice of part-ners as to exclude normal playfulness or reasonable anger from their ideal. One woman, whose parental divorce was caused by her father's infidelity and abusive behavior toward her mother, said that she wanted to choose a part-ner based on characters in French romantic novels—essentially white knights intent upon saving damsels in distress—rather than upon any of her father's characteristics. Her goal was to avoid anybody who resembled her father in any way. Her negative model was a powerful source of anxiety when a roman-tic partner resembled her father in even the slightest degree with respect to anger and flirtatiousness toward women.

In general, if their parents fought a good deal, disagreement with their partners often signals anxiety about the permanence of their own relation-ship, and elicits a stronger emotional reaction than the disagreement itself warrants. Similarly, for adults from divorced families with low conflict, emotional distance between themselves and their partners is often the trigger for worry and concern about their own relationship ending. Any symptom or dysfunction that was perceived to be the catalyst for parental divorce could serve as an alarm bell for anxiety, magnify their emotional response, and create undue concern about their own romantic relationships. As Wallerstein[41] wrote, "Anxiety leads many into making bad choices in relationships, giving up hastily when problems arise, or avoiding relationships altogether."

One middle-aged man, age forty-two, whose parents divorced when he was in his teens because of his father's infidelity, was hypersensitive to his wife's mildly flirtatious behavior when at a social gathering with mixed company. Identifying primarily with his mother, with whom he had an unusually close relationship (she treated him as her primary confidante), he felt that somehow he and his wife were destined to repeat the mistakes his parents made. However, he reversed the roles from his parents' divorce drama in that he saw himself as the victim and his wife as the adulterous spouse. His jealousy of his wife's smiling, joking behavior with men at parties, while it did not lead to any overt infidelity on her part, created much conflict and unhappiness for them both.

How the relationship anxiety of children of divorce is handled will be an important factor in determining whether the anxiety will be resolved or become part of a self-fulfilling prophecy. For example, when anxiety about the relationship leads to lengthy bouts of accusatory discussions, which are often misguided attempts to gain reassurance, the partner often feels attacked, misunderstood, and motivationally depleted. As a result, the partner is more likely to behave in maladaptive ways that are likely to lead to an intensification of the conflict. The partner may withdraw and become emotionally unavailable, or become emotionally abusive in a counterattack. Repeated accusations of emotional neglect, for instance, often lead to the very behavior being criticized. In the familiar demand/withdrawal pattern, the wife's demands for closeness frequently result in the opposite, that is, more distance from a beleaguered spouse who doesn't know how to respond. In contrast, when the anxious spouse acknowledges his or her own insecurity, is less blaming, and seeks reassurance in a reasoned manner, there is a greater probability that the partner can provide the support that is needed.

Unfortunately, adult children of dysfunctional relationships, including divorce, lack perspective on what certain partner-behaviors mean and what is important or trivial in successful relationships. Thus, they are hypersensitive to minor negative behaviors and quick to interpret even neutral behaviors as problematic. For example, when a partner is angry, disloyal, forgetful, sexually apathetic for a time, or desirous of some time apart, they are more likely to interpret such behaviors as indicative of defective love rather than as minor flaws in the human condition. In other words, they are quick to see their own romantic relationships as irrevocably damaged or severely limited and in need of termination way before reality so dictates.

In Bartell's[42] review of the literature on parental divorce and romantic relationships, she discusses the concept of cognitive representations, which are defined as "organized knowledge structures about relationships that result from prior relational experiences and consist of autobiographical memories of past relational experiences (e.g., parental divorce experiences) as well as beliefs, attitudes, and expectations about the self and others in relationships." Similar to the psychoanalytic concept of *transference*, cognitive representations are believed to be activated during relevant situations, such as serious dating encounters, for instance, and affect the way new information is processed, that is, how the experience is attended to, interpreted, and stored in memory. Furthermore, she maintains that individuals are likely to appraise and explain new relationship experiences of the same type in ways that are consistent with their representations, and that once formed, these representations are somewhat resistant to change and influence the kind of behavioral responses used in these situations. Moreover, she proposes that these cognitive representations are changed primarily by significant new experiences, such as direct romantic relationships that are inconsistent with existing expectations.

In addition, Bartell and others[43] believe that parental divorce may exert a stronger influence on attitudes about and behaviors in marriage than on premarital romantic relationships. Whereas young adults from divorced families are cautious, fearful, and distrustful about marital relationships, they are less so about their romantic relationships, which in modern Western society, are distanced in time from marriage. Therefore, it may be that there are two separate, and yet interconnected cognitive representations—one on premarital romantic relationships and a second on marital relationships—that are affected differentially by parental divorce with the more negative effects occurring on the marital representation.

Another factor related to successful marriage is commitment; happy couples are highly committed to their marriages and give their marital relationship top priority in their lives. Highly committed couples tend to adopt a long-term orientation that reduces the pain that would otherwise accompany rough spots in their relationship. Because they feel they're in it for a long haul, they are able to tolerate episodes that are difficult and unrewarding in much the same way long-term investors tolerate the up and down swings of the stock market. Most importantly, however, highly committed couples take action to protect and maintain the relationship, even when it's difficult to do so. For example, they may refrain from responding to provocation from their partners with similar anger and instead allow their partner's bad mood to dissipate. Or, they may sacrifice their own self-interest for the good of the relationship by doing some things they wouldn't do if they were alone.[44] In contrast, as a result of negative experiences observing their parents' marriages, children from divorced families have more difficulty in committing themselves to romantic relationships and are more accepting of divorce as a solution when rough spots occur. Amato and DeBoer[45] have concluded that children of divorce have a weak commitment to the norm of lifelong marriage.

Since parental divorce exerts its negative influence in a variety of ways, how can the marital expectations, perspective, and commitment hesitancy of these adult children be changed? Shulman, Scharf, Lumer, and Maurer[46] proposed that three types of processes should be associated with better relationship outcomes: (a) being able to discuss coherently any negative experiences, (b) recognizing the changes that have occurred since the parental divorce, and (c) understanding the complexity of the divorce experience, which includes being able to see the divorce from multiple perspectives rather than blaming only one parent. Individuals who are successfully able to do these things are said to have developed an "integrated perspective," which enables them to alter their views about the self and others in a positive direction. In support of this, Shulman and colleagues found that young adults from divorced families who developed an integrated perspective reported fewer problems and more friendship and enjoyment in their romantic relationships. However, it is not easy to predict who will develop such a complex perspective (nor how it develops) because neither age at divorce, gender, parental marital conflict, nor post-divorce parental romantic involvements were associated with its development.

HOW MUCH SIMILARITY IS IMPORTANT?

While it's been long known that similar values represent the foundation of a happy marriage, the extent to which similarity is important in determining marital satisfaction has not been widely publicized. Instead people tend to believe that "opposites attract," which has some truth to the statement. People are initially drawn to qualities in others they value but do not possess (the Need for Completion that was discussed in Chapter 2), but longer-lasting relationships tend to be based on similarity across a wide range of dimensions.

Happy couples tend to be more similar than dissimilar in personality, attitudes, physical attractiveness, and demographics (age, race, education, religion, and social class).[47] With respect to attitudes, the relationship between attitude similarity and attraction is straightforward and linear, that is, the more two people have in common, the more they like each other. As for personalities, husbands and wives with similar personalities have happier marriages than spouses with different styles.[48] "Moreover, the effects of personality similarity on attraction can be observed in both cognitive and emotional domains. People who think in similar ways—who resemble each other in 'cognitive complexity,' the way that they structure and organize their thoughts and perceptions—are more attracted to each other than are those who differ in cognitive complexity."[49]

People are also attracted to others who have similar moods and similar attachment styles,[50] that is, happy people are drawn to happy individuals, and vice versa. Similarly, insecurely attached individuals, characterized by anxiety, ambivalence, and neediness when it comes to relationships, gravitate to comparable souls, while the securely attached individuals seek out equally comfortable types.

In addition, surveys of marital satisfaction show that traditional marriages in which spouses adhere to stereotyped gender roles are generally less happy than nontraditional couples.[51] Insofar as shared interests and mutually enjoyable activities are concerned, the traditional couple may have little in common with each other besides values. While shared values, such as religion and family, affect marital stability, they do not necessarily influence the degree of enjoyment spouses experience with one another.

Even with interethnic marriages, which have increased fourfold in the last thirty-five years, that is, they represented 2 percent of marriages in the United States in 1970 but 7.5 percent in 2005,[52] partners tend to be similar in age, education, and attractiveness.[53] In addition, their marriages are based on common interests and personal compatibility[54] just like successful same-ethnic marriages. According to Brehm,[55] the difference between same-ethnic and interethnic relationships may be in the circumstances. In interethnic romances, circumstances (high school, college, work) provided them with a large number of interethnic potential partners, which increased their chances of falling in love with someone who looked different. Ultimately, however, it was their similarities that seemed to fuel their attraction with their differences adding some spice to the mix.

While not much is known about the similarity or dissimilarity of adult children of divorce and their romantic partners, available research suggests that birds of a feather flocking together may not be the wisest option, at least for certain factors, such as parental divorce. Amato[56] for example, reported that the risk of divorce increased substantially if both partners came from divorced families, that is, the risk increased by almost 190 percent if both partners experienced parental divorce (by 70% if only the wife's family was divorced). Wolfinger[57] also concluded that marriages between two children of divorce are especially likely to fail. It follows that if both spouses were exposed to maladaptive communication patterns in their families and confused about effective relationship strategies, then the likelihood of their developing a satisfying relationship will be reduced. Similarly, if both have insecure attachment styles, then the opportunity for uncertainty and conflict in their marital relationship is increased.

There is some supporting research evidence that adults from divorced families are more likely to have insecure attachment styles[58] but the results are far from conclusive. What does emerge with certainty, however, from the research literature is the finding that adult children of divorce are more hesitant, more pessimistic, less trusting, and less altruistic toward their partners, characteristics that are likely to lead to marital unhappiness.

OTHER MARITAL SATISFACTION FACTORS: SEX AND HOUSEHOLD EQUITY

It is not too surprising to find that in general married people are happy with their sex lives, and the happier they are in their marriages, the happier they are with sex, and vice versa. Even international studies, such as the report of 233 married Russian couples[59] found that the two most important predictors of marital satisfaction were the positive regard of spouses toward one another and satisfaction with their sexual relationship. In addition, in comparing love marriages with arranged marriages, Kumar and Dhyani[60] found that the sexual satisfaction contributed significantly to marital adjustment, not the kind of marriage. In other words, it didn't matter if people picked their own partners or they were picked by families, what mattered most was the quality of their sex lives insofar as marital happiness was concerned.

Frequency of sex has also been found to correlate with marital happiness but more specific refinements to that finding suggest that the relationship between sex and relational satisfaction is more complicated than it appears at first glance. For instance, Howard and Dawes[61] reported that the specific factor that predicted marital happiness was the rate of sexual interaction minus the number of arguments. From this study, it appeared that even couples who argued a lot can be happy with one another, provided they have more positive interactions (sexual and otherwise) to balance the negativity. Other writers have suggested that rather than frequency of sex being the critical variable, it was having sex as often as desired that was the critical determinant of relational happiness.

As for adult children of divorce and their sex lives, not much is known. A number of studies[62] have shown that children from divorced families, while initially hesitant about involvement, do get involved more quickly in romantic relationships, both emotionally and sexually, have more sexual partners, and marry younger than those from intact families. In trying to understand their finding of heightened sexual desire and behavior among children of divorce, Gabardi and Rosen[63] proposed that either children of divorce were needier of physical/sexual affection than those from intact families, or they were trying to have more loving relationships, which they mistakenly believed would be achieved with sex.

One young woman, whose parents divorced when she was prepubertal (aged eleven) and whose father emotionally abandoned the family, witnessed a string of her mother's post-divorce sexual liaisons firsthand by regularly peeking through her mother's bedroom window when she had male company. While she was titillated by her observations of her mother's sexual responsiveness, she was also quite ashamed of her mother's promiscuous behavior. Her conflict about her mother's sexuality led to early sexual experimentation on her part with little accompanying sexual pleasure and a search for partners who could provide a great deal of sexual excitement. Unfortunately, her sexual inhibitions resulted in her prematurely ending relationships with partners who were otherwise promising but lacked the kind of sexual adventurousness she desired. Whether she and other young women like her, who are sexually inhibited as a function of factors related to parental divorce, eventually resolve their conflicts on their own, without professional assistance, is not known.

Another factor related to marital satisfaction is perceived equity of household chores. Dual-career couples who perceive their spouses as doing their share of housework experience greater marital satisfaction than those who don't. This finding has been substantiated by a number of studies, which propose that unfair division of household tasks creates tension and resentment between spouses that lead to decreased marital quality for both men and women. In the Frisco and Williams study[64] using a nationally representative sample of dual-career couples, they found that inequity indeed was associated with reduced marital happiness for both men and women, but the unfair distribution of household tasks led to increased probability of divorce for wives only. Women who are trying to do it all often suffer from stress and role strain that make them more likely to end unsatisfying marriages.

Major factors that are correlated with marital satisfaction and worth serious examination by adult children of divorce are (a) positive communication patterns, (b) positive expectations, a balanced perspective and high commitment to maintain the marriage, (c) similarity in background, interests, and values,

(d) a satisfying sexual relationship, and (e) equity with respect to the performance of household tasks. Of these, communication, which includes a whole host of positive and negative response styles, that is, the demand/withdrawal pattern, negative-affect reciprocity (escalation in disagreements), and Gottman's[65] four major roadblocks to marital harmony (criticism, contempt, stonewalling, and defensiveness), has received the strongest research support. How partners talk to each other, handle disagreements, and resolve conflicts are of vital importance in maintaining the marital emotional bond. Of related significance are attributions (the positive and negative interpretations of each other's behavior), standards (or ideals), and expectations that often function as self-fulfilling prophecies.

In one interesting study,[66] it was found that intimate partners who idealized one another created the kind of relationship they idealized over time, and that idealized partners changed their self-images in the direction of the idealization. Burgoyne and Hames[67] also found that adult children with married parents (in contrast to those from divorced homes) were more "romantic" in talking about their own future marriages. Positive illusions about marriage are also believed to be adaptive as they result in greater marital satisfaction at least initially. Thus, it may be that some idealization is better than none, but too much is likely to lead to its own brand of difficulty, namely, that of disillusionment. As Brehm[68] wrote, " . . . by choosing to look on the bright side—perceiving our partners as the best they can be—and by editing our ideals and hopes so that they fit what we've got, we can increase the chances that we'll be happy with our present partners." Unfortunately, for children of divorce, the lack of much opportunity to observe parents interacting positively puts them at a disadvantage—both for learning positive communication strategies, and also for developing positive, slightly idealistic expectations regarding intimate partners—at least compared to children growing up in happy, intact families.

WHAT ELSE IS KNOWN ABOUT THE EFFECTS OF PARENTAL DIVORCE?

Divorce tends to have a long reach that extends not only into the second generation but also into the third. Amato and Cheadle[69] found that divorce in the first generation was associated with the third generation having lower education, more marital discord, and weaker ties with both mothers and fathers. All of these results were mediated (or transmitted) by lower education, more marital discord, more divorce, and greater tension in early parent–child relationships in the second generation. Parental jealousy, moodiness, criticalness, low frustration tolerance (being angered easily), infidelity, alcohol/drug use, not being home enough, and foolish spending habits accounted for the relation be-tween parental and offspring divorce.[70] Their conclusion regarding the long arm of divorce is sobering—they believe that divorce has long-term conse-quences for subsequent generations, including individuals not yet born at the time of the original divorce.

Besides the fact that divorce begets divorce via less education, marital dis-cord, and disruptions in the parent–child relationship, what else does divorce beget? Children from divorced families score significantly lower on measures of academic achievement, conduct, psychological adjustment, self-concept, and social relations than children with continuously married parents.[71] And because difficulties with interpersonal relationships result in lower levels of general happiness, it is safe to assume that parental divorce begets unhappi-ness for its children and its children's children.

In addition, young adult children of divorce have more problems with over control, or needing to control relationships, perhaps as a response to the lack of control they experienced in their families of origin.[72] They also have more difficulty maintaining a separate sense of self, or autonomy, without emotion-ally withdrawing from significant others.[73] The years of pre- and post-divorce conflict in which they were frequently embroiled appear to have led to the development of a protective shell that's difficult to shed in adult intimacy. For example, it has been found that higher levels of post-divorce conflict corre-late with higher levels of perceived risk in adult intimacy,[74] suggesting that emotionally disturbed family relationships predispose children of divorce to see romantic love as a dangerous journey to be avoided at all costs or pursued with ample protection.

Who is most affected by parental divorce in adulthood? In a number of stud-ies, the impact of parental divorce was found to be greater on adult women than on adult men in that greater intimacy conflicts[75] and greater number of sexual partners[76] were found for women only. Also, Amato[77] found signifi-cant associations between parental and offspring divorce among wives but not among husbands. In a somewhat different but fundamentally similar vein, it was found that a wife's understanding of her husband plays a greater role in enhancing marital happiness than a husband's understanding does toward his wife.[78] However, the findings attesting to the greater impact of divorce upon women were not supported by all the research studies in this area. In spite of this, it makes sense theoretically that women, whose self-esteem is tied into relationship success more than men's, would be most affected by intimacy fail-ures in their families, and that the absence of the father in the home (the most typical scenario after divorce) would affect romantic relationships for women more than for men.

The age of children at the time of divorce also appears to be an important issue affecting adult intimacy, but here, too, the results are not conclusive.[79] Younger children, whose psychic structures are in the process of formation, (hence, they are more vulnerable to traumas such as abandonment and loss), and who are less likely to have outside support systems, appear to be most affected negatively by parental divorce. Amato[80] found that parental divorce occurring when children are under the age of twelve was associated with a 60 percent increase in the probability of divorce, as opposed to a 23 percent increase for children ages thirteen to nineteen years. Children over the age of twenty when their parents divorced actually showed a decrease in the risk of divorce. Gabardi and Rosen[81] found that the greater the number of years since the divorce, the greater the risk of forming unrealistic beliefs about close relationships, such as interpreting disagreements catastrophically or believing that sex has to be perfect all the time.

A number of factors specific to marital attitudes have also been linked to parental divorce. Tasker,[82] for example, found that adults from divorced families in the United Kingdom generally do not want to marry and prefer cohabitation to marriage. In addition, Tasker also found that although they have more negative views of marriage than those from intact families, they tend to put themselves in situations that promote marriage, such as leaving school, leaving home, and being in steady relationships. In other words, adult children of divorce are emotionally conflicted about intimate relationships. On the one hand, they have a greater need for intimacy, but on the other hand, they are more fearful and pessimistic about marriage.

Wolfinger[83] attributes some of the conflicting results about whether children of divorce are more or less likely to marry to historical periods. He reported that in 1973 parental divorce greatly increased the chances of marriage (possibly because marriage was highly regarded by society at that time), but that in 1994 it produced the opposite result, that is, people from divorced families were less likely to marry than those from intact families. Furthermore, he maintains that parental divorce raises the likelihood of teenage marriage, but if the children of divorce remain single past age twenty, they are disproportionately likely to avoid marriage altogether.

Apart from parental divorce, the cultural values and national characteristics of a country influence divorce rates. In collectivistic societies, for example, where family allegiance and partner similarity are of paramount importance, divorce rates tend to be lower than in individualistic societies, where the primary emphasis is on individual happiness and freedom of partner choice. The presence of strong overarching motives in a society, such as religion, patriotism, group loyalty, and/or love of family, also serve to lower divorce rates by strengthening the marriage commitment. Paradoxically, in individualistic societies where romantic love is regarded as the *sine qua non* ingredient in marriage and the basis for a high degree of personal fulfillment within its hallowed halls, excessive individualism actually makes intimacy harder to achieve.[84]

Other national characteristics that influence divorce rates are the social stability of a society, including employment, poverty, and violence rates, and the valued qualities in a particular culture. For example, when materialism, monetary success, and hedonism are esteemed more than hard work, honor, and seriousness of purpose, divorce rates tend to be high (e.g. Russia and the United States). If parental divorce is added to the picture, the mixture of personal and cultural accelerants will further increase the likelihood of divorce.

IN CONCLUSION

Adults who grew up in divorced and other unhappy homes have difficulty in knowing what romantic love is; without parental examples to pave the way, they are confused about what love requires and how to distinguish love from related needs. In addition, their love choices are often based on the roles they played in their families or on mastery motivation, that is, the need to gain control of childhood traumas, and as such represent unhealthy attempts to redo the past with little regard for their current emotional and/or intellectual needs. For example, if they had to take care of their siblings and/or their mothers in their nuclear families, the caretaking role, as a significant source of self-esteem, becomes ingrained and leads to its continuation by the choice of helpless or inadequate partners. In addition, adults from conflict-ridden homes often learned unhealthy communication and conflict-resolution strategies in their families that they carry with them into their own romantic relationships.

While adults who grew up in unhappy, intact families are similar to adult children of divorce with respect to love confusion, inappropriate partner choice, and maladaptive interpersonal learning, divorce has its own unique lens that magnifies the significance of each parent's dysfunctional behavior with each other. Because of the serious outcome their parent's problematic behavior led to, namely the marital dissolution, their parent's interpersonal behaviors become emotionally loaded and a source of hypervigilance in their own romantic relationships. In addition, infidelity, domestic violence, and alcohol/drug abuse, all of which occur in higher percentages in divorced families, create their own unique problems for family members. Also the sense of abandonment by one or both parents as they become embroiled in divorce and post-divorce-related issues, and the disruptions to the child's life brought about by a geographical move, loss of friends, and the noncustodial parent's departure are all highly stressful, especially to younger and more vulnerable children. The strain of experiencing such a major disruption of parenting, as divorce often necessitates, is believed to be one of the major factors behind the negative consequences of divorce.[85] An exception to the oft-described injurious divorce may be the "good divorce," where the divorce itself alleviates a tension-filled or abusive situation and restores a sense of normalcy to a chaotic world.

While Constance Ahrons,[86] author of *The Good Divorce*, defines a good divorce "as one in which both the adults and the children emerge at least as emotionally well as they were before the divorce," a more appropriate definition would refer to improved functioning as a result of ameliorations in a negative situation of abuse or dysfunction. And a number of studies have pointed to positive outcomes for children as a result of their parents' divorces, such as increased maturity, enhanced self-esteem, increased empathy, and androgynous attitudes.[87] However, because divorce creates its own set of problems for almost all family members, that is, losses of all kinds, the post-divorce world ideally should be an upgrade over pre-divorce conditions. Nevertheless, in Ahrons' view, the absence of clear-cut psychopathology in children and the restoration of pre-divorce relationships constitute a good divorce.

In her defense of divorce, Ahrons[88] focuses on those children of divorce who do not manifest long-term psychological damage—the majority of adults in her twenty-year follow-up study who feel positively about their parents' divorce and appear to be leading productive and healthy lives. Unfortunately, because the average age of Ahron's sample of middle-class adults is only thirty-one, it is too early to tell the ultimate outcome of this group with respect to romantic love, marriage, and/or divorce. While it is certainly true that not all children of divorce have career and social difficulties, intimacy problems in adulthood are more subtle and difficult to discern. Lack of trust, propensity to disappointment, negative expectations about the longevity of romantic relationships, and fears of abandonment, betrayal, and rejection—some of the precursors to emotional disconnection and disengagement—are less tangible indicators of emotional conflicts regarding intimacy.

One of the primary reasons cited by divorced couples for their divorce—lack of love—is difficult to measure in any concrete or behavioral manner. And yet, experientially, loss of love is a phenomenon as powerful in uprooting marriages as a gale-sized storm is in toppling gigantic oaks. In one study,[89] 80 percent of divorced men and women said their marriages broke up because they grew apart and lost a sense of closeness. Insidious and slow-growing, loss of love, fed by hundreds of disappointments, often surprises its victims by its sudden appearance. Once it takes hold, however, lack of love is hard to pluck out or transform into something benign. The hundreds of disappointments and disillusionments, ranging from the trivial to the sublime, have undermined the very foundation of the relationship, leaving not much in its wake besides fissures and overgrown weeds. The journey from disappointment to disengagement to lack of love, while typically very painful and acrimonious, ends up with an even more soul-wrenching period of trying to decide whether to divorce or not—a decision fueled by many factors, including religious, moral, and financial barriers to divorce, the strength of one's commitment to marriage, the ages of children, and the appeal of alternatives to the current marital state.

Disappointment in romantic relationships flourishes in Western society because of skewed expectations regarding romantic love. Often too idealistic, too unrealistic, or too pessimistic (likely to be self-fulfilling prophecies), romantic expectations are overly burdened by a culture's shallow portrayals of romantic love. Adult children of divorce lacking a template of marital fulfillment derived from their own families are often unduly influenced by the culture's seductive renditions of romantic bliss and more likely to be disappointed by its false promises. Unless they adopt another more realistic model of romantic love that provides a balanced perspective of its joys and sufferings, adult children of divorce are likely to be the unwitting transmitters of their parents' unhappiness to another generation of love seekers. However, with a lifelike portrayal of marriage in hand along with a portfolio of adaptive communication strategies, their chances of wandering down dangerous pathways in pursuit of romantic love are greatly reduced. In addition, choosing a lifelong partner based upon compatible personality traits and solid values rather than on bedazzling superficialities will add to the likelihood of a companionable, emotionally gratifying, and durable union.

Notes

INTRODUCTION

1. Paul R. Amato and Shelley Irving, "Historical Trends in Divorce in the United States," in M. A. Fine and J. H. Harvey (eds.), *Handbook of Divorce and Relationship Dissolution* (Mahwah, NJ: Lawrence Erlbaum Associates, 2006), 41–57.

2. Paul R. Amato, "Children of Divorce in the 1990s: An Update of the Amato and Keith 1991 Meta-Analysis," *Journal of Family Psychology* 15(3) (2001), 355–370.

3. E. Mavis Hetherington, *For Better or Worse: Divorce Reconsidered* (New York: W. W. Norton, 2002).

4. Elizabeth Marquardt, *Between Two Worlds: The Inner Lives of Children of Divorce* (New York: Three Rivers Press, 2005).

5. E. Hetherington, *For Better or* ... (see note 3).

6. Constance Ahrons, *The Good Divorce: Keeping Your Family Together When Your Marriage Comes Apart* (New York: HarperCollins, 1994).

7. M. B. Conway, T. M. Christensen, and B. Herlihy, "Adult Children of Divorce and Intimate Relationships: Implications for Counseling," *The Family Journal* 11 (4) (2003): 364–373.

8. Judith S. Wallerstein, Julia M. Lewis, and Sandra Blakeslee, *The Unexpected Legacy of Divorce: A 25-Year Landmark Study* (New York: Hyperion, 2000).

9. P. R. Amato and D. D. DeBoer, "The Transition of Marital Instability Across Generations: Relationship Skills or Commitment to Marriage?" *Journal of Marriage and the Family* 63 (4) (2001): 1,038–1,051.

10. P. R. Amato and J. Cheadle, "The Long Reach of Divorce: Divorce and Child Well-Being Across Three Generations," *Journal of Marriage and Family* 67 (1) (2005): 191–206.

11. Judith S. Wallerstein and Julia M. Lewis, "Sibling Outcomes and Disparate Parenting and Step-Parenting After Divorce: Report from a 10-Year Longitudinal Study," *Psychoanalytic Psychology* 24 (3) (2007): 445–458.

12. J. Wallerstein, *The Unexpected Legacy of Divorce* . . . p. 299 (see note 8)

13. Mary-Lou Galician, *Sex, Love, and Romance in the Mass Media: Analysis and Criticism of Unrealistic Portrayals and Their Influence* (Mahwah, NJ: Lawrence Erlbaum Associates, 2004).

CHAPTER 1

1. Geraldine K. Piorkowski, "Back Off," *Psychology Today*, Jan/Feb 1995, 50–53.

2. Sir Walter Scott, *The Lay of the Last Minstrel*, Canto III, Stanza 2.

3. William Shakespeare, *Sonnet 116*.

4. Elizabeth Barret Browning, *Sonnets From the Portuguese*, XLIII.

5. Robert Burns, *My Love is Like a Red, Red Rose*.

6. Edgar Allan Poe, *Annabel Lee*.

7. Ralph Waldo Emerson, *Give All to Love*.

8. George Noel Gordon, Lord Byron, *Hebrew Melodies, She Walks in Beauty, Stanza I*.

9. William Shakespeare, *Sonnet 18*.

10. Roy Croft, *Love*.

11. Robert D. Putnam, *Bowling Alone: America's Collapse and Revival of the American Community* (New York: Simon and Schuster, 2000).

12. Stephanie Coontz, *Marriage, a History: From Obedience to Intimacy or How Love Conquered Marriage* (New York: Viking, 2005).

13. E. W. Burgess, H. J. Locke, and M. Thomas, *The Family: From Institution to Companionship.* (New York: American Book Company, 1963).

14. Ellen Berscheid, "The Changing Reasons for Marriage and Divorce," in M. A. Fine and J. H. Harvey (eds.) *Handbook of Divorce and Relationship Dissolution* (Mahwah, NJ: Lawrence Erlbaum Associates, 2006), 613–618.

15. William Jankowiak, ed., *Romantic Passion* (New York: Columbia University Press, 1995), 4–5.

16. Robert J. Sternberg, *The Triangle of Love* (New York: Basic Books, 1988).

17. S. Roberts, "The Shelf Life of Bliss," *New York Times*, July 1, 2007.

18. J. Collins and T. Gregor, "Boundaries of Love," in *Romantic Passion* (see note 15), 4.

19. J. W. White and M. P. Koss, "Courtship Violence: Incidence in a National Sample of Higher Education Students," *Violence and Victims* 6 (1991), 247–256.

20. M. A. Straus and R. J. Gelles, *Physical Violence in American Families: Risk Factors and Adaptations to Family Violence in 9,145 Families* (New Brunswick, NJ: Transaction Publishers, 1990); M. Straus, R. Gelles, and S. Steinmetz, *Behind Closed Doors: Violence in the American Family* (Garden City, NY: Doubleday, 1980).

21. K. E. Leonard and L. J. Roberts, "Marital Aggression, Adjustment, and Stability in the First Year of Marriage: Findings from the Buffalo Newlywed Study," in T. N. Bradbury (ed.) *The Developmental Course of Marital Dysfunction* (New York: Cambridge University Press, 1998), 44–73.

22. M. Straus and R. Gelles, *Physical Violence* . . . (see note 20).

23. Andrew J. Cherlin, *Marriage, Divorce, and Remarriage* (Cambridge, MA: Harvard University Press, 1992).

24. B. Brunner (Editor), *The Time Almanac* (Boston, MA: Information Please LLC, 1999).

25. The U. S. Census Bureau, *Statistical Abstract of the United States 1998: The National Data Book* (Lanham, MD: Bernan Press, 1998).

26. L. L. Bumpass, T. C. Martin, and J. A. Sweet, "The Impact of Family Background and Early Marital Factors on Marital Disruption," *Journal of Family Issues* 12(1991), 22–42.

27. A. E. Rodrigues, J. H. Hall, and F. D. Fincham, "What Predicts Divorce and Relationship Dissolution?" in M. A. Fine and J. H. Harvey (eds.) *Handbook of Divorce and Relationship Dissolution* (Mahwah, NJ: Lawrence Erlbaum Associates, 2006), 85–112.

28. L. A. Kurdek, "Predicting Marital Dissolution: A 5-Year Prospective Longitudinal Study of Newlywed Couples." *Journal of Personality and Social Psychology* 64 (1993), 221–242.

29. G. C. Kitson, *Portrait of Divorce: Adjustment to Marital Breakdown* (New York: Guilford, 1992).

30. Rodrigues, Hall, and Fincham, *Handbook of Divorce* . . . (see note 27).

31. A. Clarke-Stewart and C. Brentano, *Divorce: Causes and Consequences* (New Haven, CT: Yale University Press, 2006), 40.

32. P. R. Amato, "Explaining the Intergenerational Transmission of Divorce," *Journal of Marriage and the Family* 58 (1996), 628–640.

33. P. R. Amato, and A. Booth, "The Legacy of Parents' Marital Discord: Consequences for Children's Marital Quality." *Journal of Personality and Social Psychology* 81 (2001), 627–638.

34. Clarke-Stewart and Brentano, *Divorce: Causes* . . . (see note 31), 41.

35. J. M. Gottman, *What Predicts Divorce? The Relationship Between Marital Processes and Marital Outcomes* (Hillsdale, NJ: Lawrence Erlbaum Associates, 1994).

36. Kurdek (see note 28).

37. Rodrigues, Hall, and Finchman, *Handbook of Divorce* . . . (see note 27).

38. J. M. Gottman and R. W. Levenson, "Marital Processes Predictive of Later Dissolution: Behavior, Physiology, and Health," *Journal of Personality and Social Psychology* 63 (1992), 221–233.

39. J. M. Gottman, H. J. Markman, F. J. Floyd, S. M. Stanley, and R. D. Storaaski, "Prevention of Marital Distress: A Longitudinal Investigation," *Journal of Consulting and Clinical Psychology* 56 (1994), 210–217.

40. Clarke-Stewart and Brentano, *Divorce: Causes* . . . (see note 31), 42.

41. Rodriques, Hall, and Finchman, *Handbook of Divorce* . . . (see note 27).

42. L. A. Kurdek, (see note 27); V. Jockin, M. McGue, and D. T. Lykken, "Personality and Divorce: A Genetic Analysis." *Journal of Personality and Social Psychology* 71 (1996), 288–299.

43. E. L. Kelly and J. J. Conley, "Personality and Compatibility: A Prospective Analysis of Marital Stability and Marital Satisfaction," *Journal of Personality and Social Psychology* 52 (1987), 27–40.

44. Jockin, McGue, and Lykken (see note 42).

45. Kurdek (see note 27).

46. Clarke-Stewart and Brentano (see note 31), 47.

47. R. C. Kessler, E. E. Walter, and M. S. Forthofer, "The Social Consequences of Psychiatric Disorders, III: Probability of Marital Stability," *The American Journal of Psychiatry* 155 (1998), 1092–1096.

48. P. R. Amato, and D. Previti, "People's Reasons for Divorcing: Gender, Social Class, the Life Course, and Adjustment," *Journal of Family Issues* 24 (2003), 602–626.

49. L. Beitzig, "Causes of Conjugal Dissolution: A Cross-Cultural Study," *Current Anthropology* 30 (1989), 654–676; G. C. Kitson, K. B. Babri, and M. J. Roach, "Who Divorces and Why: A Review," *Journal of Family Issues* 6 (1985), 255–293.

50. J. H. Hall and F. D. Fincham, "Relationship Dissolution Following Infidelity," in M. Fine and J. Harvey (eds) *Handbook of Divorce and Relationship Dissolution* (Mahwah, NJ: Erlbaum, 2006), 153–168.

51. D. Buss, *The Evolution of Desire: Strategies of Human Mating* (New York: Basic Books, 1994).

52. Hall and Fincham, *Handbook of Divorce* . . . (see note 50), 155.

53. T. J. Paolino, B. S. McCrady, and S. Diamond, "Statistics on Alcoholic Marriages: An Overview," *International Journal of Addictions* 13 (1979), 1285–1293.

54. D. Lester, "The Effect of Alcohol Consumption on Marriage and Divorce at the National Level," *Journal of Divorce and Remarriage* 27 (1997) (3–4), 159–161.

55. James Milam and Katherine Ketcham, *Under the Influence*, cited in C. D. Weddle and P. M. Wishon, "Children of Alcoholics: What We Should Know; How We Can Help," *Children Today* 15 (January–February 1986), 8.

56. Claudia Black, *It Will Never Happen to Me* (Denver, CO: M. A. C. Printing and Publication, 1981).

57. Geraldine K. Piorkowski, *Too Close for Comfort: Exploring the Risks of Intimacy* (New York: Plenum Press, 1994), 171.

58. Amato and Previti (see note 48).

59. D. Kurz, "Separation, Divorce, and Woman Abuse," *Violence Against Women* 2 (1996), 63–81.

60. E. Lawrence, and T. N. Bradbury, "Physical Aggression and Marital Dysfunction: A Longitudinal Analysis," *Journal of Family Psychology* 15 (2001), 135–154.

61. Clarke-Stewart and Brentano, *Divorce: Causes* . . . (see note 31), 49.

62. L. C. Sayer, and S. M. Bianchi, "Women's Economic Independence and the Probability of Divorce: A Review and Reexamination," *Journal of Family Issues* 21 (2000), 906–943.

63. E. Lawrence, E. Ro, R. Barry, and M. Bunde, "Mechanisms of Distress and Dissolution in Physically Aggressive Romantic Relationships," in *Handbook of Divorce and Relationship Dissolution* (see note 50), (2006), 271.

64. Alessandra Stanley, "Say, Darling, Is it Frigid in Here?" *New York Times*, August 19, 2007.

65. C. Mort and G. Polone (producers), *Tell Me You Love Me* (Television Series), (Chicago, IL: HARPO Productions; New York: Home Box Office, 2007).

66. Gary Chapman, *Five Love Languages: How to Express Heartfelt Commitment to Your Mate* (Chicago, IL: Northfield Publishing, 1992).

CHAPTER 2

1. Billie Letts, *Where the Heart Is* (Boston, MA: Warner Books, 1996).

2. Janet Fitch, *White Oleander* (Boston, MA: Little Brown & Company, 1999), 362–363.

3. Susan Isaacs. *Any Place I Hang My Hat* (New York: Scribner, 2004).

4. Robert Sternberg, *The Triangle of Love* (New York: Basic Books, 1988).

5. S. F. Dingfelder, "The Love Drug: More Than a Feeling," *Monitor on Psychology* (Washington, DC: American Psychological Association, February 2007), 40–41.

6. P. D. James, *Original Sin* (New York: Time Warner Books, 1994).

7. Elizabeth Marquardt, *Between Two Worlds: The Inner Lives of Children of Divorce* (New York: Three Rivers Press, 2005) p. xx.

8. Heinz Kohut, *How Does Analysis Cure* (Chicago, IL: University of Chicago Press, 1984), 49–54.

9. Claudia Black, *It Will Never Happen to Me* (Denver, CO: MAC, 1981); Sharon Wegscheider, *The Family Trap: No One Escapes from a Chemically Dependent Family* (St. Paul, MN: Nurturing Networks, 1976).

10. E. Marquardt, *Between Two Worlds:* . . . (see note 7).

11. G. J. Jurkovic, A. Thirkield, and R. Morrell, "Parentification of Adult Children of Divorce: A Multidimensional Analysis," *Journal of Youth and Adolescence* 30 (2) (2001), 245–257.

12. J. S. Wallerstein and J. M. Lewis, "The Unexpected Legacy of Divorce: Report of a 25-Year Study," *Psychoanalytic Psychology* 21 (3), (2004), 353–370.

13. Bernard Shaw, *Pygmalion* (New York: Brentano, 1916).

14. Vladimir Nabokov, *Lolita* (New York: G. P. Putnam's Sons, 1955).

15. Dante Alighieri, *Inferno*, Canto V, Line 103.

16. R. Bolgar, H. Zweig-Frank, and J. Paris, "Childhood Antecedents of Interpersonal Problems in Young Adult Children of Divorce," *Journal of the American Academy of Child & Adolescent Psychiatry* 34 (2) (1995), 143–150.

17. D. G. Dutton and A. P. Aron, "Some Evidence for Heightened Sexual Attraction Under Conditions of High Anxiety," *Journal of Personality and Social Psychology* 30 (1974), 510–517.

18. G. L. White, S. Fishbein, and J. Rutstin, "Passionate Love: The Misattribution of Arousal," *Journal of Personality and Social Psychology* 41 (1981), 56–62.

19. Jeffery Kluger, "Why We Love," *Time*, January 28, 2008.

20. S. Schachter, "The Interaction of Cognitive and Physiological Determinants of Emotional State," in L. Berkowitz (ed.) *Advances in Experimental Social Psychology*, Volume 1 (New York: Academic Press, 1964); White et al. (1981) (see note 18).

21. P. R. Amato and A. Booth, *A Generation at Risk: Growing Up in an Era of Family Upheaval* (Cambridge, MA: Harvard University Press, 1997); P. R. Amato, "Children of Divorce in the 1990s: An Update of the Amato and Keith 1991 Meta-analysis," *Journal of Family Psychology* 15 (3), 355–370; F. F. Furstenberg, and J. J. Cherlin, *Divided Families: What Happens to Children When Parents Part* (Cambridge, MA: Harvard University Press, 1991).

22. E. Marquardt, *Between Two Worlds* (see note 7).

23. J. A. Holdnack, "The Long-Term Effects of Parental Divorce on Family Relationships and the Effects on Adult Children's Self-Concept," in C. C. Everett (ed.) *Divorce and the Next Generation: Effects on Young Adults' Patterns of Intimacy and Expectations for Marriage* (New York: The Haworth Press, Inc., 1992), 137–155.

24. C. Hazan and P. Shaver, "Romantic Love Conceptualized as an Attachment Process," *Journal of Personality and Social Psychology* 52 (No. 3) (1987), 511–524.

25. K. Bartholomew and L. Horowitz, "Attachment Styles Among Young Adults: A Test of a Four Category Model," *Journal of Personality and Social Psychology* 61(1991): 226–244.

CHAPTER 3

1. *Stedman's Medical Dictionary*, 27th Edition (Baltimore, MD: Lippincott, Williams & Wilkins, 2000).

2. C. Duran-Aydintug, "Adult Children of Divorce Revisited: When They Speak Up," *Journal of Divorce and Remarriage* 27 (1/2) (1997), 71–83.

3. Geraldine K. Piorkowski, *Too Close for Comfort: Exploring the Risks of Intimacy* (New York: Plenum Press, 1994), 169.

4. Ibid.

5. R. W. Firestone and J. Catlett, *Fear of Intimacy* (Washington, DC: American Psychological Association, 1999), 79.

6. Diagnostic and Statistical Manual of Mental Disorders, 4th Edition (DSMIV).

7. Scott Wetzler, *Living with the Passive-Aggressive Man* (New York: Simon & Schuster, 1992).

8. P. R. Amato and A. Booth, "The Legacy of Parents' Marital Discord: Consequences for Children's Marital Quality," *Journal of Personality and Social Psychology* 81 (2001), 627–638.

9. G. Levinger, "A Social Psychological Perspective on Marital Dissolution," *Journal of Social Issues* 32 (1) (1976), 21–47.

CHAPTER 4

1. "You Always Hurt the One You Love," music and lyrics by Allan Roberts and Doris Fisher.

2. Judith S. Wallerstein, Julia M. Lewis, and Sandra Blakeslee, *The Unexpected Legacy of Divorce: A 25-Year Landmark Study* (New York: Hyperion, 2000), 300–301.

3. Geraldine K. Piorkowski, *Too Close for Comfort: Exploring the Risks of Intimacy* (New York: Plenum Press, 1994), 39–81.

4. Elaine Hatfield, "The Dangers of Intimacy," in V. J. Derlega (ed.), *Communication, Intimacy, and Close Relationships* (Orlando, FL: Academic Press, Inc., 1984), 207–220.

5. M. J. Levitt, M. E. Silver, and N. Franco, "Troublesome Relationships: A Part of Human Experience," *Journal of Social and Personal Relationships* 13 (1996), 523–536.

6. C. J. Descutner and M. H. Thelen, "Development and Validation of a Fear-of-Intimacy Scale," *Journal of Consulting and Clinical Psychology* 3 (1991), 218–225.

7. K. Bartholemew, "Avoidance of Intimacy: An Attachment Perspective," *Journal of Social and Person Relationships* 7 (1990), 147–178.

8. M. H. Thelen, J. S. Vander Wal, A. Muir Thomas, and R. Harmon, "Fear of Intimacy among Dating Couples," *Behavior Modification* 24 (2000), 223–240.

9. H. K. Klein, "Investigation of Variables Influencing College Students' Marital Attitudes and Fear of Intimacy," *ProQuest Information & Learning* (Electronic Print), 2006.

10. T. S. Scheffler and P. J. Naus, "The Relationship between Fatherly Affirmation and a Woman's Self-Esteem, Fear of Intimacy, Comfort with Womanhood and Comfort with Sexuality," *Canadian Journal of Human Sexuality* 8 (1), (1999), 39–45.

11. A. Kirk, "The Effects of Divorce on Young Adults' Relationship Competence: The Influence of Intimate Friendships," *Journal of Divorce and Remarriage* 38 (1–2), (2000), 61–90.

12. R. Bolgar, H. Zweig-Frank, and J. Paris, "Childhood Antecedents of Interpersonal Problems in Young Adult Children of Divorce," *Journal of the American Academy of Child and Adolescent Psychiatry* 34 (2), (1995), 143–150.

13. N. Lutwak, J. Panish, and J. Ferrari, "Shame and Guilt: Characterological vs. Behavioral Self-Blame and Their Relationship to Fear of Intimacy," *Personality and Individual Differences* 35 (4) (2003), 909–916.

14. R. W. Firestone and J. Catlett, *Fear of Intimacy* (Washington, DC: American Psychological Association, 1999).

15. Randal W. Summers and Allan M. Hoffman (eds.), *Domestic Violence: A Global View* (Westport, CT: Greenwood Press, 2002), xii.

16. G. Piorkowski, *Too Close for Comfort* (see note 3), 41.

17. Oprah Winfrey TV Show, *Adult Children of Divorce*, Channel 7 (ABC-Chicago), January 25, 2008.

18. P. S. Webster and A. R. Herzog, "Effects of Parental Divorce and Memories of Family Problems on Relationships between Adult Children and Their Parents,"

Journal of Gerontology: Series B: Psychological Sciences and Social Sciences 50 (1), (1995), S24–S34.

19. P. Johnson, J. M. Thorngren, and A. J. Smith, "Parental Divorce and Family Functioning: Effects on Differentiation Levels of Young Adults," *The Family Journal* 9 (3) (2001), 265–272.

20. Claudia Black, *It Will Never Happen to Me* (Denver, CO: MAC, 1981); Sharon Wegscheider-Cruse, *The Family Trap: No One Escapes from a Chemically Dependent Family* (St. Paul, MN: Nurturing Networks, 1976).

21. M. B. Conway, T. M. Christensen, and B. Herlihy, "Adult Children of Divorce and Intimate Relationships: Implications for Counseling," *The Family Journal: Counseling and Therapy for Couples and Families* 11(4) (2003), 364–373.

22. *Fatal Attraction* (Motion picture), Directed by S. R. Jaffe and S. Lansing, Hollywood, CA: Paramount Pictures, 1987.

23. G. Piorkowski, *Too Close for Comfort* (see note 3), 48–49.

24. C. Black, *It Will Never Happen to Me* (see note 20).

25. G. Piorkowski, *Too Close for Comfort* (see note 3), 61.

26. G. Piorkowski, *Too Close for Comfort* (see note 3), 78.

CHAPTER 5

1. Tori DeAngelis, "America: A Toxic Lifestyle?" *Monitor on Psychology*, 38 (4) April 2007, 50–52.

2. J. Banks, M. Marmont, Z. Oldfield, and J. P. Smith, "Disease and Disadvantage in the United States and England," *Journal of the American Medical Association* 295 (2006), 2038–2045.

3. Madeline Levine, *The Price of Privilege: How Parental Pressure and Material Advantage Are Creating a Generation of Disconnected and Unhappy Kids.* (New York: HarperCollins, 2006).

4. T. DeAngelis, "America: A Toxic Lifestyle?" (see note 1), 52.

5. Michael Bugeja, *Interpersonal Divide: The Search for Community in a Technological Age* (New York: Oxford University Press, 2005), 19–20.

6. Kelley Kazek, "'1' is No Longer the Loneliest Number as Single Households Now In Majority," *Athens News Courier*, September 24, 2006.

7. Robert D. Putnam, *Bowling Alone: The Collapse and Revival of American Community* (New York: Simon & Schuster, 2000), 370–372.

8. Mark Twain, (1867) quoted in Bayrd Still, *Urban America: A History with Documents* (Boston, MA: Little Brown, 1974), 198.

9. Larry Frolick, *Splitting Up: Divorce, Culture, and the Search for a Real Life* (New York: Random House, 1988).

10. Mary Pipher, *The Shelter of Each Other: Rebuilding Our Families* (New York: Ballantine Books. 1997), 25.

11. R. Putnam, *Bowling Alone* (see note 7), 207.

12. Ibid., 213.

13. Ibid., 206–207.

14. M. Pipher, *The Shelter*... (see note 10), 8.

15. Ibid., 14.

16. James Howard Kunstler, cited in Robert Putnam, *Bowling Alone* (see note 7), 224.

17. R. Putnam, *Bowling Alone* (see note 7), 224.

18. "TV or not TV (Editorial)," *Chicago Tribune*, May 11, 2007, 28.

19. R. Putnam, *Bowling Alone* (see note 7), 227.

20. Albert Gore, "Book Excerpt: The Assault on Reason," *Time Magazine*, May 28, 2007, 40–42.

21. Albert Mehrabian, *Silent Messages* (Belmont, CA: Wadsworth, 1971).

22. K. S. Young, "Internet Addiction: A New Clinical Phenomenon and its Consequences," *American Behavioral Scientist* 48 (4) (2004), 402–415.

23. Y. Lin, C. Wang, and C. Wu, "The Influence of Attachment Style and Internet Interpersonal Interactions on Internet Addiction," *Chinese Journal of Psychology* 47 (3) (2005), 309.

24. E. B. Weiser, "The Functions of Internet Use and their Social and Psychological Consequences," *CyberPsychology and Behavior* 4 (6) (2001), 723–743.

25. E. J. Moody, "Internet Use and its Relationship to Loneliness," *CyberPsychology and Behavior* 4 (3) (2001), 393–401.

26. G. S. Mesch and I. Talmud, "Similarity and Quality of Online and Offline Social Relationships Among Adolescents in Israel," *Journal of Research on Adolescence* 17 (2) (2007), 455–466.

27. M. A. Stefanone and C. Jang, "Writing for Friends and Family: The Interpersonal Nature of Blogs," *Journal of Computer-Mediated Communication* 13 (1) (2007), 123–140.

28. E. Hargittai, "Whose Space? Differences Among Users and Non-Users of Social Network Sites," *Journal of Computer-Mediated Communications* 13 (1) (2008), 276–297.

29. S. B. Stevens and T. L. Morris, "College Dating and Social Anxiety: Using the Internet as a Means of Connecting to Others," *CyberPsychology & Behavior* 10 (5) (2007), 680–688.

30. J. Peter and P. M. Valkenburg, "Who Looks for Casual Dates on the Internet? A Test of the Compensation and the Recreation Hypotheses," *New Media & Society* 9 (3) (2007), 455–474.

31. A. T. Fiore, M. Hearst, C. Cheshire, L. S. Taylor, and G. A. Mendelsohn "Online Dating Research at Berkeley," www.ischool.berkeley.edu, June 2007.

32. J. B. Walther, C. L. Slovacek, and L. C. Tidwell, "Is a Picture Worth a Thousand Words? Photographic Images in Long-Term and Short-Term Computer-Mediated Communication," *Communication Research* 28 (1) (2001), 105–134.

33. Robert Reich, *The Future of Success* (New York: Alfred A. Knopf, 2000).

34. Douglas W. Kmiec, "Overworked in America," *Chicago Tribune*, November 17, 1997, Section 1, 17.

35. Jerry A. Jacobs and Kathleen Gerson, "Understanding Changes in American Working Time: A Synthesis" in C. F. Epstein and A. L. Kalleberg (eds.), *Fighting for Time: Shifting Boundaries of Work and Social Life* (New York: Russell Sage Foundation, 2004), 27.

36. International Labor Organization Report cited in Steven Greenhouse "In U. S. Workers Toil Even Longer," *Chicago Tribune*, September 1, 2001.

37. John P. Robinson and Geoffrey Godbey, *Time for Life: The Surprising Ways Americans Use Their Time* (University Park, PA: Pennsylvania State University Press, 1997).

38. J. Jacobs and K. Gerson, "Understanding Changes in American Working Time..." (see note 35).

39. Michele A. Paludi and Presha E. Neidermeyer, *Work, Life, and Family Imbalance: How to Level the Playing Field* (Westport, CT: Praeger, 2007), 10.

40. J. Brooks-Gunn, W. Han, and J. Waldogel, "Maternal Employment and Child Cognitive Outcomes in the First Three Years of Life: the NICHD Study of Early Child Care," *Child Development* 73 (73) (2000), 1053–1072.

41. J. Heymann, A. Earle, and A. Hanchate, "Bringing a Global Perspective to Community Work and Family: An Examination of Extended Work Hours in Families in Four Countries," *Community, Work and Family* 7 (2004), 247–272.

42. R. Putnam, *Bowling Alone* (see note 7), 195.

43. M. Paludi and P. Neidermeyer, *Work, Life...* (see note 39), xv.

44. Kunz Center for the Study of Work and Family, *Ohio Wives Still Stuck with Most of the Housework, Finds Statewide Survey by University of Cincinnati* (1998), www.asweb.artsci.uc.edu/sociology/kunzctr/jun398.htm.

45. S. M. Bianchi, M. A. Milkie, L. C. Sayer, and J. P. Robinson, "Is Anyone Doing the Housework? Trends in the Division of Household Labor," *Social Forces* 7 (2000), 191–228.

46. M. Gonzalez-Morales, J. Peiro, and E. Greenglass, "Coping and Distress in Organizations: The Role of Gender in Work Stress," *International Journal of Stress Management* 13 (2006), 228–248.

47. M. Paludi and P. Neidermeyer, *Work, Life...* (see note 39), 26.

48. J. S. Dikkers, S. A. Geurts, U. Kinnunen, M. A. Kompier, and T. W. Taris, "Crossover between Work and Home in Dyadic Partner Relationships," *Scandinavian Journal of Psychology* 48 (6) (2007), 529–538.

49. S. Hewlett and C. Luce, "Extreme Jobs: The Dangerous Allure of the 70-Hour Workweek," *Harvard Business Review* (December 2006), 49–59.

50. R. Putnam, *Bowling Alone...* (see note 7), 42–56.

51. Ibid.

52. Margaret Ramirez, "Many in U.S. Leave Their Churches," *Chicago Tribune*, February 26, 2008, Section 1, 4.

53. Putnam, *Bowling Alone* (see note 7), 100.

54. Ibid.

55. Irvin D. Yalom, *The Theory and Practice of Group Psychotherapy* (New York: Basic Books, Inc., 1970).

56. R. F. Baumeister and M. R. Leary, "The Need to Belong: Desire for Interpersonal Attachments as a Fundamental Human Motivation," *Psychological Bulletin* 117 (3) (1995), 497–529.

57. Miller McPherson and Lynn Smith-Lovin, "Social Isolation in America: Changes in Core Discussion Networks Over Two Decades," *American Sociological Review* 71 (2006), 353–375.

58. Ami Rokach, Miguel C. Moya, Tricia Orzeck, and Francesca Exposito, "Loneliness in North America and Spain," *Social Behavior and Personality* 29 (5) (2001), 477–490.

59. Banks et al. "Disease and Disadvantage . . ." (see note 2).

60. Emile Durkheim, *Suicide: A Study in Sociology* (London, England: Tavistock Publications, 1982).

61. R. Putnam, *Bowling Alone* . . . (see note 7), 326.

62. Martin Seligman, cited in R. Putnam (see note 7), 264–265.

CHAPTER 6

1. Toni Morrison, *Love* (New York: Vintage Books, 2003), 63 (paperback).

2. Anita Shreve, *Fortune's Rocks* (New York: Little, Brown & Co., 1999), 204 (paperback).

3. *Waitress* (Motion picture), Directed by A. Shelly (Century City, CA: Fox Searchlight, 2007).

4. *Georgia Rule* (Motion picture), Directed by G. Marshall (Universal City, CA: Universal Pictures, 2007).

5. Raelene Wilding, "Romantic Love and 'Getting Married': Narratives of the Wedding In and Out of Cinema Texts," *Journal of Sociology* 39 (4) (2003), 373–389.

6. *Four Weddings and a Funeral* (Motion picture), Directed by M. Newell (London, England: Poly Gram Filmed Entertainment, 1994).

7. *The Wedding Singer* (Motion picture), Directed by F. Coraci (New York, NY: New Line Cinema, 1998).

8. *Father of the Bride* (Motion picture), Directed by C. Shyer (Burbank, CA: Touchstone Pictures, 1991).

9. Stephanie Coontz, *Marriage, a History: From Obedience to Intimacy or How Love Conquered Marriage* (New York: Viking Press, 2005), 15.

10. William Jankowiak (ed.), *Romantic Passion* (New York: Columbia University Press, 1995), 4.

11. Ira Reiss & Gary Lee, *Family Systems in America* (New York: Holt, Rinehart, and Winston, 1988), 91–93.

12. Ovid cited in Jankowiak, *Romantic Passion* (see note 10), 6–7.

13. Schopenhauer cited in Jankowiak, *Romantic Passion* (see note 10), 7.

14. Coontz, *Marriage, a History* (see note 9), 16–17.

15. Jankowiak, *Romantic Passion* (see note 10), 161.

16. Coontz, *Marriage, a History* (see note 9).

17. *Kate and Leopold* (Motion picture), Directed by J. Mangold (New York, NY: Miramax, 2001).

18. Roger Moore, "Romancing the Fantasy: Hollywood Love Sets Impossible Standards for Real People," *Chicago Tribune*, February 28, 2002, Section 5, 8A.

19. *Pretty Woman* (Motion picture), Directed by G. Marshall (Burbank, CA: Touchstone Pictures, 1990).

20. Mary McNamara, "Fame's Fleeting Embrace: Open Big, Succeed Quickly or It's Adios," *Chicago Tribune*, December 21, 2007, Section 5, 3.

21. Belinda Luscombe, "Who Killed the Love Story? On the Lost Art of Making a Great Romantic Movie," *Time Magazine*, August 20, 2007, 65–68.

22. *Titanic* (Motion picture), Directed by J. Cameron (Hollywood, CA: Paramount Pictures, 1997).

23. *Ghost* (Motion picture), Directed by J. Zucker (Hollywood, CA: Paramount Pictures, 1990).

24. *Pretty Woman* (see note 19).

25. *Gone With the Wind* (Motion picture), Directed by V. Fleming (Los Angeles, CA: Metro-Goldwyn-Mayer, 1939).

26. *Four Weddings and a Funeral* (see note 6).

27. *Notting Hill* (Motion picture), Directed by R. Mitchell (London, England: Poly-Gram Filmed Entertainment, 1999).

28. B. Luscombe, "Who Killed the Love . . . (see note 21).

29. *The Bachelor* (Television series), Produced by S. Thomas, G. Galligani, and C. Stream (Hollywood, CA: Next Entertainment, 2002).

30. *The Bachelorette* (Television series), Produced by R. Eisen (Hollywood, CA: Next Entertainment, 2003).

31. *A Wedding Story* (Television series), Produced by R. Branch, T. Baldrick, C. Cimino, S. Garra, and N. Laving (Hollywood, CA: Film Garden Entertainment, 1996).

32. *Real Weddings from the Knot* (Television series), Produced by K. Laybourne and K. Minton Catapano (Hollywood, CA: Oxygen Media, 2003).

33. *Joe Versus the Volcano* (Motion picture), Directed by J. P. Shanley (Burbank, CA: Warner Bros. Pictures, 1990).

34. *When Harry Meets Sally* (Motion picture), Directed by R. Reiner (Culver City, CA: Castle Rock Entertainment/Columbia, 1989).

35. *Sleepless in Seattle* (Motion picture), Directed by N. Ephron (Culver City, CA: TriStar Pictures, 1993).

36. *French Kiss* (Motion picture), Directed by L. Kasdan (London, England: Polygram Filmed Entertainment, 1995).

37. *When a Man Loves a Woman* (Motion picture), Directed by L. Mandoki (Burbank, CA: Touchstone Pictures, 1994).

38. *You've Got Mail* (Motion picture), Directed by N. Ephron (Burbank, CA: Warner Bros. Production, 1997).

39. Roger Moore, "Romancing the Fantasy . . . " (see note 18).

40. *Friends* (Television series), Produced by T. Stevens (Hollywood, CA: Warner Bros. Television, 1994).

41. *The Break Up* (Motion picture), Directed by P. Reed (Universal City, CA: Universal Pictures, 2006).

42. *Music and Lyrics* (Motion picture), Directed by M. Lawrence (Culver City, CA: Castle Rock Entertainment, 2007).

43. Helen Fisher, *The Anatomy of Love: A Natural History of Mating, Marriage, and Why We Stray* (New York: Fawcett Columbine, 1992), 48.

44. S. J. Katz and A. E. Liu. *False Love and Other Romantic Illusions* (New York: Pocket Books, 1988), 329.

45. *All in the Family* (Television series), Produced by M. Josefsberg (Hollywood, CA: CBS Television, 1971).

46. Regina Barreca, *Perfect Husbands: And Other Fairy Tales* (New York: Anchor Books, 1993), 194.

47. *Rebel Without a Cause* (Motion picture), Directed by N. Ray (Burbank, CA: Warner Bros. Productions, 1995).

48. *On the Waterfront* (Motion picture), Directed by E. Kazan (Culver City, CA: Columbia Pictures Corporation, 1954).

49. *Streetcar Named Desire* (Motion picture), Directed by E. Kazan (Burbank, CA: Warner Bros. Productions, 1951).

50. *Gone With the Wind* (see note 25).

51. Regina Barreca, *Perfect Husbands*...(see note 46), 252.

52. Ibid., 192–193.

53. Gustave Flaubert, *Madame Bovary—A Story of Provincial Life* (New York: Penguin, 1950).

54. Mary-Lou Galician, *Sex, Love, and Romance in the Mass Media: Analysis and Criticism of Unrealistic Portrayals and Their Influence* (Mahwah, NJ: Lawrence Erlbaum Associates, 2004).

55. C. Segrin and R. L. Nabi, "Does Television Viewing Cultivate Unrealistic Expectations About Marriage?" *Journal of Communication* 52 (2) (June 2002), 247–263.

56. C. M. Bachen and E. Illouz, "Imagining Romance: Young People's Cultural Models of Romance and Love," *Critical Studies in Mass Communication* 13 (4) (1996), 279–308.

57. J. Shapiro and L. Kroeger. "Is Life Just a Romantic Novel: The Relationship Between Attitudes About Intimate Relationships and the Popular Media," *American Journal of Family Therapy* 19 (3) (1991), 226–236.

58. L. M. Ward and R. Rivadeneyra, "Contributions of Entertainment Television to Adolescents' Sexual Attitudes and Expectations: The Role of Viewing Amount Versus Viewer Involvement," *The Journal of Sex Research* 36 (3) (1999), 237–249.

59. Mary-Lou Galician, *Sex, Love, and Romance*...(see note 54).

60. *Knocked Up* (Motion picture), Directed by J. Apatow (Universal City, CA: Universal Pictures, 2007).

61. Mary-Lou Galician, *Sex, Love, and Romance*...(see note 54).

62. M. Mayer and M. Mayer, *Beauty and the Beast* (San Francisco, CA: Chronicle Books, 2002).

63. Sharon S. Brehm, Rowland S. Miller, Daniel Perlman, and Susan M. Campbell, *Intimate Relationships* (3rd Edition) (Boston, MA: McGraw Hill, 2002).

64. *Pretty Woman* (see note 19).

65. *An Officer and a Gentleman* (Motion picture), Directed by T. Hackford (Hollywood, CA: Lorimar Film Entertainment, 1982).

66. *A Wedding Story* (see note 31).

67. E. Engstrom, "The 'Reality' of Reality Television Wedding Programs," in Mary-Lou Galician and Debra L. Merskin (eds.) *Critical Thinking About Sex, Love, and Mass Media: Media Literacy Applications* (Mahwah, NJ: Lawrence Erlbaum Associates, 2007), 335–354.

68. D. Ackerman, *A Natural History of Love* (New York: Vintage Books, 1995), 95–99.

69. Robert J. Sternberg, *The Triangle of Love* (New York: Basic Books, 1988).

70. Dorothy Tennov, *Love and Limerence: The Experience of Being in Love* (New York: Stein & Day, 1979).

71. *The Bachelorette* (see note 30).

72. L. M. Glebatis, "Real" Love Myths and Magnified Media Effects," in Mary-Lou Galician and Debra L. Merskin (eds.), *Critical Thinking About Sex, Love, and Romance in the Mass Media: Media Literacy Applications* (Mahwah, NJ: Lawrence Erlbaum Associates, 2007), 319–334.

73. *Serendipity* (Motion picture), Directed by P. Chelsom (New York, NY: Simon Fields Productions, 2001).

74. *Kate and Leopold* (see note 17).

75. Mary-Lou Galician, *Sex, Love, and Romance* . . . (see note 54).

76. S. Johnson, "Promoting Easy Sex Without Genuine Intimacy: Maxim and Cosmopolitan Cover Lines and Cover Images," in Mary-Lou Galician and Debra Merskin (eds.) *Critical Thinking About Sex, Love, and Romance in the Mass Media: Media Literacy Applications* (Mahwah, NJ: Lawrence Erlbaum Associates, 2007), 55–74.

77. Mary-Lou Galician, *Sex, Love, and Romance* . . . (see note 54), 145.

78. D. T. Lowry, G. Love, and M. Kirby, "Sex on the Soap Operas: Patterns of Intimacy," *Journal of Communication* 31 (3) (1981), 90–96.

79. *Two and a Half Men* (Television series), Produced by M. Collier (Hollywood, CA: Warner Bros. Television, 2003).

80. *Desperate Housewives* (Television series), Produced by C. Skouras (Hollywood, CA: Touchstone Television, 2004).

CHAPTER 7

1. Khaled Hosseini, *A Thousand Splendid Suns.* (New York: Riverhead Books, 2007), 47–49.

2. Victor C. DeMunck, "Lust, Love, and Arranged Marriages in Sri Lanka," in V. C. DeMunck (ed.) *Romantic Love and Sexual Behavior: Perspectives from the Social Sciences* (Westport, CT: Praeger, 1998), 285–300.

3. *60 Minutes* (Television series), Produced by D. Hewitt (New York: CBS News Productions, 1968).

4. *20/20* (Television series), Produced by T. Smith (New York: American Broadcasting Company, 1978).

5. *Oprah Winfrey Show* (Television series), Produced by D. Hewitt (Chicago, IL: HARPO Productions, 1986).

6. Sue Lloyd Roberts, "Fighting Arranged Marriage Abuse," *BBC News*, July 12, 1999.

7. DeMunck "Lust, Love, and Arranged Marriages in Sri Lanka" (see note 2), 287.

8. S. Sprecher and R. Chandak, "Attitudes About Arranged Marriages and Dating among Men and Women from India," *Free Inquiry in Creative Sociology* 20 (1992), 1–11.

9. B. B. Ingoldsby, "Mate Selection and Marriage," in B. B. Ingoldsby and S. Smith (eds.) *Families in Multicultural Perspective* (New York: Guilford Press (1995), 143–160.

10. C. H. Hui and H. C. Triandis, "Individualism-Collectivism: A Study of Cross-Cultural Researchers," *Journal of Cross-Cultural Psychology* 17 (1986), 222–248.

11. Nilufer P. Medora, "Mate Selection in Contemporary India: Love Marriages versus Arranged Marriages," in R. R. Hamon and B. B. Ingoldsby (eds.) *Mate Selections Across Cultures* (Chicago, IL: The University of Chicago Press, 1995).

12. A. Schlegel, "The Cultural Management of Adolescent Sexuality," in P. R. Abramson and S. D. Pickerton (eds.) *Sexual Nature, Sexual Culture* (Chicago, IL: The University of Chicago Press, 1995).

13. Robin Goodwin, *Personal Relationships Across Cultures* (New York: Routledge, 1999).

14. Ibid., 50.

15. "{From Abroad}: What the U. S. Missed In Iraq," in *Chicago Tribune, Parade*, April 29, 2007, 18.

16. Rao Prakasa, *Marriage, the Family and Women in India* (Printox: South Asia Books, 1982).

17. Ibid., p. 15.

18. G. Gupta, "Love, Arranged Marriage, and the Indian Social Structure," *Journal of Comparative Family Studies* 7 (1976), 75–85.

19. Ibid.

20. Jhumpa Lahiri, *Interpreter of Maladies* (New York: Houghton Mifflin, 1999), 165.

21. Nilufer P. Medora, Mate Selection in Contemporary India (see note 11).

22. Ibid., 218.

23. J. Lessinger, "Asian Indian Marriages: Arranged, Semi-Arranged, or Based on Love?" in N. V. Benokraitis (ed.) *Contemporary Ethnic Families in the United States: Characteristics, Variations, and Dynamics* (Upper Saddle River, NJ: Prentice Hall, 2002), 103.

24. Nilufer P. Medora, Mate Selection in Contemporary India (see note 11), 220.

25. D. Nanda, "Arranging a Marriage in India," in J. K. Norton (ed.), *India and South Asia*. (New York: Guilford, 1995), 113.

26. M. D. Bramlett and W. D. Mosher, "Cohabitation, Marriage, Divorce, and Remarriage in the United States," *Vital and Health Statistics*, Series 23, No. 22 (Washington, DC: U. S. Government Printing Office, 2002).

27. L. L. Bumpass, T. C. Martin, and J. A. Sweet, "The Impact of Family Background and Early Marital Factors in Marital Disruption," *Journal of Family Issues* 12 (1991), 22–42.

28. T. B. Heaton, "Factors Contributing to Increasing Stability in the United States," *Journal of Family Issues* 23 (2002), 392–409.

29. U. Gupta and P. Singh, "Exploratory Study of Love and Liking and Type of Marriages," *Indian Journal of Applied Psychology* 19 (1982), 92–97.

30. P. Yelsma and K. Althappilly, "Marital Satisfaction and Communication Practices: Comparisons among India and American Couples," *Journal of Comparative Family Studies* 19 (1988), 37–54.

31. P. Kumar and J. Dhyani, "Marital Adjustment: A Study of Some Related Factors." *Indian Journal of Clinical Psychology* 23 (2) (1996), 112–116.

32. "44 Percent Women Abused," *The Times of India*, December 9, 2006.

33. Leela Visaria, "Violence against Women in India: Evidence from Rural Gujarat," *Domestic Violence in India: A Summary Report*, prepared by the International Center for Research on Women (Washington, DC: ICRW, 2004).

34. Carolyn Mordecai, *Weddings, Dating and Love Customs of Cultures Worldwide* (Dexter, MI: Thompson-Shore, Inc., 1999).

35. James Estrin, "It's Muslim Boy Meets Girl, But Don't Call It Dating," *New York Times*, September 19, 2006.

36. Victor C. DeMunck, "Lust, Love, and Arranged Marriages in Sri Lanka," (see note 2), 297–298.

37. Nuran Hortacsu, "Marriage in Turkey," R. R. Hamon and B. B. Ingoldsby (eds.) *Mate Selection Across Cultures* (Thousand Oaks, CA: Sage Publications, 2003), 155–171.

38. Jenny B. White, "Two Weddings" in Donna Lee Bowen and Evelyn A. Early (eds.) *Everyday Life in the Muslim Middle East* (Bloomington, IN: Indiana University Press, 2002), 63–77.

39. Nuran Hortacsu, "Marriage in Turkey" (see note 37).

40. Bahira Sherif-Trask, "Love, Courtship, and Marriage from a Cross-Cultural Perspective: The Upper Middle Class Egyptian Example" in *Mate Selection Across Cultures* (Thousand Oaks, CA: Sage Publications, 2003), 121–136.

41. Nuran Hortacsu, "Marriage in Turkey" (see note 37).

42. Stephen M. Wilson, Lucy W. Ngige, and Linda J. Trollinger, "Connecting Generations: Kamba and Maasai Paths to Marriage in Kenya" in *Mate Selection Across Cultures*, 95–118.

43. Ibid.

44. Centers for Disease Control and Prevention (2008). *National Center for Health Statistics 2006*. Retrieved April 13, 2008 from Department of Health and Human Services Centers for Disease Control and Prevention. http://www.cdc.gov/nchs/.

45. Gulnar Nugman, "World Divorce Rates," Nugman Gulnar of the Heritage Foundation, 2002 http://www.divorcereform.org/gul.html.

46. U. Gupta and P. Singh, "Exploratory Study of Love and Liking and Type of Marriages" (see note 29); P.Yelsma and K. Althappilly, Marital Satisfaction and Communication Practices (see note 30).

47. Robert O. Blood, *Love Match and Arranged Marriage* (New York: Free Press, 1967).

48. X. Xu and M. K. Whyte, "Love Matches and Arranged Marriages: A Chinese Replication." *Journal of Marriage and the Family* 52 (1990), 709–722.

49. L. Heise, M. Ellsberg, and M. Gottemoeller, "Ending Violence against Women," *Population Reports*, Series L, No. 11, December 1999.

50. "Domestic Violence against Women and Girls," *Innocenti Digest*, UNICEF, No. 6, June 2000.

51. Rhonda Roumani, "Study Reveals Domestic Abuse is Widespread in Syria," *Christian Science Monitor*, April 25, 2006.

52. Elizabeth Marquardt, *Between Two Worlds: The Inner Lives of Children of Divorce* (New York: Three Rivers Press, Random House, 2005).

CHAPTER 8

1. Kelley Kazek, "'1' is No Longer the Loneliest Number as Single Households Now in Majority," *Athens News Courier*, September 24, 2006.

2. U. Bronfenbrenner, "Ecology of the Family as a Context for Human Development: Research Perspectives," *Developmental Psychology* 22 (1986), 723–742.

3. Ann Swidler, *Talk of Love: How Culture Matters* (Chicago, IL: The University of Chicago Press, 2001).

4. Randal W. Summers and Alan M. Hoffman, (eds.) *Domestic Violence: A Global View*. (Westport, CT: Greenwood Press, 2002), p. xiv.

5. Lydia Voight and William E. Thornton, "Russia" in Randal W. Summers and Allan M. Hoffman (eds.) *Domestic Violence: A Global View* (Westport, CT: Greenwood Press, 2002), 99.

6. United Nations, (2002), Divorces and Crude Divorce Rates by Urban/Rural Residence: 1998–2002. Retrieved March 4, 2008, from http://unstats.un.org/unsd/demographic/products/dyb/DYB2002/Table25.pdf.

7. D. S. Ballard-Reisch, M. Zaguidoulline, and D. J. Weigel, "Maintaining Marriages in Russia: Managing Social Influences and Communication Dynamics" in D. J. Canary, and M. Dainton, *Maintaining Relationships Through Communication: Relational, Contextual, and Cultural Variations* (Mahwah, NJ: Lawrence Erlbaum Associates Publishers, 2003), 255–275.

8. D. Vannoy, N. Rimashevskaya, L. Cubbins, M. Malysheva, E. Meshterkina, and M. Pisklakova, *Marriages in Russia: Couples during the Economic Transition* (Westport, CT: Praeger, 1999).

9. L. Voight and W. Thornton, W., "Russia" (see note 5), 104.

10. L. A. Cubbins and D. Vannoy, "Division of Household Labor as a Source of Contention for Married and Cohabiting Couples in Metropolitan Moscow," *Journal of Family Issues* 25 (20) (2004), 182–215.

11. Sara Yogev, "Relationship between Stress and Marital Satisfaction among Dual Career Couples," *Women and Therapy* 5 (Summer/Fall 1986), 313–329.

12. D. Vannoy, et al. *Marriages in Russia . . .* (see note 8).

13. D. Vannoy, et al. *Marriages in Russia . . .* (see note 8), 182.

14. F. F. Furstenberg and A. J. Cherlin, *Divided Families: What Happens to Children When Parents Part* (Cambridge, MA: Harvard University Press, 1991).

15. D. H. Olson and M. S. Matskovsky, "Soviet and American Families: A Comparative Overview" in J. W. Maddock, M. J. Hogan, A. I. Antonov, and M. S. Matskovsky (eds.) *Families Before and After Perestroika* (New York: The Guilford Press, 1994), 9–35.

16. L. Voight and W. Thornton, "Russia" (see note 5).

17. Elliot Currie (ed.) "A Recipe for a Violent Society" in *Confronting Crime: New Directions* (New York: Pantheon Books, 1996).

18. D. Vannoy et al. *Marriages in Russia: Couples . . .* (see note 8), 179–181.

19. A. Jasilioniene, "Premarital Conception and Divorce Risk in Russia in Light of the GGS Data." *MPIDR Working Papers WP-2007-025* (Rostock, Germany: Max Planck Institute for Demographic Research, 2007).

20. A. Avdeev, and A. Monnier, "Marriage in Russia: A Complex Phenomenon Poorly Understood," *Population: An English Selection* 12 (2000), 7–49.

21. D. Vannoy et al. *Marriages in Russia: Couples . . .* (see note 8), 180.

22. A. Avdeev and A. Monnier, "Marriage in Russia: A Complex Phenomenon Poorly Understood" (see note 20).

23. L. Y. Gozman and Y. A. Aleshin, "Contacts and Development of Spousal Relations" in G. M. Andreeva and J. Janousek (eds.) *Communication and Optimization in Joint Activities* (Moscow, Soviet Union: Moscow State University, 1987), 30–42.

24. A. Avdeev and A. Monnier, "Marriage in Russia: A Complex Phenomenon Poorly Understood" (see note 20), 19.

25. D. Vannoy et al. Marriages *in Russia: Couples . . .* (see note 8), 41.

26. NationMaster (2007), *Religion Statistics: Religions (most recent) by Country.* (Electronic version). Retrieved April 6, 2008, from http://www.nationmaster.com/graph/rel_religion-religions.

27. Yan R. Xia and Zhi G Zhou, "The Transition of Courtship, Mate Selection, and Marriage in China" in Raeann R. Hamon and Bron B. Ingoldsby (eds.) *Mate Selection Across Cultures* (Thousand Oaks, CA: Sage Publications, 2003), 231–246.

28. A. Xu, "Love and Marriage of the Chinese at the Time of Transition" in A. B. Fan (ed.) *Zhuanxingqi Zhongguoren de Aiqing he Hunyin* (Beijing, China: Chinese Women's Press, 1998).

29. Y. Xia and Z. Zhou, "The Transition of Courtship, Mate Selection, and Marriage in China" (see note 27), 237.

30. United Nations, 2002 (see note 6).

31. D. Liu, D. *Sexual Behavior in Modern China: Report of the Nationwide "Sex Civilization" Survey in China*, Third Edition (Shanghai, China: Sanlian Press, 1998).

32. Y. Xia, and Z. Zhou, "The Transition of Courtship, Mate Selection, and Marriage in China" (see note 26).

33. Robert L. Moore, "Love and Limerence with Chinese Characteristics: Student Romance in the PRC" in Victor C. DeMunck (ed.) *Romantic Love and Sexual Behavior: Perspectives from the Social Sciences* (Westport, CN: Praeger, 1998), 257–260.

34. Ibid., 258–260.

35. Robin Goodwin, *Personal Relationships Across Cultures* (New York: Routledge, 1999).

36. R. Goodwin and C. Findlay, "We Were Just Fated Together: Chinese Love and the Concept of *Yuan* in Hong Kong and England," *Personal Relationships* 4 (1997), 85–92.

37. X. Xu and M. K. Whyte, "Love Matches and Arranged Marriages: A Chinese Replication," *Journal of Marriage and the Family*, 52 (1990), 709–722.

38. Zhu Zhe, "Domestic Violence in Spotlight," *Daily China*, August 2, 2007.

39. NationMaster (2007), *Religion Statistics* (see note 26).

40. Yan Xia and Zhi Zhou, "The Transition of Courtship, Mate Selection, and Marriage in China" (see note 27), 240.

41. Marcus Rebick and Ayumi Takenaka (eds.) *The Changing Japanese Family* (New York: Routledge, 2006), 5–9.

42. Ibid., 8.

43. Ibid., 8.

44. Yoshinori Kamo, "Determinants of Marital Satisfaction: A Comparison of the United States and Japan," *Journal of Social and Personal Relationships* 10 (1993), 551–568.

45. M. Rebick and A. Takenaka, *The Changing Japanese Family* (see note 41), 9

46. E. Ochiai, *The Japanese Family System in Transition: A Sociological Analysis of Family Change in Postwar Japan* (Tokyo: LTCB International Library Foundation, 1997).

47. Colleen I. Murray and Naoko Kimura, "Multiplicity of Paths to Couple Formation in Japan," in R. R. Hamon and B. B. Ingoldsby (eds.) *Mate Selection Across Cultures* (Thousand Oaks, CA: Sage Publications, 2003), 247–268.

48. Ibid., 253.

49. M. Rebick and A. Takenaka, *The Changing Japanese Family* (see note 41), 3.

50. United Nations, 2002 (see note 6).

51. "Domestic Violence Against Women and Girls," *Innocenti Digest*, Unicef, No. 6, June 2000.

52. Roger Goodman, "Policing the Japanese Family: Child Abuse, Domestic Violence, and the Changing Role of the State," in M. Rebick and A. Takenaka (eds.) The Changing Japanese Family (2006), 147–160 (see note 41).

53. "More Women Seeking Help for Domestic Violence in Japan, Survey Finds," *International Herald Tribune*, June 13, 2007.

54. Ken Y-N, "Domestic Violence in Japan: Part 1 of 3," April 3, 2006. http://whatjapanthinks.com.

55. R. Goodman, "Policing the Japanese Family ... (see note 52), 153.

56. H. M. Gaspar-Pereira, *Patterns of Family Violence in Japan*, Wellesley Centers for Women, Working Paper Series, Working Paper No. 411 (Wellesley, MA: Wellesley Centers for Women, 2003).

57. Justin McCurry, "Japan's Virgin Wives Turn to Sex Volunteers," *The Guardian*, Tokyo, April 4, 2005.

58. Y. Kamo, Determinants of Marital Satisfaction: (see note 44).

59. J. Crouch, M. Scoville, R. Beaulieu, A. Sharpe, K. Thrine, S. Dukat, and S. Williams, *Divorce Rates and Laws: USA and Europe* (Westport, CN: Praeger, 2007).

60. M. Rebick and A. Takenaka, *The Changing Japanese Family* (see note 41), 3.

61. Francesca Bettio, "Strong in Tradition and Yet Innovative: The Puzzles of the Italian Family," in M. Rebick and A. Takenaka (eds.) *The Changing*... (see note 41), 54–71.

62. Ibid., 62–63.

63. Ibid., 61–62.

64. Ibid., 64.

65. J. Roberto Reyes, "Couple Formation Practices in Spain," in *Mate Selection Across Cultures* (2003), 175–190.

66. I. Alberdi, L. Flaquer, and J. Iglesias de Ussel, *Couples and Marriages: Contemporary Attitudes and Experiences* (Madrid, Spain: Centro de Asuntos Sociales, Centro de Publicaciones, 1994).

67. Encarta (2008), *Marriage and Divorce Rates* (Electronic version). Retrieved April 5, 2008, from http://encarta.msn.com/media_701500518_761574825_-1_1/marriage_and_divorce-rates.html.

68. Centro de Investigaciones Sociologicas. "Today's Youth," *Datos de Opinion*, Boletin 19, Study Nos. 2257, 2262, and 2265, January–March 1999 (online). Retrieved January 9, 2002, from www.cis.es/boletin/19/familia.html.

69. J. R. Reyes, "Couple Formation Practices in Spain" (see note 65), 183–185.

70. Ibid., 183.

71. NationMaster (2007) *Religion Statistics* (see note 26).

72. Ibid., 185.

73. United Nations (2002) (see note 6).

74. Manfred H. M. van Dulmen, "The Development of Intimate Relationships in the Netherlands," in *Mate Selection Across Cultures* (2003), 191–206.

75. C. S. van Praag and M. Niphuis-Nell, *The Family Report* (Rijswijk, the Netherlands: Sociaal en Cultureel Planbureau, 1997).

76. M. van Dulmen, *Mate Selection*... (see note 74), 195–196.

77. *Social and Cultural Report 2000: The Netherlands in Europe*. The Hague, the Netherlands: Sociaal en Cultureel Planbureau (2000).

78. G. Kraaykamp, "Trends and Countertrends in Sexual Permissiveness: Three Decades of Attitude Change in the Netherlands 1965–1995," *Journal of Marriage and Family* 64 (2002), 225–239.

79. M. van Dulmen, *Mate Selection Across Cultures* (see note 74), 198.

80. C. van Praag and M. Niphuis-Nell, *The Family Report* (see note 75).

81. M. van Dulmen, *Mate Selection . . .* (see note 74).

82. Steven Stack and J. Ross Eshleman, "Marital Status and Happiness: A 17 Nation Study," *Journal of Marriage and the Family* 60 (1998), 527–536.

83. "The European Men Profeminist Network," *Domestic Violence in the Netherlands: Government and Private Sector Interventions* (2008, Electronic version). Retrieved April 5, 2008, from http://www.europrofem.org/contri/2_09_nl/nl-vio/01nl_vio.html.

CHAPTER 9

1. B. R. Karney and T. N. Bradbury, "Neuroticism, Marital Interaction and the Trajectory of Marital Satisfaction," *Journal of Personality and Social Psychology* 72 (1997), 1075–1092.

2. Sam Roberts, "The Shelf Life of Bliss," *New York Times*, July 1, 2007, 1 & 9.

3. T. L. Huston and A. F. Chorost, "Behavioral Buffers on the Effect of Negativity on Marital Satisfaction: A Longitudinal Study," *Personal Relationships* 1 (1994), 223–239.

4. H. Fisher, "The Nature and Evolution of Romantic Love" in W. Jankowiak (ed.) *Romantic Passion: A Universal Experience* (New York: Columbia University Press, 1995), 23–41.

5. Sharon S. Brehm, Rowland S. Miller, Daniel Perlman, and Susan M. Campbell, *Intimate Relationships* (3rd ed.) (Boston, MA: McGraw Hill, 2002), 243.

6. Robert J. Sternberg, *The Triangle of Love: Intimacy, Passion, Commitment* (New York: Basic Books, 1988).

7. J. Lauer and R. Lauer, "Marriages Made to Last," *Psychology Today* (June 1985), 22–26.

8. U. Gupta and P. Singh, "Exploratory Study of Love and Liking and Type of Marriages, *Indian Journal of Applied Psychology* 19 (1982), 92–97.

9. X. Xiaohe and M. K. Whyte, "Love Matches and Arranged Marriages: A Chinese Replication," *Journal of Marriage and the Family* 52 (1990), 709–722.

10. S. Sprecher and P. C. Regan, "Passionate and Companionate Love in Courting and Young Married Couples," *Sociological Inquiry* 68 (1998), 163–185.

11. Madeleine L'Engle cited by Terry Nelson-Johnson, "Resurrection in July . . . What a Concept," *Crossroads, Old St. Patrick's Catholic Church Bulletin*, July 15, 2007, 3 (Chicago, IL).

12. B. S. Meeks, S. S. Hendrick, and C. Hendrick, "Communication, Love, and Relationship Satisfaction," *Journal of Social and Personal Relationships* 15 (1998), 755–773.

13. Denise S. Bartell, "Influence of Parental Divorce on Romantic Relationships in Young Adulthood: A Cognitive-Developmental Perspective," in M. A. Fine and J. H. Harvey (eds.) *Handbook of Divorce and Relationship Dissolution* (Mahwah, NJ: Lawrence Erlbaum Associates, 2006), 339–360.

14. K. M. Macie, "The Influence of Co-Parenting and Parental Marital Status on the Long-Term Adjustment of Young Adults: ProQuest Information and Learning,"

Dissertation Abstracts International: Section B: The Sciences and Engineering 63 (10-B) (2003) (Electronic Print).

15. A. Christensen, K. Eldridge, A. B. Catta-Preta, V. R. Lim, and R. Santagata, "Cross-Cultural Consistency of the Demand/Withdraw Interaction Pattern in Couples," *Journal of Marriage and Family* 68 (4) (2006), 1029–1044.

16. Sharon S. Brehm et al., *Intimate Relationships*, 134–135 (see note 5).

17. J. M. Gottman, *Why Marriages Succeed or Fail* (New York: Simon & Schuster, 1994).

18. P. Noller, "Gender and Marital Adjustment Level Differences in Decoding Messages from Spouses and Strangers," *Journal of Personality and Social Psychology* 41(1981), 272–278.

19. Sharon S. Brehm et al., *Intimate Relationships*, 341 (see note 5).

20. N. B. Epstein, D. H. Baucom, and A. Daiuto, "Cognitive-Behavioral Couples Therapy," in W. K. Halford, H. J. Markman (eds.) *Clinical Handbook of Marriage and Couples Interventions* (Hoboken, NJ: John Wiley & Sons, Inc., 1997), 415–449.

21. J. M. Gottman, *Why Marriages Succeed or Fail* (see note 17).

22. W. K. Halford, K. Hahlweg, and M. Dunne "The Cross-Cultural Consistency of Marital Communication Associated with Marital Distress," *Journal of Marriage and the Family* 52 (2) (1990), 487–500.

23. J. M. Gottman and R. W. Levenson, "Marital Processes Predictive of Later Dissolution: Behavior, Physiology and Health," *Journal of Personality and Social Psychology* 63 (1992), 221–233.

24. A. Christensen and C. L. Heavey, "Intervention for Couples," *Annual Review of Psychology* 50 (1999), 165–190.

25. P. R. Amato and D. D. DeBoer, "The Transmission of Marital Instability Across Generations: Relationship Skills or Commitment to Marriage," *Journal of Marriage and the Family* 63 (4) (2001), 1038–1051.

26. C. Duran-Aydintug, "Adult Children of Divorce Revisited: When they Speak Up," *Journal of Divorce and Remarriage* 27 (1–2) (1997), 71–83.

27. Denise S. Bartell, and C. A. Surra, "Family Background Characteristics and Stability of Commitment to Premarital Romantic Relationships," paper presented at the *Meeting of the National Council on Family Relations* (Milwaukee, WI, November 1998).

28. Denise S. Bartell, *Handbook of Divorce . . .* (see note 13).

29. M. Snyder, E. D. Tanke, and E. Berscheid, "Social Perception and Interpersonal Behavior: On the Self-Fulfilling Nature of Social Stereotypes," *Journal of Personality and Social Psychology* 35 (1977), 656–666; R. C. Curtis and K. Miller, "Believing Another Likes or Dislikes You: Behaviors Making the Beliefs Come True," *Journal of Personality and Social Psychology* 51 (1986), 284–290.

30. Mary-Lou Galician, *Sex, Love and Romance in the Mass Media: Analysis and Criticism of Unrealistic Portrayals and Their Influence* (Mahway, NJ: Lawrence Erlbaum Associates, Inc., 2004).

31. N. B. Epstein et al., *Clinical Handbook . . .* (see note 20.)

32. N. B. Epstein, F. Chen, and I. Beyder-Kamjou, "Relationship Standards and Marital Satisfaction in Chinese and American Couples," *Journal of Marital and Family Therapy* 31/1 (2005), 59–74.

33. G. J. Fletcher, J. A. Simpson, G, Thomas, and L. Giles, "Ideals in Intimate Relationships," *Journal of Personality and Social Psychology* 76 (1) (1990), 72–89.

34. R. J. Eidelson and N. Epstein, "Cognition and Relationship Maladjustment: Development of a Measure of Dysfunctional Relationship Beliefs," *Journal of Consulting and Clinical Psychology* 50 (1982), 715–720.

35. Denise S. Bartell, *Handbook of Divorce* . . . (see note 13).

36. P. R. Amato and A. Booth, "The Legacy of Parents' Marital Discord: Consequences for Children's Marital Quality," *Journal of Personality and Social Psychology* 81 (4) (2001), 627–638.

37. L. C. Kurdek and C. Kennedy, "Differences Between Couples Who End Their Marriage by Fault or No-Fault Legal Procedures," *Journal of Family Psychology* 15 (2001), 241–253.

38. M. B. Conway, T. M. Christensen, and B. Herlihy, "Adult Children of Divorce and Intimate Relationships: Implications for Counseling," *The Family Journal* 11 (4) (2003), 364–373.

39. M. E. Boyer-Pennington, J. Pennington, and C. Spink, "Students' Expectations and Optimism Towards Marriage as a Function of Parental Divorce," *Journal of Divorce and Remarriage* 34 (3/4) (2001), 71–87.

40. S. G. Johnston and A. M. Thomas, "Divorce versus Intact Parental Marriage and Perceived Risk and Dyadic Trust in Present Heterosexual Relationships," *Psychological Reports* 78 (1996), 387–390.

41. Judith S. Wallerstein, Julia M. Lewis, and Sandra Blakeslee, *"The Unexpected Legacy of Divorce: A 25-Year Landmark Study"* (New York: Hyperion, 2000), p. xxix.

42. Denise S. Bartell. *Handbook of Divorce* . . . , 345 (see note 13).

43. K. M. Franklin, R. Janoff-Bulman, and J. E. Roberts, "Long-Term Impact of Parental Divorce on Optimism and Trust: Changes in General Assumptions or Narrow Beliefs?" *Journal of Personality and Social Psychology* 59 (1990), 743–755.

44. Sharon S Brehm et al., *Intimate Relationships*, 184 (see note 5).

45. P. R. Amato and DeBoer, 2001 (see note 25).

46. S. Shulman, M. Scharf, D. Lumer, and O. Maurer, "Parental Divorce and Young Adult Children's Romantic Relationships: Resolution of the Divorce Experience," *American Journal of Orthopsychiatry* 71 (2001), 473–478.

47. Geraldine K. Piorkowski, *Too Close for Comfort: Exploring the Risks of Intimacy* (New York: Plenum Press, 1994), 267; Sharon S Brehm et al., *Intimate Relationships* (see note 5).

48. A. Caspi and E. S. Herbener, "Continuity and Change: Assortative Marriage and the Consistency of Personality in Adulthood," *Journal of Personality and Social Psychology* 58 (1990), 250–258.

49. Sharon S Brehm et al., *Intimate Relationships*, 85 (see note 5).

50. K. D. Locke and L. M. Horowitz, "Satisfaction in Interpersonal Interactions as a Function of Similarity in Level of Dysphoria," *Journal of Personality and Social Psychology* 58 (1990), 823–831; P. A. Frazier, A. L. Byer, A. R. Fischer, D. M. Wright, and K. A. DeBord, "Adult Attachment Style and Partner Choice: Correlational and Experimental Findings," *Personal Relationships* 3 (1996), 117–136.

51. M. E. Zammichielli, F. D. Gilroy, and M. F. Sherman, "Relation Between Sex-Role Orientation and Marital Satisfaction," *Personality and Social Psychology Bulletin* 14 (1988), 747–754.

52. Kathryn Masterson, "A Personal Look at '*The Namesake*': Amid Cultural Differences, Does Love Conquer All?" *Chicago Tribune*, April 8, 2007, 1 (Perspective section).

53. K. M. Kouri and M. Lasswell, "Black-White Marriages: Social Change and Intergenerational Mobility," *Marriage and Family Review* 19 (1993), 241–255; R. Lewis, Jr., G. Yancey, and S. S. Bletzer, "Racial and Nonracial Factors that Influence Spouse Choice in Black/White Marriages," *Journal of Black Studies* 28 (1997), 60–78.

54. K. Shibazaki and K. A. Brennan, "When Birds of Different Feathers Flock Together: A Preliminary Comparison of Intra-Ethnic and Inter-Ethnic Dating Relationships," *Journal of Social and Personal Relationships* 15 (1998), 248–256.

55. Sharon S Brehm et al., *Intimate Relationships*, 87 (see note 5).

56. P. R. Amato, "Explaining the Intergenerational Transmission of Divorce," *Journal of Marriage and the Family* 58 (1996), 628–640.

57. N. H. Wolfinger, "Family Structure Homogamy: The Effects of Parental Divorce on Partner Selection and Marital Stability," *Social Science Research* 32 (1) (2003), 80–97.

58. T. R. Walker and M. F. Ehrenberg, "An Exploratory Study of Young Persons' Attachment Styles and Perceived Reasons for Parental Divorce," *Journal of Adolescent Research* 13 (3) (1998), 320–342; S. Sprecher, R. Cate, and L. Levin, "Parental Divorce and Young Adults' Beliefs About Love," *Journal of Divorce and Remarriage* 28 (3–4) (1998), 107–120.

59. P. G. Boss and T. A. Gurko, "The Relationships of Men and Women in Marriage," in J. Maddock, M. Hogan, A. Antonov, and M. Matskovsky (eds.) *Families Before and After Perestroika: Russian and U. S. Perspectives. Perspectives on Marriage and the Family* (New York: Guilford, 1994), 36–75.

60. P. Kumar and J. Dhyani, "Marital Adjustment: A Study of Some Related Factors," *Indian Journal of Clinical Psychology* 23 (2) (1996), 112–116.

61. J. W. Howard and R. M. Dawes, "Linear Prediction of Marital Happiness," *Personality and Social Psychology Bulletin* 2 (1976), 478–480.

62. Denise S. Bartell, *Handbook of Divorce* . . . (see note 13).

63. L. Gabardi and L. A. Rosen, "Intimate Relationships: College Students from Divorced and Intact Families," *Journal of Divorce and Remarriage* 18 (1992), 25–56.

64. M. L. Frisco and K. Williams, "Perceived Housework Equity, Marital Happiness, and Divorce in Dual-Earner Households," *Journal of Family Issues* 24 (2003), 51–73.

65. J. M. Gottman, *Why Marriages Succeed or Fail* (see note 17).

66. S. L. Murray, J. G. Holmes, and D. W. Griffin, "The Self-Fulfilling Nature of Positive Illusions in Romantic Relationships: Love is Not Blind, but Prescient," *Journal of Personality and Social Psychology* 71 (1996), 1155–1180.

67. C. Burgoyne and R. Hames, "Views of Marriage and Divorce: An In-Depth Study of Young Adults from Intact and Divorced Families," *Journal of Divorce and Remarriage* 37 (2002), 75–100.

68. Sharon S Brehm et al., *Intimate Relationships*, 102 (see note 5).

69. P. R. Amato and J. Cheadle, "The Long Reach of Divorce: Divorce and Child Well-Being Across Three Generations," *Journal of Marriage and Family* 67 (1) (2005), 191–206.

70. P. R. Amato and S. J. Rogers, "A Longitudinal Study of Marital Problems and Subsequent Divorce," *Journal of Marriage and the Family* 59 (1997), 612–624.

71. P. R. Amato, "Children of Divorce in the 1990s: An Update of the Amato and Keith Meta-Analysis," *Journal of Family Psychology* 15 (3) (2001), 355–370.

72. R. Bolgar, H. Zweig-Frank, and J. Paris, "Childhood Antecedents of Interpersonal Problems in Young Adult Children of Divorce," *Journal of the Academy of Child Psychiatry* 34 (1995), 134–150.

73. P. Johnson, J. M. Thorngren, and A. J. Smith, "Parental Divorce and Family Functioning: Effects on Differentiation Levels of Young Adults," *The Family Journal* 9 (3) (2001), 265–272.

74. M. H. Morris, and C. West, "Post-Divorce Conflict and Avoidance of Intimacy," *Journal of Divorce and Remarriage* 35 (3–4) (2001), 93–105.

75. H. M. Aro and U. K. Palosaari, "Parental Divorce, Adolescence, and Transition to Young Adulthood: A Follow-Up Study," *American Journal of Orthopsychiatry* 62 (1992), 421–429.

76. K. L. Kinnaird and M. Gerrard, "Premarital Sexual Behavior and Attitudes Toward Marriage and Divorce Among Young Women as a Function of their Mothers' Marital Status," *Journal of Marriage and the Family* 48 (1986), 757–765.

77. P. R. Amato, "Explaining the Intergenerational Transmission of Divorce," *Journal of Marriage and The Family* 58 (1996), 628–640.

78. Sharon S Brehm et al., *Intimate Relationships*, 329 (see note 5).

79. T. M. Christensen and M. C. Brooks, "Adult Children of Divorce and Intimate Relationships: A Review of the Literature," *The Family Journal* 9 (3) (2001), 289–294.

80. P. R. Amato, *Journal of Marriage and The Family* (see note 77).

81. L. Gabardi and L. A. Rosen, *Journal of Divorce and Remarriage* (see note 63).

82. F. L. Tasker, "Anti-Marriage Attitudes and Motivations to Marry Amongst Adolescents with Divorced Parents," *Journal of Divorce and Remarriage* 18 (1992), 105–119.

83. N. H. Wolfinger, "Beyond the Intergenerational Transmission of Divorce: Do People Replicate the Patterns of Marital Instability They Grew Up With?" *Journal of Family Issues* 21 (8) (2000), 1061–1086.

84. K. D. Dion and K. L. Dion, "Cultural Perspectives on Romantic Love," *Personal Relationships* 3 (1996), 5–17.

85. N. H. Wolfinger, *Journal of Family Issues* (see note 83).

86. Constance Ahrons, *The Good Divorce* (New York: HarperCollins, 1994), 2.

87. M. B. Conway et al., *The Family Journal* (see note 38).

88. Constance Ahrons, *We're Still Family: What Grown Children Have to Say About Their Parents' Divorce* (New York: HarperCollins, 2004).

89. L. Gigy, and J. Kelly, cited in J. M. Gottman and N. Silver, *The Seven Principles for Making Marriages Work* (New York: Crown Publishers, 1999), 16.

Index

About the Authors

GERALDINE K. PIORKOWSKI is Clinical Associate Professor of Psychology at the University of Illinois at Chicago, where she has also served as Interim Dean of Students and Director of the Counseling Center. She has been in private practice for 40 years, including individual and couples therapy. She has been quoted in *Cosmopolitan, Reader's Digest, Vogue, Chicago Sun Times, Boston Globe*, and *USA Today*.